2000 MOVIES
THE
1940s

ROBIN CROSS

Arlington House
New York

Published 1985 by Arlington House
Distributed by Crown Publishers, Inc

One Park Avenue, New York NY 10016

©Copyright Charles Herridge Ltd 1985

ISBN 0-517-472740

Printed in Italy

Author's Acknowledgment

The author would particularly like to thank Michelle Snapes, Jenny Sussex and Elaine Crowther of the National Film Archive for their tireless help, and their unfailing good humour, in the preparation of this book.

Picture Acknowledgments

The majority of the stills in this book were supplied by the Stills, Posters and Designs Department of the British Film Institute, and the rest were supplied by the Kobal Collection. Acknowledgments are due to the following film companies: Associated British Picture Corporation, Alliance, Allied Artists, Ambassador, Apollo, The Archers, Army, Air Force Film Units, Sydney Box, British Lion, British National, Butcher, Charter Films, Cineguild, Columbia Pictures, Crown Film Unit, John Corfield, Coronet, Eagle Lion, Ealing Studios, Enterprise, Excelsior Pictures, Film Classics, Film Craft, Robert Flaherty, Gainsborough Films, General Film Distributors, Samuel Goldwyn, Grand National Pictures, Hammer-Marylebone, Holbein, Independent Producers, Independent Sovereign, Individual Pictures, International, King Brothers, Lippert Pictures, London Films, Mayflower, Ministry of Information, Metro Goldwyn Mayer, Monogram, Monterey, Nettlefold, Niskos, Ortus Films, Paramount, Gabriel Pascal, Pilgrim, Pioneer, Producers Releasing Corporation, Premier Films, Producers-Actors, Quebec, Rank Film Distributors, Reynolds, Renown, Republic Pictures, RKO Radio Corporation, Hal Roach, David O. Selznick, Tansa, Transatlantic, Triton, Twentieth Century-Fox, Two Cities, United Artists, Universal Studios, Vanguard, Victoria, Warner Brothers, Wessex Films, World Screen Plays.

Author's Note

The dating of movies can be something of a problem, and different reference books frequently offer different dates for films. In order to remain consistent, we have followed the system used in the British National Film Archive's comprehensive Catalogue of Stills. In this Catalogue the date for each film is the year during which the film was copyrighted/registered/reviewed by the appropriate censorship authorities and is in most cases the year which appears on the copy of the film itself. This will account for the apparent time lapse between some dates for films and the year in which they received Oscar nominations or Awards.

A small number of abbreviations have been used in the captions.

Fox – Twentieth Century-Fox
UA – United Artists
GFD – General Film Distributors
PRC – Producers Releasing Corporation
Mon – Monogram

CONTENTS

INTRODUCTION

The decade opened with the Second World War and closed with the Cold War and the McCarthy witch hunt. It began with massive queues winding round cinemas to see Clark Gable and Vivien Leigh in *Gone with the Wind* and ended with the steady growth of television audiences and the first steps in the dismemberment of the vertically integrated Hollywood studio empires. In the years between, the cinema bore witness to a rapidly changing world and in the process underwent its own transformation. The sensation of 1940 was Carmen Miranda. In 1950 it was Marlon Brando.

At the beginning of the decade cinema was the most powerful medium of popular entertainment. Confirmed in their supremacy, the great Hollywood studios projected a world in which impossible glamour and absurdity competed on equal terms. It was a world both sentimental and utterly ruthless – in which Louis B Mayer would tearfully act out his favourite love scenes in his office and then turn his attention to exploiting child stars Mickey Rooney and Judy Garland to the limit and far beyond. Few could step from behind a drug store counter into the movies – just like Lana Turner – but millions cherished the dream.

In those days films were often premiered in the towns with which they were associated. Such was the power of cinema that a crowd of 100,000 turned up in South Bend, Indiana, for the premiere of *Knute Rockne – All American,* starring Pat O'Brien and Ronald Reagan. The future President was also involved in the celebrations in Tacoma which marked the premiere of *Tugboat Annie Sails Again.* All the schools were closed and the town declared a 'Tugboat Annie Day'. The crowds were swelled by 40,000 troops from nearby Army bases who were given special leave for the occasion. The cast of the movie chugged up Puget Sound escorted by a small armada of tugboats, yachts, freighters and dredgers.

At the other end of the scale was the gimmick dreamed up by Paramount's publicity department for the premiere of *The Biscuit Eater,* a boy-and-dog B picture which was one of the surprise hits of 1940. On the opening night the film's canine flavour was underlined by the presence in the front row of dogs belonging to Dorothy Lamour, Bing Crosby and other top-flight studio stars. Dress was formal – the gentlemen were in tails and the ladies were resplendent in red silk and net. It is not recorded what the humans wore.

Wartime restrictions brought an end to the more spectacular premiere junketings, but it also led to a boom in cinema audiences. Unlike some industries, the Hollywood dream factory required a minimum of conversion, effortlessly adapting all the stock genres – crime thrillers, musicals, even the B Western – to accommodate popular war themes. War workers and troops demanded escapist entertainment, and there was a vogue for exotic costume spectaculars – usually starring Maria Montez and Jon Hall – which retain much of their camp charm today. Musicals entered a golden age, emancipating themselves from the stage and climaxing in MGM's *On the Town,* which set the pattern for the musicals of the 1950s.

Technical developments were often promoted by wartime needs and the decade saw considerable advances in cinema technology – film stocks, colour and sound recording. In the big studios' B units, and in 'poverty row' outfits like Monogram and PRC, wartime rationing of building materials led to the multiple use of cheaply constructed sets which were ideally shot in low key light. In turn this was made easier by the development of more sensitive, finely grained film stock, high speed lenses and portable power units, which gave second feature geniuses like Joseph H Lewis and Edgar Ulmer the opportunity to indulge in virtuoso camera work. These very practical considerations played an integral part in the 'noir' films of the mid- and late 1940s, whose shadow-drenched sets provided the setting for Freud according to Hollywood.

Hollywood's B hives worked flat out during the war years. Series, serials, modified versions of A-feature hits came churning off the production line. Ladd and Lake topped the bill, Tom Neal and Ann Savage were on the bottom. Most of the Bs were amiable rubbish, characterized by director William Beaudine's famous remark, 'You mean somebody out there is actually waiting to see this?' But among the dross small masterpieces gleamed brightly. Second features like *Among the Living, My Name is Julia Ross, When Strangers Marry, Cat People, Thunderhoof* and *Gun Crazy* packed a bigger punch than the A features they were designed to support.

In Britain the war came to the rescue of a film industry which in 1939 was in the throes of one of its periodically recurring bouts of crisis. After a faltering start, which mirrored the nation's uncertain progress through the

'Phoney War', British film makers began to address the major themes of the conflict with a growing confidence. The influence of the realist school of film making, fostered in the 1930s at the GPO Film Unit by John Grierson, found an outlet in a stream of superb documentary and propaganda films, among them *Listen to Britain, Target for Tonight, Fires Were Started* and *Western Approaches*. The impact of the documentary approach on the waging of the 'People's War' can also be seen in feature films like *Nine Men, The Foreman Went to France, San Demetrio, London, Millions Like Us, Waterloo Road* and *The Way Ahead*, all of which focussed their attention on the lives of ordinary soldiers and civilians. More complex and romantic notions of 'Englishness' were advanced by Michael Powell and Emeric Pressburger in *The Life and Death of Colonel Blimp* and *A Canterbury Tale*.

Pure escapism was provided by Gainsborough Studios' bravura cycle of costume melodramas, initiated by *The Man in Grey*. Treated with undisguised disdain by the critics of the day, the Gainsborough output nevertheless remains an important part of the British cinema's mainstream.

The British film industry entered the postwar period in a mood of high optimism. The immense success on both sides of the Atlantic of Noel Coward's *In Which We Serve*, Olivier's *Henry V* and Anthony Asquith's *The Way to the Stars* convinced the industry's most important figure, J Arthur Rank, that he could take on the American majors in their own market. By the end of the decade Rank had come badly unstuck, but the period 1945-50 remains one of the most fertile in the history of British cinema. Carol Reed and Graham Greene pursued a fruitful collaboration in *The Fallen Idol* and *The Third Man*. David Lean was at the height of his powers, before his talent was calcified by endless preparations and mammoth budgets. Powell and Pressburger produced a series of quirky, challenging films, ranging from the bleakly pessimistic *The Small Back Room* to the extravagant fantasy of *The Red Shoes*. Ealing Studios reached a high point in 1949 with the release of *Passport to Pimlico, Whisky Galore* and *Kind Hearts and Coronets*.

In contrast with their British counterparts, European film makers – in Germany and the occupied countries – were inhibited rather than liberated by the war. The German film industry fulfilled its propaganda quota with a combination of hymns to German history and military strength, anti-Semitic tracts and frothy escapism. In occupied France the pressures of censorship channelled her finest film makers' energies into a politically neutral 'poetic romanticism' of which the finest examples are Marcel Carné's *Les Visiteurs du Soir* and *Les Enfants du Paradis*.

In Italy the film output of the war years was dominated by smooth, empty entertainments – popularly dubbed 'white telephone films'. The reaction against them was signalled by Luchino Visconti's *Ossessione*, a melodrama adapted from James M Cain's novel *The Postman Always Rings Twice* and a harbinger of the 'neo-realist' cycle of films which began with Roberto Rossellini's *Rome, Open City*. With the end of the hollow bombast of Mussolini's regime the neo-realists set about using non-professional actors to reproduce actual experience in authentic conditions, regardless of technical imperfections. Necessity was to a great extent the mother of invention as finance, decent equipment and studio space were all in short supply in the immediate postwar period. The subsequent international success of neo-realism brought different problems in its wake. When Vittorio de Sica was raising money for *Bicycle Thieves*, he received a generous offer from David O Selznick, who was prepared to back the film if Cary Grant was cast in the central role. By the end of the decade the influence of the European realist movement could be seen at work in films as diverse as the Japanese *Drunken Angel* and *Stray Dog* and hardnosed American thrillers like *The Naked City, Side Street* and *He Walked by Night*, which took their cameras out of the studio and into the city streets.

This book pulls all these strands together to provide the unfolding story of the decade's cinema: Judy Garland and Mickey Rooney in full flight in *Babes on Broadway*; a young Robert Mitchum lurking as the third heavy on the left in Hopalong Cassidy oaters; Hope and Crosby taking *The Road to Singapore* and Gene Kelly taking the musical to the top of the Empire State Building in *On the Town*; Joan Crawford suffering mightily in *Mildred Pierce*; Spencer Tracy introducing Katharine Hepburn to the joys of baseball in *Woman of the Year*; Dennis Price elegantly murdering his way to a dukedom in *Kind Hearts and Coronets*; and James Cagney making one of the most spectacular exits in movie history in *White Heat*. Here you will find a gallery of films in all their forms, from the Oscar winners to the lowliest products of 'poverty row', all of them celebrating ten crowded years of cinema.

1940

The outbreak of World War II, and the inexorable spread of hostilities, had a serious effect in Hollywood, closing eleven countries to American movies. One important individual casualty was Greta Garbo, whose films were far more popular in Europe than in the United States. Her career came to an end a year later with *Two-Faced Woman* (1941).

Studios could take some comfort from the increased business in Latin America, but profits still took a nosedive, with Fox and RKO recording losses. MGM stayed in profit thanks to the revenue rolling in from *Gone With the Wind* (1939). Nevertheless, RKO had already taken a step which would secure the studio's place in the cinema history of the 1940s. In 1939 they signed the boy wonder Orson Welles on an unprecendented contract which gave him the freedom to write, direct, produce and act.

Although the United States was still neutral, films like *The Mortal Storm*, *Escape* and Chaplin's *The Great Dictator* took a strong anti-Nazi line. The last was Chaplin's first all-talking picture, an ambitious attempt to mock Nazism out of existence which was flawed by its overly-sentimental conclusion.

Eighteen pictures were made in Technicolor, not exactly galloping progress as it was now five years since the release of the first movie in the perfected three-colour process, *Becky Sharp* (1935). The most colourful film of the year was undoubtedly Walt Disney's *Fantasia*, filmed in multiplane Technicolor and recorded with the advanced RCA Fantasound system, which combined three sound tracks on the film. The other Disney triumph of 1940 was *Pinocchio*, which had been three years in the making.

Also outstanding were John Ford's *The Grapes of Wrath* (voted best picture of the year by the New York Critics), *The Great McGinty* – Preston Sturges' directorial debut – and *Abe Lincoln in Illinois*, which contained a central performance of massive integrity from Raymond Massey. Classic comedy was provided by *The Philadelphia Story*, which won James Stewart an Academy Award as Best Actor. The Oscar for Best Film was scooped by Alfred Hitchcock's *Rebecca*, a masterly interpretation of Daphne du Maurier's romantic melodrama. Ginger Rogers won the Best Actress Award for *Kitty Foyle;* Jane Darwell's moving performance in *The Grapes of Wrath* won her the Best Supporting Actress Award; Walter Brennan was voted Best Supporting Actor for *The Westerner*.

At the more modest end of the scale Stuart Heisler's *The Biscuit Eater* proved to be the 'sleeper' of the year, while Boris Ingster's moody *Stranger on the Third Floor* was a shadow-splashed signpost to the *films noirs* of the later 1940s.

. Among those who died in 1940 were silent comedian Ben Turpin, and Marguerite Clark, who in her heyday had briefly rivalled Mary Pickford. Cowboy star Tom Mix met a characteristically flamboyant end in a spectacular car crash. He was killed instantly, reputedly by a blow on the head from a suitcase crammed with silver dollars. Anne Baxter made her screen debut in *20 Mule Team* as did Gene Tierney in *The Return of Frank James*. A nondescript Universal comedy, *One Night in the Tropics*, featured a pair of comedians who would soon be the studio's biggest money-earners – Abbott and Costello. Laird Cregar turned up in a bit part in *Granny Get Your Gun*.

In Britain the outbreak of war had temporarily threatened to close down the film industry. For two weeks in September 1939 the cinemas were shut, a measure prompted by fears of mass death at the height of an air raid. Like the nation itself, the British film industry went through a kind of Phoney War before finding its feet and a fresh sense of purpose. Among the better movies of the year were Carol Reed's *Night Train to Munich* – a chase thriller in the style of *The Lady Vanishes* (1938) – the Boultings' thoughtful *Pastor Hall* and Penrose Tennyson's *The Proud Valley*, in which Paul Robeson gave one of his best performances on film. Many years later he remarked that *The Proud Valley* was the one film in which he was proud to have appeared.

ACTION

Torrid Zone (Warner) d.William Keighley:
Ann Sheridan, James Cagney. Bananas and
badinage aplenty in zesty South of the
Border actioner

Typhoon (Paramount) d.Louis King:
Robert Preston, Dorothy Lamour. Sarong
girl Lamour is shipwrecked, meets Preston
and chimpanzee. Good comic support from
Lynne Overman

Strange Cargo (MGM) d.Frank Borzage:
Clark Gable, Joan Crawford, Peter Lorre.
Intriguing metaphysical tale of convicts'
escape from Devil's Island, aided by
Christ-figure Ian Hunter

Diamond Frontier (Universal) d.Harold
Schuster: Cecil Kellaway, John Loder.
Western law'n' order plot grafted on to tale
of South African gold rush

Green Hell (Universal) d.James Whale:
John Howard, Douglas Fairbanks, Jr.
Expedition in search of Inca treasure
hacks its way grimly through forest of
jungle clichés

Seven Sinners (Universal) d.Tay Garnett:
Marlene Dietrich, Albert Dekker. Dietrich is
the sultry Bijou for whom Lieutenant John
Wayne almost jumps ship. Wayne-Dietrich
chemistry enthralling

Moon over Burma (Paramount) d.Louis
King: Preston Foster, Dorothy Lamour.
Singer Lamour attracts attention of Foster,
Robert Preston, hooded cobra, giant ghost
tigers and other jungle denizens

City for Conquest (Warner) d.Anatole
Litvak: Frank McHugh, James Cagney,
Anthony Quinn. Superlative New York
drama with Cagney as truckdriver turned
prizefighter

Boom Town (MGM) d.Jack Conway: Hedy
Lamarr, Clark Gable, Spencer Tracy,
Claudette Colbert. Star names turn routine
oilwell saga into box-office gusher. B-movie
with big-budget gloss

Raffles (Goldwyn) d.Sam Wood: Olivia de Havilland, Dudley Digges, David Niven. Niven is the cricketing gentleman thief in stolid third film version of E W Hornung novel

Flowing Gold (Warner) d.Alfred E Green: Frances Farmer. Farmer, Pat O'Brien and John Garfield flounder in oilfield melodrama. Climactic avalanche comes none too soon

Castle on the Hudson (Warner) d.Anatole Litvak: Pat O'Brien, John Garfield. Potboiling remake of 1933 Spencer Tracy vehicle *20,000 Years in Sing Sing*

They Drive by Night (Warner) d.Raoul Walsh: Humphrey Bogart, Ann Sheridan, George Raft. Livewire performances and sparkling dialogue as trucking brothers Raft and Bogart battle crooked haulage barons

Johnny Apollo (Fox) d.Henry Hathaway: Tyrone Power, Dorothy Lamour. College boy Power turns crook after father Edward Arnold is jailed. Winds up in same prison

Devil's Island (Warner) d.William Clemens: Boris Karloff. Pulsating drama with Karloff playing surgeon sent to penal colony after treating wounds of escaped convict

The Trial of Mary Dugan (MGM) d.Norman Z McLeod: Laraine Day, Robert Young. Remake of studio's first all-dialogue movie with Day cast in the Norma Shearer role

East of the River (Warner) d.Alfred E Green: John Garfield, Brenda Marshall. Perennial programmer about two guys growing up on different sides of the law: Garfield on wrong side

Ski Patrol (International) d.Lew Landers:
Philip Dorn, Reed Hadley. Low-budget
actioner dealing with incident in
Russo-Finnish war. A curiosity for students
of war films

Busman's Honeymoon (MGM) d.Arthur
Woods: Aubrey Mallalieu, Robert
Montgomery, Seymour Hicks, Constance
Cummings. Murder mystery with
Montgomery miscast as Lord Peter Wimsey.

Escape (MGM) d.Mervyn Le Roy: Conrad
Veidt, Robert Taylor. Taylor rescues
Nazimova from concentration camp with
help of Countess Norma Shearer

Earl of Chicago (MGM) d.Richard Thorpe:
Robert Montgomery, Edward Arnold, E E
Clive. Montgomery is US mobster who
inherits title then kills sidekick and is tried
in the House of Lords

The Mortal Storm (MGM) d.Frank
Borzage: Maria Ouspenskaya, Ward Bond,
Margaret Sullavan. A family is torn apart
when the Nazis come to power. Frank
Morgan moving as Jewish academic

Men Against the Sky (RKO) d.Leslie
Goodwins: Wendy Barrie, Richard Dix. Dix
is washed-up pilot designing revolutionary
new 'plane in workmanlike aerial
programmer

Foreign Correspondent (UA) d.Alfred
Hitchcock: Joel McCrea, Charles
Wagenheim, Eduardo Ciannelli. Immensely
stylish espionage thriller with Herbert
Marshall outstanding as master spy

Flight Command (MGM) d.Frank Borzage:
Walter Pidgeon, Robert Taylor. Tribute to
US Navy Air Corps soars in aerial
sequences, flags badly on the ground

The Fighting 69th (Warner) d.William
Keighley: James Cagney, Pat O'Brien. Box-
office smash with Cagney a cowardly
soldier in a famous World War I regiment

The Leather Pushers (Universal) d.John Rawlins: Richard Arlen. Rock-bottom slugfest – another entry in the threadbare Arlen-Devine action series

The Quarterback (Paramount) d.H Bruce Humberstone: William Frawley, Wayne Morris. Morris in dual role of identical twins – one is a swot, the other a brash football hero

Knute Rockne – All American (Warner) d.Lloyd Bacon: Pat O'Brien. Story of legendary Notre Dame football coach; Ronald Reagan is his star player George Gipp – 'Let's hear it for the Gipper!'

ADVENTURE

The Sea Hawk (Warner) d.Michael Curtiz: Flora Robson, Errol Flynn. Robson repeats role of Good Queen Bess in high, wide and handsome blend of romance, piracy and swordplay

The Mark of Zorro (Fox) d.Rouben Mamoulian: Tyrone Power, Basil Rathbone. Power's flickering rapier wipes the sneer off Rathbone's face in fluent remake of Fairbanks silent classic

Santa Fe Trail (Warner) d.Michael Curtiz: Ronald Reagan, Olivia de Havilland, Errol Flynn. Flynn is Jeb Stuart in simplistic but spectacular reconstruction of Harper's Ferry massacre

Northwest Passage (MGM) d.King Vidor: Spencer Tracy, Robert Young. Rogers' Rangers open up the great outdoors in robust Technicolor epic filled with spectacular location shooting

The Sea Wolf (Warner) d.Michael Curtiz: Edward G Robinson, John Garfield, Ida Lupino. Fog-shrouded version of the much-filmed Jack London novel with Robinson as the sadistic master of *The Ghost*

The Howards of Virginia (Columbia)
d.Frank Lloyd: Cary Grant, Richard Carlson.
Uneasy Grant hopelessly miscast in
ponderous historical romance set at time
of American Revolution

The House of Seven Gables (Universal)
d.Joe May: George Sanders, Vincent Price,
Margaret Lindsay. A family curse leads to
murder in overwrought version of
Hawthorne novel

Chad Hanna (Fox) d.Henry King: Henry
Fonda, Guy Kibbee. Hayseed Fonda joins
circus, falls head over heels for bareback
rider Linda Darnell

Swiss Family Robinson (RKO) d.Edward
Ludwig: Thomas Mitchell, Edna Best,
Freddie Bartholomew. Well-crafted
adaptation of Johann Wyss' tale of family
on remote island paradise

Tom Brown's School Days (RKO)
d.Robert Stevenson: Freddie Bartholomew,
Cedric Hardwicke. Enjoyably hokey
Hollywood version of British public school
life. Freddie's last big starring role

Dr Ehrlich's Magic Bullet (Warner)
d.William Dieterle: Donald Crisp, Edward G
Robinson, John Hamilton. Medical
adventure as Edward G finds a cure for
syphilis in superior biopic

MELODRAMA

Hudson's Bay (Fox) d.Irving Pichel: Laird
Cregar, Paul Muni. Expansive historical
drama with Muni as fur-trapping founder of
Hudson's Bay Company

Rebecca (Selznick) d.Alfred Hitchcock:
Laurence Olivier, Joan Fontaine, Judith
Anderson. Ingenue Fontaine marries
moody aristocrat Olivier but cannot
exorcise the ghost of his first wife

My Son, My Son (UA) d. Charles Vidor: Brian Aherne, Madeleine Carroll. Carroll rises above banal script to give fine performance in tear-splashed family drama

The Letter (Warner) d. William Wyler: Sen Yung, Bette Davis, James Stephenson. Queen bitch Davis empties revolver into lover, pleads self-defence in second version of Somerset Maugham colonial tale

Susan and God (MGM) d. George Cukor: Joan Crawford, Rita Quigley, Fredric March. Socialite Crawford finds God, loses love of her family. Patchy version of Gertrude Lawrence stage hit

Angels Over Broadway (Columbia) d. Ben Hecht, Lee Garmes: Rita Hayworth, Douglas Fairbanks, Jr. Con-man Fairbanks teams with no-talent chorus girl Hayworth in turgid tale of New York no-hopers

And One Was Beautiful (MGM) d. Robert B Sinclair: Robert Cummings, Laraine Day, Jean Muir. Sisters Day and Muir both yearn for bland Bob. Heaven knows why

A Bill of Divorcement (RKO) d. John Farrow: Maureen O'Hara, Adolphe Menjou. Despite Menjou's skill, this remake of Hepburn/Barrymore classic is pale shadow of original

We Who Are Young (MGM) d. Harold S Bucquet: John Shelton, Lana Turner. Early straight role for Lana in tinny drama of young couple in The Big City

COMEDY

My Favourite Wife (RKO) d. Garson Kanin: Gail Patrick, Cary Grant. Marital mix-up when Irene Dunne 'returns from the dead' to find Grant wed to Patrick. Remade as *Move Over Darling* (1963)

He Married His Wife (Fox) d. Roy Del Ruth: Elisha Cook, Jr. Nancy Kelly, Mary Boland, Barnett Parker, Joel McCrea. Divorce can't keep racehorse owner McCrea apart from pretty Nancy Kelly

Hired Wife (Universal) d. William Seiter: Virginia Bruce, Brian Aherne. Frothy fun as secretary Rosalind Russell marries and then tames philandering boss Aherne

His Girl Friday (Columbia) d. Howard Hawks: Cary Grant, Rosalind Russell. High point of screwball comedy in sparkling remake of *The Front Page* (1931). Grant the cynical editor, Russell his star reporter

You Can't Fool Your Wife (RKO) d. Ray McCarey: Lucille Ball, Robert Coote. Disillusioned Ball leaves husband James Ellison and then tries to patch things up at a masquerade party

The Great McGinty (Paramount) d. Preston Sturges: Brian Donlevy (c). Donlevy perfectly cast as the hobo who becomes a state governor in Sturges' first outing as director. Oscar-winning screenplay

Brother Orchid (Warner) d. Lloyd Bacon: Edward G Robinson. Deft, amusing performance by Robinson as mobster-turned-monk in entertaining spoof of studio's gangster cycle

The Great Profile (Fox) d. Walter Lang: John Barrymore, Mary Beth Hughes. Barrymore reduced to parodying himself as has-been ham. A deeply melancholy exercise

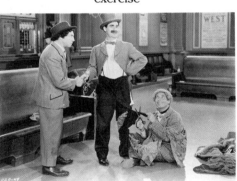

Go West (MGM) d. Edward Buzzell: Chico, Groucho, Harpo Marx. The Brothers' humour becomes increasingly mechanical despite hilarious train ride sequence

I Love You Again (MGM) d. W S Van Dyke: Myrna Loy, William Powell. Dull stick Powell gets knock on the head, reverts to former self – a wild-living con-man. Farcical complications ensue

Hullabaloo (MGM) d. Edwin L Marin: Virginia Grey, Dan Dailey. Muddled musical comedy starring Frank Morgan notable as the first film to show TV set as home furniture

A Chump at Oxford (UA) d. Alfred Goulding: Stan Laurel, Oliver Hardy. Concussion turns Stan into academic and athletic genius Lord Paddington. Harry Langdon had hand in screenplay

Third Finger Left Hand (Fox) d.Robert Z
Leonard: Donald Meek, Myrna Loy, Melvyn
Douglas. Stars' warm skills animate
featherweight offering in which Loy
pretends to be Douglas' wife

Love Thy Neighbour (Paramount) d.Mark
Sandrich: Fred Allen, Jack Benny.
Celebrated Benny-Allen radio feud
translates disappointingly to the screen

Lucky Partners (RKO) d.Lewis Milestone:
Ginger Rogers, Jack Carson, Ronald
Colman. Artist Colman becomes Ginger's
good luck charm in racily paced
box-office hit

L'il Abner (RKO) d.Albert Rogell: Charles
A Post, Granville Owen, Johnny Arthur,
Mona Ray. Al Capp's Dogpatch characters
brought scrappily to life in welter of
unconvincing accents

Alias the Deacon (Universal) d.Christy
Cabanne: Bennie Bartlett, Peggy Moran
Dennis O'Keefe. Modest effort in which
card sharp Bob Burns poses as a man
of the cloth

The Philadelphia Story (MGM) d.George
Cukor: James Stewart, Cary Grant,
Katharine Hepburn. Scintillating comedy
won Oscar for Stewart and screenplay
award for Donald Ogden Stewart

Three Cheers for the Irish (Warner)
d.Lloyd Bacon: Henry Armetta, Thomas
Mitchell. Retired cop Mitchell spends much
time feuding with son-in-law Dennis
Morgan, who's replaced him in the force

Misbehaving Husbands (PRC) d.William
Beaudine: Harry Langdon. Forgotten silent
star Langdon excellent as hen-pecked
husband in low-budget return to feature-
length comedy

No Time for Comedy (Warner) d.William
Keighley: Allyn Joslyn, Rosalind Russell,
James Stewart. Dramatist Stewart is
married to actress Russell, who tries to
stop him taking himself too seriously

Tugboat Annie Sails Again (Warner)
d.Lewis Seiler: Ronald Reagan, Marjorie
Rambeau. Rambeau steps into Marie
Dressler's capacious boots; Reagan and
Jane Wyman provide love interest

Brother Rat and a Baby (Warner) d.Ray Enright: Priscilla Lane, Ronald Reagan, Jane Wyman. Madcap sequel to *Brother Rat* (1938) with Reagan graduating from military academy

The Great Dictator (UA) d.Charles Chaplin: Henry Daniell, Charles Chaplin. Satirical assault on fascism slithers into sentimentality. Chaplin in dual role as Jewish barber and dictator Adenoid Hynkel

Road to Singapore (Paramount) d.Victor Schertzinger: Bing Crosby, Dorothy Lamour, Bob Hope. First in the long, winding, money-making series

The Ghost Comes Home (MGM) d.William Thiele: Frank Morgan, Billie Burke. Morgan returns from the dead to find family has managed perfectly well without him. Burke flutters and flutes away

My Little Chickadee (Universal) d.Edward Cline: Mae West, W C Fields. Comedy equivalent of *King Kong versus Godzilla* never quite achieves lift-off. Fields and West just too wary of each other

The Bank Dick (Universal) d.Edward Cline: Grady Sutton, W C Fields. Fields is Egbert Souse – 'with accent grave' – patron of the Black Pussy saloon and unlikely security man of the title

WESTERNS

20 Mule Team (MGM) d.Richard Thorpe: Wallace Beery. Leo Carrillo and Beery are brawling borax miners staking a claim in robust oater. Film marked Anne Baxter's screen debut

Dark Command (Republic) d.Raoul Walsh: John Wayne, Claire Trevor. Marshal John Wayne deals with renegade Walter Pidgeon in actioner loosely based on the tale of Quantrell's Raiders

Buck Benny Rides Again (Paramount) d.Mark Sandrich: Edward 'Rochester' Anderson, Jack Benny. Would-be cowpoke Benny transfers radio show to the range with moderately comic results

Virginia City (Warner) d.Michael Curtiz: Randolph Scott, Miriam Hopkins, Errol Flynn. Uneven follow-up to *Dodge City* (1939) with Humphrey Bogart cast as a most improbable Mexican bandit

The Westerner (Paramount) d.William Wyler: Walter Brennan, Gary Cooper. Oscar-winning performance by Brennan as Judge Roy Bean. Cooper the drifter who brings him to book

Return of Frank James (Fox) d.Fritz Lang: Jackie Cooper, Henry Fonda. Despite the revenge theme, Lang's first Western is handsomely mounted celebration of the Old West. Gene Tierney's debut

Northwest Mounted Police (Paramount) d.Cecil B DeMille: Gary Cooper, Madeleine Carroll. Cooper is Texas Ranger Dusty Rivers in overblown Canadian epic, much of it filmed on the sound stage

Melody Ranch (Republic) d.Joseph Santley: Jimmy Durante, Gene Autry, Ann Miller. More of a musical than a Western with range warbling winning out over shootin' and a sluggin'

ROMANCE

Comrade X (MGM) d.King Vidor: Hedy Lamarr, Clark Gable. Cast as an icy Russian, Lamarr displays a surprisingly deft comic touch in heavily contrived reworking of the *Ninotchka* (1939) theme

The Shop Around the Corner (MGM) d.Ernst Lubitsch: Margaret Sullavan, Frank Morgan, James Stewart. Sullavan and Stewart delightfully matched by Lubitsch in period tale of budding romance

Dance Girl Dance (RKO) d.Dorothy Arzner: Lucille Ball, Louis Hayward. Chorus girl Ball falls for Hayward, so does aspiring ballerina Maureen O'Hara. Interesting Arzner film latterly taken up by feminists

Arise My Love (Paramount) d.Mitchell Leisen: Ray Milland, Claudette Colbert. War-torn Spain provides background to romance between pilot Milland, reporter Colbert. Starts stylishly but fails to deliver

They Knew What They Wanted (RKO) d.Garson Kanin: Charles Laughton, Carole Lombard. Laughton secures mail-order bride Lombard on the strength of his handsome foreman's photograph

Vigil in the Night (RKO) d. George Stevens: Carole Lombard, Anne Shirley, Peter Cushing. Nurse Lombard and doctor Brian Aherne are star-crossed lovers in turgid medical melodrama

Waterloo Bridge (MGM) d. Mervyn Le Roy: Robert Taylor, Vivien Leigh. World War I weepie as Taylor's ballerina wife Leigh takes to (tasteful) prostitution after he's reported missing in action

'Til We Meet Again (Warner) d. Edmund Goulding: Merle Oberon, George Brent. Smooth crook Brent is smitten by fatally ill (though not so's you'd notice) Oberon. Remake of *One-Way Passage* (1932)

I'm Still Alive (RKO) d. Irving Reis: Linda Hayes, Kent Taylor. Stunt flier's nerve cracks, closely followed by his marriage. Can he pull himself together and fly back into his wife's life?

Saturday's Children (Warner) d. Vincent Sherman: Anne Shirley, John Garfield, Claude Rains. Depression drama with Shirley luring Garfield into poverty-stricken marriage

Little Old New York (Fox) d. Henry King: Fred MacMurray, Alice Faye. The story of Robert Fulton's revolutionary steamboat is framework for standard romantic tale. Fulton is played by Richard Greene

The Primrose Path (RKO) d. Gregory La Cava: Ginger Rogers, Joel McCrea, Henry Travers. Ginger from the wrong side of the tracks falls for ambitious McCrea. Marjorie Rambeau is her trollop of a mother

Kitty Foyle (RKO) d. Sam Wood: Ginger Rogers, Dennis Morgan. Oscar-winning performance by Rogers as working girl who marries into money but not happiness. Great cameo from Eduardo Ciannelli

My Love Came Back (Warner) d. Curtis Bernhardt: Jane Wyman, Eddie Albert. Romantic comedy set in music academy and starring Olivia de Havilland as aspiring violinist on the look-out for a husband

Pride and Prejudice (MGM) d.Robert Z
Leonard: Frieda Inescort, Laurence Olivier,
Edward Ashley, Greer Garson. Olivier's Mr
Darcy is the only character Jane Austen
would find remotely recognizable

It All Came True (Warner) d.Lewis Seiler:
Ann Sheridan, Humphrey Bogart, Felix
Bressart. Sheridan sings in oddball mixture
of drama, comedy and romance as gangster
Bogart hides out in boarding house

All This and Heaven Too (Warner)
d.Anatole Litvak: Charles Boyer, Bette
Davis. Aristocrat Boyer woos governess
Davis with tragic results in weepie based
on a Rachel Field novel

Irene (RKO) d.Herbert Wilcox: Anna
Neagle, Ray Milland. Technicolor ball
sequence is highlight of old-fashioned
'Long Island set' romantic musical

Star Dust (Fox) d.Walter Lang: John Payne,
Linda Darnell. Star-struck shopgirl Darnell
fails screen test but agent Roland Young
still manages to make her a star, naturally

MUSICALS

Down Argentine Way (Fox) d.Irving
Cummings: Carmen Miranda. Technicolor
Betty Grable vehicle hijacked by the
Brazilian bombshell, who has no
discernible connection with the flimsy plot

I Can't Give You Anything But Love
(Universal) d.Albert Rogell: Peggy Moran,
Johnny Downs. Composer Downs is
kidnapped by mobster Broderick Crawford
to pen song for missing sweetheart

If I Had My Way (Paramount) d.David
Butler: Gloria Jean, Bing Crosby.
Construction worker Bing adopts fatherless
Gloria Jean in box-office flop with
vaudeville background

Broadway Melody of 1940 (MGM)
d.Norman Taurog: Fred Astaire, Eleanor
Powell. Fred and Eleanor 'Begin the
Beguine' in their only film together. Superb
score by Cole Porter

The Boys from Syracuse (Universal) d.Edward Sutherland: Allan Jones, Rosemary Lane, Martha Raye. Inept screen version of Rodgers and Hart Broadway hit based on Shakespeare's 'Comedy of Errors'

Strike up the Band (MGM) d.Busby Berkeley: Judy Garland, Mickey Rooney. Wistful Garland perfect foil for dynamic Rooney whose high school band competes in Paul Whiteman's radio contest

Little Nellie Kelly (MGM) d.Norman Taurog: Judy Garland, George Murphy. Garland almost buried beneath an avalanche of blarney in adaptation of old George M Cohan Broadway smash

No No, Nanette (RKO) d.Herbert Wilcox: Anna Neagle. Marvellous score is pushed into background as Neagle simpers coyly through watered-down version of 1925 Broadway success

It's a Date (Universal) d.William Seiter: Deanna Durbin, Lewis Howard. Durbin plays rising star (Kay Francis her fading actress mother) and also treats us to rendering of Schubert's 'Ave Maria'

Young People (Fox) d.Allan Dwan: Jack Oakie, Shirley Temple, Charlotte Greenwood. A pair of vaudevillians take in an orphan. The dimpled one's last film for Fox for nine years. Senility struck at 12

One Night in the Tropics (Universal) d.Edward Sutherland: Robert Cummings, Nancy Kelly, Mary Boland. Box-office turkey based on Earl derr Biggers story. Abbott and Costello's screen debut

Music in My Heart (Columbia) d.Joseph Santley: Don Brodie, Rita Hayworth, Tony Martin. Brisk programmer with foreign singer Martin battling deportation. Hayworth looks stunning

Bitter Sweet (MGM) d.W S Van Dyke: George Sanders, Jeanette MacDonald, Edward Ashley, Diana Lewis. MGM's treatment of Noel Coward's ironic operetta apparently reduced him to tears

FANTASY

Tin Pan Alley (Fox) d. Walter Lang: Alice Faye, Betty Grable. Faye and Grable are dancing sisters in tuneful celebration of music publishing business. Remade as *I'll Get By* (1950)

Too Many Girls (RKO) d. George Abbott: Richard Carlson, Lucille Ball, Desi Arnaz. Heiress Ball acquires footballing bodyguards in zippy Rodgers and Hart-scored campus romp

New Moon (MGM) d. Robert Z Leonard: Nelson Eddy. French aristocrat Jeanette MacDonald falls for buccaneer Eddy in Romberg-scored operetta. Buster Keaton in tiny role

The Blue Bird (Fox) d. Walter Lang: Johnny Russell, Helen Ericson, Shirley Temple. A visual delight but the German gingerbread sticks firmly in the craw. First Temple box-office flop

One Million BC (Roach) d. Hal Roach: Carole Landis, Lon Chaney, Jr. One-eyed Chaney outshines prettier co-stars Landis and Victor Mature in caveman saga, part of which was directed by D W Griffith

AMERICANA

Brigham Young – Frontiersman (Fox) d. Henry Hathaway: Dean Jagger, Vincent Price (r). Dull account of Mormon trek to Utah takes back seat to romance between Tyrone Power and Linda Darnell

Blondie on a Budget (Columbia) d. Frank Strayer: Arthur Lake, Penny Singleton, Rita Hayworth. Series based on Chic Young's comic strip lasted from 1938 to 1951 with Lake as Dagwood, Singleton as Blondie

Fantasia (RKO) d. Ben Sharpsteen, Ford Beebe, Norman Ferguson, Bill Roberts, James Algar, Paul Satterfield, Samuel Armstrong. Disney's richly imaginative interpretation of a classical music concert

Pinocchio (RKO) d. Ben Sharpsteen, Hamilton Luske. A puppet comes to life but has to prove himself to turn into a real boy. Both charming and scaring in turns

Edison the Man (MGM) d. Clarence Brown: Spencer Tracy. Tracy well cast as the earnest inventor in smooth biopic with sentimental streak down the middle

Abe Lincoln in Illinois (RKO) d.John Cromwell: Raymond Massey. Massey repeats celebrated stage role in craggy, intense performance ably supported by Ruth Gordon as Mary Todd

Our Town (UA) d.Sam Wood: Beulah Bondi, Martha Scott. Serviceable adaptation of Thornton Wilder play about the families who live in a small New England town

Young Tom Edison (MGM) d.Norman Taurog: Virginia Weidler, Mickey Rooney, George Bancroft. Companion piece to *Edison the Man.* Rooney pleasantly restrained

Andy Hardy Meets Debutante (MGM) d.George B Seitz: Mickey Rooney, Judy Garland. The teenage embodiment of Middle America sets his cap on classy Diana Lewis (soon to marry William Powell)

The Grapes of Wrath (Fox) d.John Ford: Henry Fonda, John Carradine, John Qualen. Moving tale of the Depression dispossessed burnished by Gregg Toland's photography

Of Mice and Men (UA) d.Lewis Milestone: Lon Chaney, Jr. Burgess Meredith Chaney's finest performance as the feeble-minded Lenny in John Steinbeck's powerful morality play

Men of Boy's Town (MGM) d.Norman Taurog: Mickey Rooney. Sequel to *Boy's Town* (1938) rapidly gets bogged down in the syrup narrowly avoided by its predecessor

HORROR

Dr Cyclops (RKO) d.Ernest B Schoedsack: Albert Dekker. Dekker in superb form as sinister Dr Thorkel shrinking troupe of small-part actors even smaller. All in glorious Technicolor

The Invisible Man Returns (Universal) d.Joe May: Nan Grey, Vincent Price. The urbane Price goes invisible to clear himself of a murder charge. First entry in a Universal B series

The Mummy's Hand (Universal) d.Christy Cabanne: Tom Tyler, Peggy Moran. Cost-conscious sequel to *The Mummy* (1932) used sets built for *Green Hell* (1940). George Zucco in fine form as the heavy

The Devil Bat (PRC) d.Jean Yarbrough: Bela Lugosi. Bela lets loose a swarm of electrically enlarged killer bats. Glorious rubbish made for about six bucks

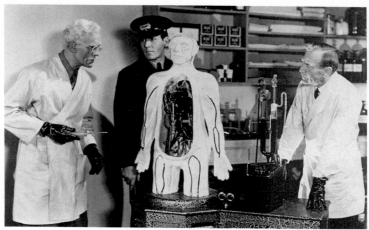

Before I Hang (Columbia) d.Nick Grinde: Boris Karloff, Edward Van Sloan. Scientist Karloff's 'cure for death' serum only succeeds in transforming him into a demented strangler

B MOVIES

The Lone Wolf Meets a Lady (Columbia) d.Sidney Salkow: Warren William, Jean Muir. William as sophisticated gumshoe Michael Lanyard outwitting the cops and the crooks in jewel heist thriller

Michael Shayne, Private Detective (Fox) d.Eugene Forde: Lloyd Nolan, Charles Coleman, Marjorie Weaver. Nolan as Brett Halliday's slick Irish-American sleuth in gambling racket mystery.

Charlie Chan at the Wax Museum (Fox) d.Lynn Shores: Hilda Vaughn, Sidney Toler, Sen Yung. Difficult to distinguish dummies from cast as Toler tracks down master criminal in chamber of horrors

Turnabout (UA) d.Hal Roach: George Renavent, Carole Landis, John Hubbard. Idiotic comedy from Thorne Smith tale in which statue causes husband and wife to exchange personalities. Risqué in its day

Congo Maisie (MGM) d.H C Potter: John Carroll, Ann Sothern. Sothern is hardboiled, heart-of-gold chorus girl heroine stranded in jungle. Second in lively series was *Red Dust* (1932) retread

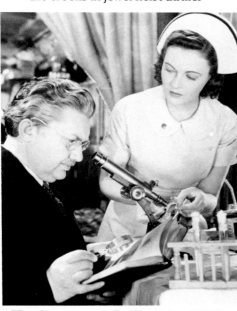

The Courageous Dr Christian (RKO) d.Bernard Vorhaus: Jean Hersholt, Dorothy Lovett. Anodyne entry in medical series with saintly sawbones Hersholt curing everything in sight. Sleep-inducing

The Saint Takes Over (RKO) d.Jack Hively: Jonathan Hale, Robert Emmett Keane, Paul Guilfoyle, George Sanders. Svelte Sanders clears Inspector Fernack (Jonathan Hale) of bribery charge

San Francisco Docks (Universal) d.Arthur Lubin: Joe Downing, Burgess Meredith, Raymond Walburn, Irene Hervey. Pacy drama in which longshoreman Meredith clears himself of murder rap

Blonde Inspiration (MGM) d.Busby Berkeley: John Shelton, Virginia Grey. Disarming satire on the shady side of the book publishing business adapted from a play by John Cecil Holm

Stranger on the Third Floor (RKO) d.Boris Ingster: John McGuire, Peter Lorre. Brooding, expressionist harbinger of the 'film noir' with Lorre cast as second-feature echo of M

Fugitive from Justice (Warner) d.Terry Morse: Roger Pryor (r). Insurance investigator Pryor foils the mob's plans to rub out a criminal lawyer

Framed (Universal) d.Harold Schuster: Frank Albertson, Constance Moore. Reporter Albertson is fingered on murder charge but ends up with a scoop for his newspaper

The Golden Fleecing (MGM) d.Leslie Fenton: Virginia Grey, Nat Pendleton, Lew Ayres. Insurance man Ayres has to protect mobster client from the attentions of gangsters and cops

Gambling on the High Seas (Warner) d.George Amy: Wayne Morris, Jane Wyman. Romance and melodrama on a casino ship with Gilbert Roland providing a dose of smooth villainy

The Biscuit Eater (Paramount) d.Stuart Heisler: Cordell Hickman, Billy Lee. Classic sleeper. Simple Georgia-set boy and dog tale directed with unobtrusive skill by Heisler

Mexican Spitfire (RKO) d.Leslie Goodwins: Leon Errol, Lupe Velez. Firecracker Lupe in sequel to *Girl from Mexico* (1939) and the first in freewheeling low-budget comedy series

Mysterious Dr Satan (Republic) d.William Witney, John English: Robert Wilcox (c). Eduardo Ciannelli builds a robot army (well, one robot actually) but his plans for world conquest are foiled by 'Copperhead'

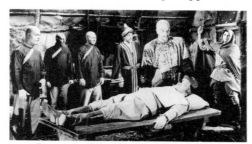

Little Orvie (MGM) d.Ray McCarey: Johnny Sheffield. Get your Kleenex out as curly-haired moppet Sheffield takes in a stray and hides it from hard-hearted father

Drums of Fu Manchu (Republic) d.William Witney, John English: Henry Brandon. Brandon in superlative form as evil Oriental mastermind in search of the long-lost sceptre of Genghis Khan

La Conga Nights (Universal) d.Lew Landers: Hugh Herbert. Slaphappy comedy with Herbert as cab-driving vaudevillian putting on a show in his boarding house

Sporting Blood (MGM) d.S Sylvan Simon: Robert Young, William Gargan, Maureen O'Sullivan. Modest drama set in the world of horse racing. Bears no relation to the 1931 Clark Gable vehicle

The Green Archer (Columbia) d.James W Horne: Victor Jory (r). Who is the mysterious masked bowman in risible remake of 1925 chapter play? Above-average serial cast sink without trace

Flash Gordon Conquers the Universe (Universal) d.Ford Beebe, Ray Taylor: Frank Shannon, Buster Crabbe, Carol Hughes, Roland Drew. Can Flash save Earth from Ming's purple death dust?

BRITISH & FOREIGN

Contraband (British National) d.Michael Powell: Conrad Veidt, Valerie Hobson. Sea captain Veidt and passenger Hobson entangled in well-paced espionage thriller with exciting black-out chase

Convoy (Ealing) d.Penrose Tennyson: John Clements, Clive Brook, Stewart Granger. Stiff upper lip naval drama leavened by Tennyson's sympathetic direction and some salty below decks cameos

Inspector Hornleigh Goes to It (Twentieth Century) d.Walter Forde: Alastair Sim, Raymond Huntley, Phyllis Calvert. Third entry in breezy detective series starring Gordon Harker in title role

Night Train to Munich (Twentieth Century) d.Carol Reed: Margaret Lockwood, Albert Lieven. Jaunty agent Rex Harrison whisks Lockwood from under the noses of the Nazis

For Freedom (Gainsborough) d.Maurice Elvey: Billy Russell (as Hitler). Dramatized account of the *Altmark* incident and the sinking of the *Graf Spee*

Freedom Radio (Two Cities) d.Anthony Asquith: Reginald Beckwith (on ground). An anti-Nazi surgeon (Clive Brook) establishes secret radio transmitter to broadcast the truth about Hitler's Germany

Pastor Hall (Charter) d.Roy Boulting: Wilfred Lawson (c). Thoughtful morality tale based on the life of Martin Niemöller with Lawson convincing in title role

The Proud Valley (Ealing) d.Penrose Tennyson: Paul Robeson, Edward Chapman. Robeson lends massive dignity to coal mining saga with patriotic twist. His favourite film role

Gaslight (British National) d.Thorold Dickinson: Diana Wynyard, Anton Walbrook. Cultivated Walbrook sets out to drive wife Wynyard mad in the first film version of this melodrama. Tremendously stylish

John Smith Wakes Up (Pioneer) d.Jiri Weiss: Eliot Makeham, Amy Veness. Fantasy in which meek Makeham wakes up to find Britain occupied by the Nazis

They Came By Night (Twentieth Century) d.Harry Lachman: Will Fyffe, Phyllis Calvert. Scottish jeweller poses as thief to trap a gang responsible for his brother's suicide. Calvert's debut

Bulldog Sees it Through (ABPC) d.Harold Huth: Greta Gynt, Robert Newton, Jack Buchanan. London society types outwit the beastly Hun. Utterly fatuous and Buchanan's last film for 13 years

Kipps (Twentieth Century) d.Carol Reed: Michael Redgrave. Redgrave in fine form as Victorian draper's assistant trying to move up in the world. Adapted from the novel by H G Wells

Band Wagon (Gainsborough) d.Marcel Varnel: Arthur Askey, Richard Murdoch. 'Big Hearted' Arthur and 'Stinker' Murdoch acquire a haunted house full of Nazi spies. Radio spin-off

The Thief of Bagdad (UA) d.Ludwig Berger, Tim Whelan, Michael Powell: Sabu. Spellbinding fantasy with Academy Award-winning special effects. Rex Ingram as outsize genie

So This is London (Fox) d.Thornton Freeland: George Sanders. Remake of 1930 Will Rogers comedy with cantankerous Brits and Yanks at cultural odds with each other

Saloon Bar (Ealing) d.Walter Forde: Judy Campbell, Gordon Harker. Broad comedy thriller with bookmaker Harker solving a murder mystery. Adapted from a play by Frank Harvey, Jr

Shipyard Sally (Fox) d.Monty Banks: Gracie Fields, Oliver Wakefield. Robust comedy in which singing publican Fields comes to the rescue of a shipyard

Old Mother Riley in Society (British National) d.John Baxter: Arthur Lucan. Complete chaos breaks out when Lucan's demented Irish washerwoman crashes the world of the toffs

Crooks Tour (British National) d.John Baxter: Basil Radford, Naunton Wayne. Cricket-loving stalwarts Charters and Caldicott get the better of Nazi master spy in chase across Europe

Sailors Three (Ealing) d.Walter Forde: Tommy Trinder, Claude Hulbert, Michael Wilding (r). Tipsy Trinder staggers aboard German pocket battleship and captures it. Propaganda with anti-pacifist slant

Let George Do It (Ealing) d.Marcel Varnel: George Formby, Phyllis Calvert. In between bouts of ferocious ukelele bashing gormless George breaks up a spy ring in Norway

Gasbags (Gainsborough) d.Marcel Varnel: The Crazy Gang. The Gang are blown to Germany on a barrage balloon, wind up in a concentration camp (sic), tunnel their way home in mad inventor's machine

Jeannie (Tansa) d.Harold French: Michael Redgrave, Barbara Mullen. Naive Scots girl Mullen has a variety of adventures before settling down with washing machine sales-man Redgrave. Deft romantic comedy.

Die Rothschilds Aktion auf Waterloo (Germany) d.Eric Waschneck. Fabricated account of the creation of banking empire by the financing of the alliance against Napoleon

Jud Süss (Germany) d.Veit Harlan: Werner Kraus. Anti-Semitic propaganda masquerading as 18th-century history. The people rise up against a Jewish finance minister

Somewhere in England (Butcher) d.John E Blakeley: Frank Randle. Knockabout service comedy starring Harry Korris which made slack-jawed comic Randle a star and launched a series

La Comedie du Bonheur (France) d.Marcel L'Herbier. Wistful carnival-time comedy in which Michel Simon brightens up the lives of his fellow lodgers with comedians. Ramon Novarro also stars

Nous les Gosses (France) d.Louis Daquin. Some schoolchildren spend their Easter holiday raising money to pay for huge window they smashed while playing football

Friedrich Schiller (Germany) d.Herbert Maisch: Horst Caspar. Biopic of the poet concentrates on his early youth as a cadet at the Duke of Wurttemberg's military academy

L'Assedio dell' Alcazar (Italy) d.Augusto Genina: Mireille Balin, Andrea Checchi. Drama set against the background of long drawn out siege during the Spanish Civil War

1941

The year ended with the United States plunged into war and the studios back in the black. MGM-Loew's balance sheet showed a profit of $11 million, followed by Paramount with $9 million. Warner recorded a profit of $5.4 million.

Acting honours went to Gary Cooper, who had two big hits, *Meet John Doe* and *Sergeant York*, the latter winning him the Best Actor Award. Joan Fontaine won the Best Actress Oscar for her performance in Hitchcock's *Suspicion*. The Best Supporting Actress Award went to Mary Astor for her fine portrayal of a bitchy, selfish concert pianist in *The Great Lie*, a part which had been built up during filming at the insistence of co-star Bette Davis. Donald Crisp carried off the Best Supporting Actor Award for his performance in John Ford's *How Green Was My Valley*, the film chosen by the Academy as the year's best.

Also nominated but ultimately gaining only a minor award was Orson Welles' *Citizen Kane*. Because of Charles Foster Kane's thinly disguised similarity to William Randolph Hearst, the enraged press baron refused to advertise or review the movie in any of his newspapers, a move which disrupted the film's release and badly affected its box-office performance. *Citizen Kane* remains a milestone in cinema, but for Welles – its presiding genius – it has become the cinematic equivalent of Kane's Xanadu, a vast sarcophagus for the wunderkind's 'Rosebud'.

Another sensational directing debut was made by John Huston with *The Maltese Falcon*, which also gave Sydney Greenstreet his first screen role at the age of sixty-one. 'Hold me hand, m'dear,' he asked Mary Astor before he went on the set to film his first scene. Other newcomers included Turhan Bey, Janet Blair, Lloyd Bridges and Dan Duryea. *Woman of the Year* marked the first film in the magical screen partnership of Katharine Hepburn and Spencer Tracy.

There was a rash of filmed stage hits, including *The Little Foxes*, *The Man Who Came to Dinner* and *Ladies in Retirement*. Remakes also came into their own, with mixed results, in *Back Street*, *Smilin' Through*, *Blood and Sand* and *Dr Jekyll and Mr Hyde*, the last boasting a performance of great malevolence from Spencer Tracy. Among the year's outstanding films were *Here Comes Mr Jordan*, *King's Row* – which provided Ronald Reagan with his finest hour as the amputee struggling to come to terms with life – and *High Sierra*. A moment to treasure was Rita Hayworth dancing with Fred Astaire in *You'll Never Get Rich*.

The year saw British cinema lose one of its brightest prospects, the director Penrose Tennyson, who was killed in an air crash while filming a documentary. The most successful film of the year was Michael Powell's *The 49th Parallel*, which established Eric Portman as a leading film actor. *Pimpernel Smith* starred Leslie Howard in the title role, playing an unworldly academic whose *alter ego* is a brilliant secret agent. The film has its charm but its whimsical celebration of the amateur spirit was already out of step with the demands of 'Total War'. The changing public mood was reflected in Harry Watt's documentary *Target for Tonight*, a big success on both sides of the Atlantic and one of the first serious films to show the British taking the war back to the Nazis.

ACTION

Parachute Battalion (RKO) d.Lesley Goodwins: Pat Kelly, Harry Carey, Edmond O'Brien, Richard Cromwell. Miles of documentary footage spin out everyday tale of parachute jumping folk

High Sierra (Warner) d.Raoul Walsh: Ida Lupino, Humphrey Bogart. Bogie is sympathetically drawn killer Roy 'Mad Dog' Earle, Lupino his moll in moody thriller. Remade in 1949 and 1955

I Wanted Wings (Paramount) d.Mitchell Leisen: Ray Milland. Veronica Lake emerges as a star in an otherwise routine air force training drama

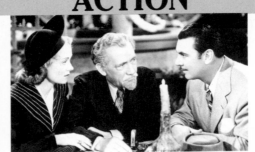

They Dare Not Love (Columbia) d.James Whale: Martha Scott, Egon Brecher, George Brent. Brent woefully miscast as Austrian princeling on the run from the Nazis, falling for commoner Scott.

Unholy Partners (MGM) d.Mervyn Le Roy: Edward G Robinson, Edward Arnold. Newspaperman Robinson falls into the clutches of racketeer Arnold in prohibition thriller

Johnny Eager (MGM) d.Mervyn Le Roy: Don Costello, Joseph Downing, Lana Turner, Robert Taylor, Van Heflin. Taylor is big-time hoodlum. Heflin won Oscar for performance as drunken hanger-on

The Penalty (MGM) d.Harold S Bucquet: Edward Arnold, Gene Reynolds, Lionel Barrymore. After a spell with kindly farmer Barrymore Gene turns against mobster Dad Arnold

Dangerously They Live (Warner) d.Robert Florey: Leo G Carroll, Nancy Coleman, Raymond Massey, Moroni Olsen. Doctor John Garfield rescues Coleman and secret information from Nazi spy ring

Manpower (Warner) d.Raoul Walsh: Edward G Robinson, Marlene Dietrich, George Raft. Diner scene outstanding in punchy reworking of studio's tried and tested *Tiger Shark* (1932) theme

Shadow of the Thin Man (MGM) d.W S Van Dyke: William Powell, Myrna Loy. In between the Martinis Nick and Nora Charles solve racetrack murder. Barry Nelson's screen debut

The Maltese Falcon (Warner) d.John Huston: Humphrey Bogart, Peter Lorre, Mary Astor, Sydney Greenstreet. Huston was told to 'Make every shot count.' He did. Greenstreet's screen debut at 61

I Wake Up Screaming (Fox) d.H Bruce Humberstone: Carole Landis, Victor Mature, Betty Grable. Psychopathic cop Laird Cregar pursues Mature and Grable in atmospheric suspense picture

Out of the Fog (Warner) d.Anatole Litvak: Eddie Albert, John Garfield, Ida Lupino. Screen version of Irwin Shaw's 'The Gentle People' with hoodlum Garfield terrorizing an innocent family, coming to sticky end

ADVENTURE

The Corsican Brothers (UA) d.Gregory Ratoff: Douglas Fairbanks, Jr. Roguish Fairbanks swashbuckles athletically through Dumas adventure. Ingenious photographic effects

Blood and Sand (Fox) d.Rouben Mamoulian: Tyrone Power. Brilliant use of Technicolor but Power leaves a vacuum in the romantic retelling of 1922 Valentino bullfighting classic

Tarzan's Secret Treasure (MGM) d.Richard Thorpe: Johnny Weissmuller, Johnny Sheffield, Maureen O'Sullivan. Jane and Boy are kidnapped by explorers searching for jungle gold

Singapore Woman (Warner) d.Jean Negulesco: David Bruce, Brenda Marshall. Rubber planter Bruce removes oriental curse from Marshall. Remake of *Dangerous* (1935)

Swamp Water (Fox) d.Jean Renoir: Walter Brennan, Dana Andrews. Brennan is fugitive living with daughter Anne Baxter in Georgia swamp. Renoir's first American film

Flame of New Orleans (Universal) d.René Clair: Bruce Cabot, Marlene Dietrich, Roland Young. Enigmatic Marlene is the prize fought for by two-fisted Cabot and wealthy Roland Young. Cabot wins

MELODRAMA

Suspicion (RKO) d.Alfred Hitchcock: Joan Fontaine, Nigel Bruce, Cary Grant. Oscar for Fontaine who believes playboy husband Grant is scheming to kill her. Bruce touching as bluff, silly-ass friend

A Woman's Face (MGM) d.George Cukor: Melvyn Douglas, Joan Crawford. Scarred gang boss Crawford falls under evil spell of Conrad Veidt in supercharged Crawford vehicle. God, she suffers

Back Street (Universal) d.Robert Stevenson: Charles Boyer, Margaret Sullavan. Sullavan is silently suffering kept woman, Boyer her rich lover, in smooth remake of 1932 weepie

King's Row (Warner) d.Sam Wood: Ann Sheridan, Ronald Reagan. Ronnie's finest hour as an amputee regaining will to live in lush, sweeping saga of life in Midwestern town. Stirring Korngold score

Penny Serenade (Columbia) d.George Stevens: Cary Grant, Edgar Buchanan, Irene Dunne. Accomplished tearjerker with Grant and Dunne adopting a baby girl after Dunne miscarries in Japanese earthquake

Ladies in Retirement (Warner) d.Charles Vidor: Ida Lupino, Elsa Lanchester, Louis Hayward, Edith Barrett. Lupino is homicidal housekeeper in Gothic tale – her favourite role

How Green Was My Valley (Fox) d.John Ford: Sara Allgood, Roddy McDowall, Donald Crisp. Wales was never like this in sentimental Oscar-laden adaptation of Richard Llewellyn's best-seller

The Little Foxes (Warner) d.William Wyler: Bette Davis, Herbert Marshall. Davis unstoppable as bitch on wheels Regina in Lillian Hellman's Southern family drama. See also *Another Part of the Forest* (1948)

The Shanghai Gesture (UA) d.Josef Von Sternberg: Victor Mature, Gene Tierney. Masterpiece of Hollywood baroque set in Mother Gin Sling's gambling hell. Plot too ludicrous to summarize

COMEDY

Two-Faced Woman (MGM) d.George Cukor: Constance Bennett, Melvyn Douglas, Greta Garbo. Garbo has dual role in her last film. A poor vehicle in which she nevertheless contrives to be quite luminous

Tall, Dark and Handsome (Fox) d.H Bruce Humberstone: Virginia Gilmore, Cesar Romero. Comedy crime drama set in the 20s with suave Cesar in the title role as gangster with social aspirations

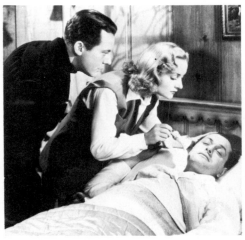

Mr and Mrs Smith (RKO) d.Alfred Hitchcock: Gene Raymond, Carole Lombard, Robert Montgomery. Lombard and Montgomery find their marriage is illegal in intriguing Hitchcock comedy

Sullivan's Travels (Paramount) d.Preston Sturges: Joel McCrea, Veronica Lake. Director McCrea takes to the road in search of real life. Hard edge marred by sentimental ending

That Uncertain Feeling (UA) d.Ernst Lubitsch: Burgess Meredith, Melvyn Douglas, Merle Oberon. Sparkling comedy in which hiccups and psychoanalysis almost wrecks marriage of Douglas and Oberon

The Man who Came to Dinner (Warner) d.William Keighley: Ann Sheridan, Richard Travis, Bette Davis, Monty Woolley. Woolley is house guest who overstays his welcome. Part originally slated for John Barrymore

The Lady Eve (Paramount) d.Preston Sturges: Charles Coburn, Barbara Stanwyck, Henry Fonda. Coburn and Stanwyck decide to fleece sappy naturalist Fonda, but romance gets in the way

Model Wife (Universal) d.Leigh Jason: Joan Blondell, Dick Powell. Dick marries fashion model Joan but they daren't let her boss know. Then she gets pregnant. Stars rise above mediocre script

My Life with Caroline (RKO) d.Lewis Milestone: Ronald Colman, Reginald Gardiner, Anna Lee. Featherweight tale of marital misunderstandings sustained solely by Colman's abundant charm

The Bride Came C.O.D. (Warner) d.William Keighley: James Cagney, Bette Davis. Pilot Cagney is on the trail of runaway heiress Davis, but comedy never gets off the runway

Design for Scandal (MGM) d.Norman Taurog: Rosalind Russell, Walter Pidgeon. Newsman Pidgeon sets out to discredit stern judge Russell, then falls for her

Nothing But the Truth (Paramount) d.Elliott Nugent: Paulette Goddard, Bob Hope. Stockbroker Hope wagers that he can tell the absolute truth for twenty-four hours

The Devil and Miss Jones (RKO) d.Sam Wood: Robert Cummings, Jean Arthur, Charles Coburn. Classy comedy of manners with Coburn masquerading as clerk in his own department store

Louisiana Purchase (Paramount) d.Irving Cummings: Victor Moore, Bob Hope. Hope sparkles in Irving Berlin's spirited satire on political corruption. Watch out for hilarious filibuster scene

The Road to Zanzibar (Paramount) d.Victor Schertzinger: Una Merkel, Bob Hope, Dorothy Lamour, Bing Crosby. Bob and Bing join a circus in a hunt for diamonds in so-so series entry

It Started With Eve (Universal) d.Henry Koster: Deanna Durbin, Charles Laughton. Deanna poses as Bob Cummings' fiancée to please his dying father Laughton. Then the old codger recovers

The Feminine Touch (MGM) d.W S Van Dyke: Kay Francis, Rosalind Russell, Don Ameche. Russell sets out to disprove professor husband Ameche's theories on jealousy, then gets jealous herself

Here Comes Mr Jordan (Columbia) d.Alexander Hall: Edward Everett Horton, Robert Montgomery, Claude Rains. Dead boxer Montgomery returns to earth in a new body. As fresh as when it was made

In the Navy (Universal) d.Arthur Lubin: Gayle Mallott, Lou Costello, Bud Abbott. Chubby Lou nearly sends the fleet to the bottom. Musical support from Dick Powell, the Andrews Sisters

Keep 'Em Flying (Universal) d.Arthur Lubin: Martha Raye, Lou Costello, Bud Abbott. A & C's 4th in 10 months found them fouling up the air force. Martha Raye sings 'Pig Foot Pete'

The Big Store (MGM) d.Charles Reisner: Harpo and Groucho Marx, Margaret Dumont. Groucho is detective Wolf J Flywheel investigating Douglass Dumbrille's shady emporium. Their last film at MGM

Charley's Aunt (Fox) d.Archie Mayo: Arleen Whelan, Jack Benny, Anne Baxter, Richard Haydn, James Ellison. Benny triumphs over apparent miscasting and displays his talent for physical comedy

Bachelor Daddy (Universal) d.Harold Young: Edward Everett Horton, Baby Sandy. A baby is left in the care of three bachelors while mother serves a prison sentence

Hellzapoppin (Universal) d.H C Potter: Ole Olsen, Chic Johnson. Gallant but only partially successful attempt to capture surreal flavour of big Broadway hit

The Wild Man of Borneo (MGM) d.Robert Sinclair: Frank Morgan, Phil Silvers. Theatrical boarding house comedy with Morgan hamming it up as hyperactive salesman

Pot O'Gold (UA) d.George Martin: James Stewart, Charles Winninger, Horace Heidt. Stewart co-stars with Paulette Goddard in tale of radio sponsor Winninger's battle with hard-up entertainers

Great Guns (Fox) d.Monty Banks: Oliver Hardy, Stan Laurel. L & H get caught in the draft and go on manoeuvres. A long way from their best. Look out for Alan Ladd passing through

Weekend for Three (RKO) d.Irving Reis: Philip Reed, Jane Wyatt, Dennis O'Keefe. Limp variation on the Man Who Came to Dinner theme. Philip Reed the pest of a guest

The Invisible Woman (Universal) d.Edward Sutherland: John Howard, John Barrymore. Barrymore hams away bemusedly as the scientist behind model Virginia Bruce's disappearing act

Unexpected Uncle (RKO) d.Tay Garnett: Charles Coburn, Anne Shirley. Farce and a touch of pathos as philanthropic tycoon Coburn encourages romance between shopgirl and playboy

The Man Who Lost Himself (Universal) d.Edward Ludwig: S Z 'Cuddles' Sakall, Brian Aherne, Kay Francis. Scatterbrained mistaken-identity romp with Aherne masquerading as recently deceased lookalike

Look Who's Laughing (RKO) d.Allan Dwan: Jim Jordan, Edgar Bergen, Lucille Ball, Marian Jordan. Ventriloquist Bergen's 'plane makes emergency landing in Wistful Valley, home of radio's Fibber and Molly McGee (the Jordans)

Father Takes a Wife (RKO) d.Jack Hively: Gloria Swanson, Adolphe Menjou. Big Gloria's umpteenth comeback appropriately playing a reluctantly retired actress married to Menjou

Ball of Fire (RKO) d.Howard Hawks: S Z 'Cuddles' Sakall, Oscar Homolka, Barbara Stanwyck. A neat twist on the tale of Snow White and the Seven Dwarfs. Gary Cooper co-stars

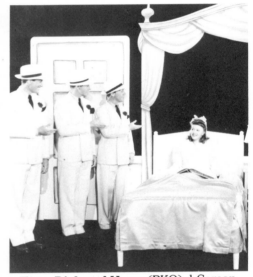

Tom, Dick and Harry (RKO) d.Garson Kanin: Alan Marshal, George Murphy, Burgess Meredith, Ginger Rogers. Comic fantasy in which small-town Cinderella Ginger has three suitors

She Knew All the Answers (Columbia) d.Richard Wallace: Joan Bennett, Eve Arden, Franchot Tone. Lightweight love tangle with stuffy stockbroker Tone succumbing to wiles of chorus girl Bennett

This Thing Called Love (Columbia) d.Alexander Hall: Rosalind Russell, Melvyn Douglas. Newlyweds Douglas and Russell agree to a three-month trial period in slickly mounted farce

Three Girls About Town (Columbia) d.Leigh Jason: Janet Blair, John Howard, Joan Blondell. Zany comedy follows three sisters' discovery of what appears to be a corpse in their New York hotel

Barnacle Bill (MGM) d.Richard Thorpe: Virginia Weidler, Wallace Beery, Leo Carrillo. Beery as loveable plug ugly fencing with the amorous Marjorie Main in routine waterfront yarn

The Richest Man in Town (Columbia) d.Charles Barton: Edgar Buchanan, Frank Craven. Two feuding citizens in a small town are united by the arrival of a con-man

Topper Returns (UA) d.Roy Del Ruth: Edward 'Rochester' Anderson, Joan Blondell, Roland Young. Last of the series in which Topper solves a murder mystery with the help of the spectral Blondell

Never Give a Sucker an Even Break (Universal) d.Edward Cline: W C Fields dives after a bottle of whisky he's dropped from a 'plane and lands on a mountain belonging to Mrs Hemoglobin. Get the picture?

Too Many Blondes (Universal) d.Thornton Freeland: Jerome Cowan, Eddie Quillan, Lon Chaney, Jr. Showbiz newlyweds nearly split up over rivalry. Rudy Vallee's warbling whiles away the time

You're in the Army Now (Warner) d.Lewis Seiler: Phil Silvers, Joseph Sawyer, Jimmy Durante. Two vacuum cleaner salesmen are drafted into the army with fairly raucous results

Love Crazy (MGM) d.Jack Conway: William Powell, Gail Patrick, Myrna Loy, Jack Carson. Loy and Powell try their hand at slapstick as the latter feigns madness to prevent Myrna from divorcing him

WESTERNS

Belle Starr (Fox) d.Irving Cummings: Gene Tierney, Randolph Scott. Tierney is the well-bred lady gunslinger, Scott her beau, in romantic but muffled biopic

Western Union (Fox) d.Fritz Lang: Robert Young. Epic film, superbly photographed by Edward Cronjagger and for good measure given a big dose of Lang's customary fatalism

The Round Up (Paramount) d.Lesley Selander: Patricia Morrison, Richard Dix. Lumbering remake of 1920s silent with Preston Foster turning up to trouble Dix's love life.

The Bad Man (MGM) d.Richard Thorpe: Laraine Day, Lionel Barrymore, Wallace Beery, Ronald Reagan. Beery's blustering Mexican bandit is a parody of his 1934 hit as Pancho Villa

Honky Tonk (MGM) d.Jack Conway: Lana Turner, Clark Gable, Albert Dekker. First pairing of Gable and Turner in overwrought western soaper. He's a con-man, she's the girl who tames him

Billy the Kid (MGM) d.David Miller: Robert Taylor, Brian Donlevy. Pedestrian biopic rewrites history to make Pat Garrett (Donlevy) and Billy (Taylor) childhood pals

Arizona Cyclone (Universal) d.Joseph H Lewis: Johnny Mack Brown, Kathryn Adams. Lewis's customary stylistic flourishes lift this routine Mack Brown oater out of the rut

Down Mexico Way (Republic) d.Joseph Santley: Fay McKenzie, Gene Autry. Gene heads South of the Border after no-good fraudsters have fleeced the honest folk of Sage City

Riders of the Purple Sage (Fox) d.James Tinling: Mary Howard, George Montgomery. Montgomery is Texas Ranger in warmed-over version of oft-filmed Zane Grey story

Doomed Caravan (Paramount) d.Lesley Selander: William Boyd. Outstanding entry in Hopalong Cassidy series as Hoppy rides to the rescue of Minna Gombell's wagon freighting business

Riders of Death Valley (Universal) d.Ford Beebe, Ray Taylor: Dick Foran, Roy Barcroft. Big-budget serial which still contrived to include footage from *Flash Gordon's Trip to Mars* (1938)

Romance of the Rio Grande (Fox) d.Herbert I Leeds: Chris Pin Martin, Ricardo Cortez, Cesar Romero. Suave Cesar is the Cisco Kid in routine yarn of land-grabbing skullduggery

ROMANCE

The Great Lie (Warner) d.Edmund Goulding: Mary Astor, George Brent, Bette Davis. Self-sacrificing Bette brings up Astor's child by lost explorer Brent as her own. Astor won Oscar as bitchy pianist

That Hamilton Woman (UA) d.Alexander Korda: Vivien Leigh, Laurence Olivier. Leigh and Olivier look exquisite in plush historical romance upholstered with piles of wartime patriotic uplift

Come Live With Me (MGM) d.Clarence Brown: Adeline De Walt Reynolds, James Stewart, Hedy Lamarr. Delicious romantic comedy with hard-up Stewart marrying Hedy to save her from deportation

Hold Back the Dawn (Paramount) d.Mitchell Leisen: Charles Boyer, Olivia de Havilland. This time it's gigolo Boyer who marries spinsterish Olivia to obtain US visa

Kathleen (MGM) d.Harold S Bucquet: Laraine Day, Shirley Temple, Herbert Marshall. Poor little rich girl Temple finds new wife for widower father. Her only film for MGM

Woman of the Year (MGM) d.George Cukor: Spencer Tracy, Katharine Hepburn. Joyous first T & H teaming. He's a grizzled sports writer. She's a political columnist. Here they are at her first baseball game

H M Pulham Esq (MGM) d.King Vidor: Robert Young, Hedy Lamarr. Young in title role as stuffy Boston blueblood meeting old flame Lamarr 20 years after they parted. Hedy's aged well

When Ladies Meet (MGM) d.Robert Z Leonard: Robert Taylor, Joan Crawford. Crawford's rivalry with rising co-star Greer Garson spices up remake of 1933 Ann Harding-Myrna Loy vehicle

Smilin' Through (MGM) d.Frank Borzage: Brian Aherne, Jeanette MacDonald. Jeanette follows Norma Talmadge and Norma Shearer in sob-sodden tale of orphan who marries son of a murderer

Blossoms in the Dust (MGM) d.Mervyn Le Roy: Greer Garson. Tastefully mounted tearjerker with Garson founding an orphanage after losing her child. First film with Walter Pidgeon

Lydia (UA) d.Julien Duvivier: Merle Oberon, Edna May Oliver, Joseph Cotten. Flashback tale of Oberon recalling her life and loves. Adapted from Duvivier's *Carnet de Bal* (1937)

One Foot in Heaven (Warner) d.Irving Rapper: Fredric March, Martha Scott. Well-observed biographical drama of turn of the century minister (March) coming to terms with changing face of America

The Men in Her Life (Columbia) d.Gregory Ratoff: Conrad Veidt, Loretta Young. If you can believe Loretta as ballerina then you'll believe anything

A Yank in the RAF (Fox) d.Henry King: Betty Grable, Tyrone Power. Cocky Power joins RAF to impress chanteuse Grable. Songs from Betty and plenty of action

Rage in Heaven (MGM) d.W S Van Dyke: Robert Montgomery, Ingrid Bergman, George Sanders. Rare romantic outing for Sanders as unhinged Montgomery plans to dispose of him and wife Bergman

They Met in Bombay (MGM) d.Clarence Brown: Clark Gable, Rosalind Russell, Peter Lorre. Jewel thieves Gable and Russell join forces in romantic adventure. Lorre droll as money-grubbing sea captain

Appointment for Love (Universal) d.William Seiter: Charles Boyer, Margaret Sullavan. Boyer and Sullavan find their respective careers take the fun out of marriage in bubbling comedy showcase

You Belong to Me (Columbia) d.Wesley Ruggles: Henry Fonda, Barbara Stanwyck, Gordon Jones. Doctor Stanwyck's male patients arouse playboy husband Fonda's suspicions in brisk comedy

MUSICALS

Birth of the Blues (Paramount) d.Victor Schertzinger: Mary Martin, Bing Crosby. One of Bing's favourite roles as the New Orleans jazzman setting the Vieux Carré alight. Schertzinger's last film

Babes on Broadway (MGM) d.Busby Berkeley: Mickey Rooney, Judy Garland. Unstoppable Rooney and Garland run the gamut from minstrel numbers to Mickey's wicked impersonation of Carmen Miranda

Blues in the Night (Warner) d.Anatole Litvak: Richard Whorf (l), Mabel Todd. Excellent Robert Rossen screenplay in tale of itinerant jazz band. Elia Kazan appears as clarinettist

Hit Parade of 1941 (Republic) d.John H Auer: Ann Miller. Struggling radio station provides background for modest mixture of music and romance

Dance Hall (Fox) d.Irving Pichel: Carole Landis, Cesar Romero. A comedy romance with some pleasant songs from Landis, including 'There's a Lull in My Life'

That Night in Rio (Fox) d.Irving Cummings: Carmen Miranda, Don Ameche. Carmen sings 'I Yi Yi Yi Yi Yi (I Like You Very Much)' in gaudy remake of *Folies Bergère* (1935)

Buck Privates (Universal) d.Arthur Lubin: The Andrews Sisters. The $190,000 army life programmer which shot Abbott and Costello to stardom. Sisters sing 'Boogie Woogie Bugle Boy from Company B'

The Chocolate Soldier (MGM) d.Roy Del Ruth: Nelson Eddy, Rise Stevens, Dorothy Gilmore. Remake of the Lunts' *The Guardsman* (1931) casts Eddy opposite opera star Stevens. He melts

Ice Capades (Republic) d.Joseph Santley: Phil Silvers, James Ellison, Dorothy Lewis. Backstage ice-skating yarn introduced Vera Hruba Ralston, soon to marry the boss and become the queen of the Republic lot

Kiss the Boys Goodbye (Paramount) d.Victor Schertzinger: Jerome Cowan, Don Ameche, Mary Martin, Virginia Dale. Clare Booth's satire on Hollywood watered down to conventional backstage musical fare

Lady Be Good (MGM) d.Norman Z McLeod: Robert Young, Ann Sothern, John Carroll, Red Skelton, Eleanor Powell. Tale of songwriters Sothern and Young. 'Fascinating Rhythm' finale

Sunny (RKO) d.Herbert Wilcox: Anna Neagle. Highlights are Kern-Hammerstein score and circus performer Neagle's eccentric dance with Ray Bolger

Ziegfeld Girl (MGM) d.Robert Z Leonard: Hedy Lamarr, Judy Garland, Lana Turner. Stunning if ever so slightly camp costumes prompt Tony Martin to croon 'You Stepped Out of a Dream' to the divine Hedy

Let's Make Music (RKO) d.Leslie Goodwins: Elisabeth Risdon, Jean Rogers. Lively programmer in which Bob Crosby turns spinster Risdon's song into hit. Includes 'Big Noise from Winnetka'

You'll Never Get Rich (Columbia) d.Sidney Lanfield: Rita Hayworth, Fred Astaire. Scored by Cole Porter, Fred and Rita's first film never quite gels despite Rita's dancing in 'So Near And Yet So Far'

Sun Valley Serenade (Fox) d.H Bruce Humberstone: Sonja Henie, John Payne. Skating spectacular with breathtaking finale performed on black ice. Support from The Glenn Miller Orchestra, Joan Davis

Moon Over Miami (Fox) d.Walter Lang: Betty Grable and the Condos Brothers. Heiress Grable hits the millionaire's playground in expansive, confident remake of *Three Blind Mice* (1938)

Second Chorus (Paramount) d.H C Potter: Fred Astaire, Paulette Goddard. Fred plays an aspiring trumpeter (dubbed by Buddy Hackett) but Paulette just can't dance. A rare Astaire failure

Time Out for Rhythm (Columbia) d.Sidney Salkow: The Three Stooges. One big yawn despite endless procession of speciality acts. Even Ann Miller and Rudy Vallee go down with the ship

Weekend in Havana (Fox) d.Walter Lang: Carmen Miranda. Carmen steals the show again in knockout finale 'The Nango' staged by Hermes Pan. Alice Faye, John Payne bring up the rear

Dumbo (RKO) d.Ben Sharpsteen. Disney fantasy about a circus elephant which can fly. The celebrated Pink Elephant sequence is a classic of the animator's art

AMERICANA

They Died With Their Boots On (Warner) d.Raoul Walsh: Errol Flynn. Historically romanticized biopic with intriguing portrait of flamboyant, insecure General Custer by Flynn

Sergeant York (Warner) d.Howard Hawks: Gary Cooper. Biopic of America's most famous World War I hero, a pacifist farm boy ultimately rewarded for killing

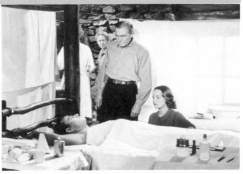

The Shepherd of the Hills (Paramount) d.Henry Hathaway: John Wayne, Harry Carey, Betty Field. Mountain man Wayne is victim of bitter Ozark blood feud

Citizen Kane (RKO) d. Orson Welles: Orson Welles. Flawed masterpiece in which Welles built the cinematic lumber room in which he has been searching for his own 'Rosebud' ever since

The Strawberry Blonde (Warner) d. Raoul Walsh: Rita Hayworth, Olivia de Havilland, James Cagney, Jack Carson. Dentist Cagney falls for gold-digger Hayworth in remake of *One Sunday Afternoon* (1933)

Cheers for Miss Bishop (UA) d. Tay Garnett: Donald Douglas, Martha Scott. Touching account of teacher Scott's life in a small Midwestern town

Meet John Doe (Warner) d. Frank Capra: Barbara Stanwyck, Rod La Rocque, Gary Cooper. Idealist Cooper becomes front for corrupt political campaign. Sentimental anti-fascist tract

Tobacco Road (Fox) d. John Ford: Charley Grapewin. Cleaned-up version of Erskine Childers' tale of poor whites in the South. Leans too heavily on comedy rather than crudeness and ignorance of characters

All That Money Can Buy (RKO) d. William Dieterle: Walter Huston, James Craig. Edward Arnold's Daniel Webster fights for James Craig's soul with Huston's diabolic Mr Scratch. Exquisitely photographed

Little Men (Play's the Thing) d. Norman Z McCleod: George Bancroft, Jack Oakie, Jimmy Lydon. Tale of orphan and three amiable swindlers in free adaptation of Louisa M Alcott novel

HORROR

The Wolf Man (Universal) d. George Waggner: Lon Chaney, Jr. Evelyn Ankers. Chaney gets the big bite from Bela Lugosi and is transformed from man to werewolf

Dr Jekyll and Mr Hyde (MGM) d. Victor Fleming: Ingrid Bergman, Spencer Tracy. Bergman miscast but Tracy revealingly menacing in lush remake of Stevenson classic

Man-Made Monster (Universal) d.George Waggner: Lon Chaney, Jr. Lionel Atwill. Sideshow attraction Chaney turned into high-voltage electrical monster by crazed scientist Atwill

The Devil Commands (Columbia) d.Edward Dmytryk: Richard Fiske, Boris Karloff. Boris' attempts to communicate with dead wife from private power station have distressing consequences

The Monster and the Girl (Paramount) d.Stuart Heisler: Ellen Drew. An ape is given condemned man Philip Terry's brain by George 'they call me a scientist' Zucco. Understandably, it runs amok

The Black Cat (Universal) d.Albert Rogell: Anne Gwynne. Comedy vies with horror in variation on Old Dark House theme – look out for Alan Ladd in small role

The Smiling Ghost (Warner) d.Lewis Seiler: Brenda Marshall, David Bruce, Wayne Morris. 'Old Dark House' thriller. Morris unravels mystery surrounding high accident rate of Alexis Smith's fiancés

B MOVIES

Among the Living (Paramount) d.Stuart Heisler: Albert Dekker, Susan Hayward. Suspenseful thriller with Dekker in dual role as murdering psychopath and twin who gets blamed

Face Behind the Mask (Columbia) d.Robert Florey: Peter Lorre, Evelyn Keyes. Powerful vehicle for Lorre as disfigured mobster hiding behind contoured rubber mask

Passport to Alcatraz (Columbia) d.Lewis D Collins: Robert Fiske, Jack Holt, Noah Beery, Jr. Iron-jawed, all-purpose action-man Holt in routine bottom-of-the bill thriller

Lady Scarface (RKO) d.Frank Woodruff: Judith Anderson. Livid scar turns Anderson into female version of Edward G. Robinson in reworking of *Wanted! Jane Turner* (1936)

Tight Shoes (Universal) d.Albert Rogell: Ed Gargan, Binnie Barnes, Broderick Crawford, Shemp Howard. Shoes of the title lead to myriad complications in sprightly Damon Runyon adaptation

Mr Dynamite (Universal) d.John Rawlins: Irene Hervey, Lloyd Nolan, Robert Armstrong. Nolan and Hervey unmask Nazi spy ring in 'Professor' J Carrol Naish's sideshow

Nine Lives Are Not Enough (Warner) d.Edward Sutherland: Howard da Silva, Ronald Reagan. Hot-shot newshound Ronnie tracks down murderer in compendium of B-thriller clichés

Washington Melodrama (MGM) d.S Sylvan Simon: Kent Taylor, Dan Dailey, Ann Rutherford. Politics, blackmail, murder and an odd water ballet seemingly lost from another movie

The Officer and the Lady (Columbia) d.Sam White: Roger Pryor, Bruce Bennett, Rochelle Hudson. Snappy cop melodrama with Bennett foiling a jewel heist, marrying schoolteacher Hudson

Mystery Ship (Columbia) d.Lew Landers: Larry Parks, Lola Lane, Dick Curtis. G-Man foils deported aliens' bid to capture ship and rendezvous with U-boat

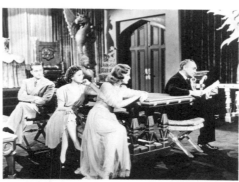

Whistling in the Dark (MGM) d.S Sylvan Simon: Red Skelton, Ann Rutherford, Virginia Grey, Conrad Veidt. Comedy thriller with Veidt trying to force crime writer Skelton to plan 'perfect murder'

Forced Landing (Paramount) d.Gordon Wiles: Eva Gabor, J Carrol Naish. Aerial espionage thriller set in mythical foreign country stays firmly on the ground

City of Chance (Fox) d.Ricardo Cortez: Lynn Bari, Donald Woods. Bari follows gambling addict boyfriend Woods to New York, saves him from life of crime

Man Who Wouldn't Talk (Fox) d.David Burton: Lloyd Nolan, Jean Rogers, Richard Clarke. Nolan clams up on murder rap in remake of early Paul Muni talkie *The Valiant* (1929)

Mutiny in the Arctic (Universal) d.John Rawlins: Richard Arlen (l). Arlen and Andy Devine go drilling for radium and run into trouble in the frozen backlot wastes

Knockout (Warner) d. William Clemens: Cliff Edwards, Arthur Kennedy, Tom Garland, Anthony Quinn. Snappy treatment of old tale of cocksure fighter riding for a fall

The Phantom Submarine (Columbia) d. Charles Barton: Anita Louise, Bruce Bennett, Oscar O'Shea. Bennett's after the gold in a sunken steamship but discovers a minefield laid by enemy agents

The Cowboy and the Blonde (Fox) d. Ray McCarey: Mary Beth Hughes, Minerva Urecal, George Montgomery. Cowboy star Montgomery tames shrewish actress Hughes in B satire on Hollywood

Steel Against the Sky (Warner) d. Edward Sutherland: Lloyd Nolan, Craig Stevens, Alexis Smith. Bridge-building brothers Stevens, Nolan, fall out over boss' daughter Smith

The Pittsburgh Kid (Republic) d. Jack Townley: Billy Conn. Real-life fighter Conn is managed by Jean Parker in entertaining boxing drama

All-American Co-Ed (UA) d. Le Roy Prinz: Frances Langford, Johnny Downs. Campus programmer in which Downs dons fetching drag outfit for rival college's beauty contest. Hm

Emergency Landing (PRC) d. William Beaudine: Forrest Tucker, Emmett Vogan. Youthful Tucker after enemy aircraft saboteurs; smouldering silent star Evelyn Brent billed third

Sis Hopkins (Republic) d. Joseph Santley: Susan Hayward, Mary Ainslee. Judy Canova moves in with snobbish cousin Hayward in remake of old Mabel Normand hit. Biggish budget but B-movie patina

The Body Disappears (Warner) d. D Ross Lederman: Willie Best, Edward Everett Horton, Jeffrey Lynn. Horton's experimental life-preserving serum renders hapless Lynn invisible. Zany comedy

Six Lessons from Madame La Zonga
(Universal) d.John Rawlins: Lupe Velez.
Lupe queens it over Cuban niterie but film
fails to live up to exotic delights promised
by the title

World Premiere (Paramount) d.Ted
Tetzlaff: Ricardo Cortez, Frances Farmer
(r). Farmer stars with fuddled John
Barrymore in chaotic tale of spies in
Hollywood

A Night at Earl Carroll's (Paramount)
d.Kurt Neumann: Rose Hobart. Gangster
kidnaps Carroll's principal performers, but
a cigarette girl saves the day

Harvard Here I Come (Columbia) d.Lew
Landers: Yvonne De Carlo, Maxie
Rosenbloom, Byron Foulger. College
professor pronounces Maxie America's No
1 Moron. Film equally moronic

Rookies on Parade (Republic) d.Joseph
Santley: Marie Wilson, Eddie Foy, Jr. Drafted
gambling show producer Bob Crosby puts
on a camp show and is reunited with
an old flame

Playmates (RKO) d.David Butler: Lupe·
Velez, Patsy Kelly, John Barrymore.
Barrymore gives Kay Kyser a crash course
in Shakespeare, Lupe is lady bullfighter in
truly awful musical

Four Jacks and a Jill (RKO) d.Jack Hively:
Anne Shirley, Ray Bolger. Ray's dancing lifts
slim tale of struggling singer Shirley trying
to get ahead by posing as European
intimate of royalty

Sweetheart of the Campus (Columbia)
d.Edward Dmytryk: Ruby Keeler, Ozzie
Nelson. Ruby's return after three-year
absence. She should have stayed away. She
did after this

Curtain Call (RKO) d.Frank Woodruff:
Alan Mowbray, Barbara Read. Mowbray
and Donald MacBride are conniving
theatrical agents in brisk Dalton Trumbo-
scripted comedy

Puddin' Head (Republic) d.Joseph
Santley: Judy Canova. Hayseed Judy's New
York farm is the apple of crooked
developers' eye

The Saint in Palm Springs (RKO) d.Jack
Hively: Paul Guilfoyle, George Sanders,
Wendy Barrie, Jack Arnold. Barrie is heir to
stamp fortune – then murder strikes

Tillie the Toiler (Columbia) d.Sidney
Salkow: Marjorie Reynolds, Kay Harris,
William Tracy. Failed attempt to turn Russ
Westover's comic-strip heroine (Harris)
into series queen

Mr Celebrity (PRC) d.William Beaudine:
James Seay (c). Sentimental horse racing
tale also features old-timers Clara Kimball
Young, Jim Jeffries and silent matinée idol
Francis X Bushman

On the Sunny Side (Fox) d.Harold
Schuster: Freddie Mercer, Ann Todd, Roddy
McDowall. Posh little Brit Roddy is shipped
across the Atlantic to escape the
London Blitz

Adventures of Captain Marvel
(Republic) d. John English, William Witney:
Tom Tyler. Handsome serial as Western
star Tyler dons cape to battle the sinister
Scorpion. Shazam!

Meet Boston Blackie (Columbia)
d.Robert Florey: Rochelle Hudson, Chester
Morris. Morris is the jaunty jewel thief
turned sleuth in first of zippy series of
thirteen

Henry Aldrich for President
(Paramount) d.Hugh Bennett: Charles
Smith, Jimmy Lydon, Mary Anderson.
Gormless Lydon in title role as studio's
answer to Andy Hardy series. First of nine

Jungle Girl (Republic) d. John English,
William Witney: Trevor Bardette, Frances
Gifford, Tom Neal. Gifford as Nyoka foils
villains in race for cache of diamonds.
Classic serial

BRITISH & FOREIGN

The 49th Parallel (Ortus) d.Michael Powell: Leslie Howard, Eric Portman. Ruthless U-boat officer Portman flees across Canada, Howard wimpish anthropologist he meets on the way

Major Barbara (GFD) d. Gabriel Pascal: Wendy Hiller, Rex Harrison. Hiller outstanding as the spirited Salvation Army heroine in faithful adaptation of George Bernard Shaw's play

Cottage to Let (Gainsborough) d.Anthony Asquith: George Cole, Muriel Aked, Jeanne de Cassalis. Junior sleuth Cole helps Alastair Sim to trap a German agent (John Mills) posing as an RAF officer

The Big Blockade (Ealing) d.Charles Frend: Robert Morley. Curious blend of fiction and documentary aimed at explaining Britain's wartime fight for economic survival

Target for Tonight (MoI) d.Harry Watt. Exemplary, influential documentary following the fortunes of a single RAF bomber 'F for Freddie'. Early attempt to show Britain hitting back

Love on the Dole (British National) d.John Baxter: Mary Merrall, Geoffrey Hibbert, Deborah Kerr. Clumsy but affecting tale of northern working-class girl Kerr set in Depression

The Prime Minister (Warner) d.Thorold Dickinson: Fay Compton, John Gielgud. Thudding historical drama following the progress of politician Benjamin Disraeli through 50 years of his life

Ships with Wings (Ealing) d.Sergei Nolbandov: Michael Rennie, John Clements. Excruciating Boy's Own tale of disgraced pilot Clements redeeming himself with kamikaze attack on vital dam

Hatter's Castle (Paramount) d.Lance Comfort: Robert Newton. Tyrannical tradesman Newton loses his mind after his assistant seduces his daughter and his wife dies of cancer. Understandable, perhaps

Dangerous Moonlight (RKO) d.Brian Desmond Hurst: Sally Gray, Anton Walbrook. Romance between journalist Gray and Polish airman Walbrook. Tosh but it gets to you

The Black Sheep of Whitehall (Ealing)
d.Will Hay, Basil Dearden: John Mills, Will
Hay. Incompetent pedagogue Hay,
mistaken for economics expert, is
embroiled in spy plot

Pimpernel Smith (British National)
d.Leslie Howard: Raymond Huntley,
Francis L Sullivan, Mary Morris. Bumbling
don Howard is also a master spy.
Performance of ironic charm from Howard

Ohm Kruger (Germany) d.Hans Steinhoff.
Goebbels-scripted account of the Boer
War. Churchill portrayed as gluttonous
concentration camp commandant

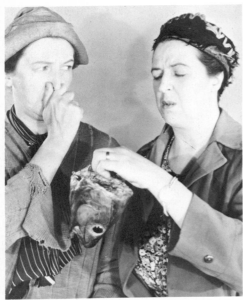

Gert and Daisy's Weekend (Butcher)
d.Maclean Rogers: Elsie and Doris Waters.
Comic Cockney sisters are placed in charge
of evacuees, then framed for the theft of a
society lady's jewels

Quiet Wedding (Paramount) d.Anthony
Asquith: Margaret Lockwood, Derek Farr.
Accomplished comedy in which family
complications almost upset a young
couple's wedding plans

Bismarck (Germany) d.Wolfgang
Liebeneiner: Paul Hartmann. Propaganda
account of the statesman's defeat of Austria
and France and proclamation of Wilhelm of
Prussia as Kaiser

Stukas (Germany) d.Karl Ritter. Wartime
aerial drama centering on the celebrated
gull-winged dive bombers and the men
who fly them

The Ghost of St Michael's (Ealing)
d.Marcel Varnel: Charles Hawtrey, Will Hay.
Hay's seedy schoolmaster teaches for
victory in a 'haunted' Scottish castle,
uncovers Nazi spy ring

Carl Peters (Germany) d.Herbert Selpin.
Hans Albers stars in a wildly inaccurate
biopic of 19th-century colonial who
grabbed large chunks of Africa for Germany

Corona di Ferro (Italy) d.Alessandro
Blasetti: Massimo Girotti. Big-budget
historical fantasy mobilizing over 7000
horses and, apparently, an entire zoo.
Crazy but watchable

1942

Hollywood's all-out war effort was approaching top gear, accompanied by record profit levels. Paramount topped the list at $13 million; MGM-Loew recorded profits of $12 million; close behind were Fox on $10.5 million and Warner on $8.5 million. Bringing up the rear were Universal and Columbia, with profits of $3 million and $1.5 million respectively. Nowadays the combined total might stretch to financing a single space opera.

The Academy Awards were dominated by *Mrs Miniver*, William Wyler's artfully glossy fantasy of wartime England. It was named Best Film and won Awards for Wyler, scriptwriters Arthur Wimperis and James Hilton (among others), photographer Joe Ruttenberg, Teresa Wright (Best Supporting Actress) and Greer Garson (Best Actress). James Cagney won the Best Actor Award for his ferociously animated impersonation of George M Cohan in *Yankee Doodle Dandy*, directed by Michael Curtiz. The Best Supporting Actor Award went to Van Heflin for his performance as the pathetic, drunken hanger-on in *Johnny Eager* (1941).

Holiday Inn bequeathed us 'White Christmas'. Among the new faces on the screen were Esther Williams, Ava Gardner, Gloria Grahame, Farley Granger, John Hodiak and Virginia Mayo. A new screen partnership was formed in *This Gun for Hire*, which shot Alan Ladd and Veronica Lake to the front rank of stars.

Wake Island was a sober attempt to come to grips with the reality of war, but romance and escapism had their part to play. Tyrone Power and Joan Fontaine tugged at the heart strings in *This Above All*. Bogart and Bergman loved and left each other in *Casablanca*. Ronald Colman lost his memory and contrived to marry Greer Garson twice in *Random Harvest*, the archetypal 'women's picture' of the 1940s. Rosalind Russell wowed them in the aisles in the breezy comedy *My Sister Eileen*. Ginger Rogers gave one of her best performances in William Wellman's *Roxie Hart*, as the gloriously brazen chorus girl going on trial for murder as a publicity stunt.

Stars were kept busy making personal appearances across America selling war bonds, and it was on one of these tours that Carole Lombard, nonpareil of screen comediennes, was killed in a 'plane crash. Her husband Clark Gable was never quite the same man again. Other deaths included showman supreme George M Cohan, cowboy star Buck Jones, and John Barrymore, now a drunken, swollen-faced shadow of the Great Profile of the 1920s. Shortly before his death he was glimpsed in a radio studio by Mary Astor, who had starred with him at his peak in *Beau Brummel* (1924). She recalled that Barrymore was alone, sagging against a wall like a man 'who just couldn't walk another step.'

In Britain the war had breathed new life into an industry which had been in deep crisis only two years before. Output was down, as a number of studios were turned over to war use, but quality was up. The most impressive British film of the year was Noel Coward's *In Which We Serve*, which won the New York Critics' Award and was given a special Academy Award. Eschewing the 'Boys Own' heroics of a number of British features of the early war years, *In Which We Serve* gave equal emphasis to the roles played by both officers and men. At the centre of the film was Coward's meticulously observed portrayal of the captain of the doomed destroyer *Torrin*. Coward wrote and produced the film and collaborated on direction with David Lean. Other British films of note included Thorold Dickinson's *Next of Kin*, a stark warning against the dangers of wartime complacency, and *The Foreman Went to France*, directed by Charles Frend, which reflected the feeling in Britain that the struggle against the Axis was a 'People's War'.

ACTION

Joe Smith, American (MGM) d.Richard Thorpe: Robert Young. Successful Dore Schary quickie in which kidnapped munitions worker Young refuses to give secrets to the Nazis

Wake Island (Paramount) d.John Farrow: Brian Donlevy, Walter Abel. Stirring semi-documentary actioner and an early attempt by Hollywood to deal seriously with the war

To the Shores of Tripoli (Fox) d.H Bruce Humberstone: John Payne, Maureen O'Hara, Randolph Scott. Cocky John Payne runs up against veteran sergeant Scott in flag-waving tribute to Marine Corps

The Commandos Strike at Dawn (Columbia) d.John Farrow: Paul Muni (l), Lillian Gish (c). Muni leads raid on German airfield in Norway in syrupy Resistance drama

Stand By for Action (MGM) d.Robert Z Leonard: Robert Taylor, Charles Laughton. Taylor's destroyer rescues boatload of mothers and children in dull Atlantic convoy drama

Wings for the Eagle (Warner) d.Lloyd Bacon: Dennis Morgan, Ann Sheridan, Jack Carson. Hardware overshadows humans in well-crafted tale of aircraft workers. Sheridan usual wise-cracking self

Nazi Agent (MGM) d.Jules Dassin: Conrad Veidt. Freedom-loving Veidt takes place of beastly Nazi twin brother to break up spy ring

Thunder Birds (Fox) d.William Wellman: John Sutton, Preston Foster. RAF man Sutton tangles with hard-bitten instructor Foster over Gene Tierney in plodding air training drama

Saboteur (Universal) d.Alfred Hitchcock: Robert Cummings, Priscilla Lane. Quintessential Hitchcock chase . Cummings framed for wartime sabotage. Nail-biting climax atop the Statue of Liberty

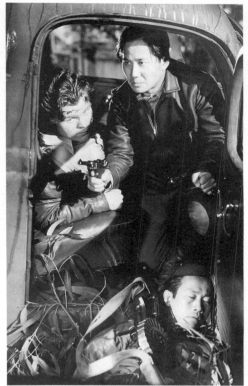

A Yank on the Burma Road (MGM)
d. George B Seitz: Barry Nelson, Keye Luke.
Nelson leads a caravan of medical supplies
to China in first Hollywood film to take
account of US entry into the war

Somewhere I'll Find You (MGM)
d. Wesley Ruggles: Lana Turner, Clark
Gable, Eleanor Sookoo. Gable and Turner
are war correspondents in Clark's last
movie before joining US Air Corps

This Gun for Hire (Paramount) d. Frank
Tuttle: Alan Ladd, Veronica Lake. Overnight
stardom for Ladd as Graham Greene's
glacial gunman Raven, waylaid by Veronica
Lake's miniature embrace

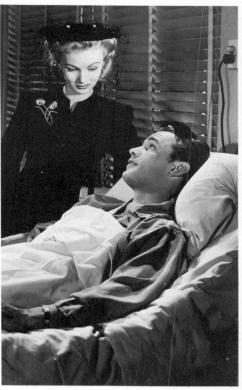

The Glass Key (Paramount) d. Stuart
Heisler: Veronica Lake, Alan Ladd. Lake
and Ladd paired in pacy version of
Hammett novel. Ladd memorably beaten
up by William Bendix

Across the Pacific (Warner) d. John
Huston: Humphrey Bogart, Mary Astor,
Sydney Greenstreet. Bogie foils a Japanese
attempt to block the Panama canal. Their
agent Greenstreet contemplates hara kiri

Eagle Squadron (Universal) d. Arthur
Lubin: Robert Stack, Diana Barrymore.
Babyface Stack is Yank in the RAF,
hijacking Nazi mystery plane in France

Desperate Journey (Warner) d. Raoul
Walsh: Arthur Kennedy, Errol Flynn, Ronald
Reagan. Downed American airmen cross
occupied Europe. Fun, but large pinch of
salt required

Flying Tigers (Republic) d. David Miller:
John Wayne. Big John is leader of famous
air group in China, John Carroll is
troublesome subordinate who makes the
supreme sacrifice

Berlin Correspondent (Fox) d. Eugene
Forde: Martin Kosleck, Dana Andrews,
Virginia Gilmore. American broadcaster
Andrews doubles as spy in Berlin prior to
Pearl Harbor

Underground (Warner) d. Vincent
Sherman: Philip Dorn, Frank Reicher. Dorn
is selfless Resistance leader, Jeffrey Lynn
the brother who betrays him to Nazis in
heavy-going melodrama

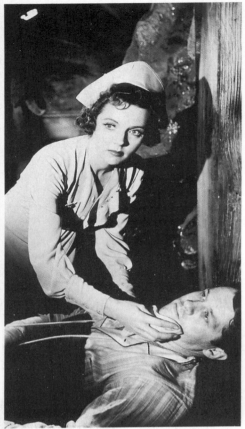

Army Surgeon (RKO) d.Edward Sutherland: Jane Wyatt. Feeble tub-thumper for Army Medical Corps with James Ellison and Kent Taylor vying for Wyatt's affections

Flying Fortress (Warner) d.Walter Forde: Richard Greene, Donald Stewart, Betty Stockfield. Canadian playboy Greene joins the RAF, knuckles down, becomes hero. Filmed in England

China Girl (Fox) d.Henry Hathaway: Gene Tierney. Eurasian girl Tierney helps newsman George Montgomery escape the clutches of the Japanese to deliver vital military secrets

The Pied Piper (Fox) d.Irving Pichel: Roddy McDowall, Monty Woolley. Elderly Englishman Woolley spirits group of children from occupied France. Otto Preminger splendid as his Nazi adversary

All Through the Night (Warner) d.Vincent Sherman: Karen Verne, Humphrey Bogart. Racketeer Bogart tracks down Nazi saboteurs planning to blow up a battleship in well-paced comedy-thriller

Nightmare (Universal) d.Tim Whelan: Diana Barrymore, Brian Donlevy. Down-on-his-luck gambler Donlevy tangles with Nazi spies, comes out on top

Lucky Jordan (Paramount) d.Frank Tuttle: Helen Walker, Alan Ladd, Sheldon Leonard, Miles Mander. Gangster Ladd is drafted, catches spies. Uneasy blend of romance, comedy, thriller

Joan of Paris (RKO) d.Robert Stevenson: Michele Morgan. Paul Henreid and Morgan make Hollywood debut in Resistance drama. Watch out for Alan Ladd in role as British airman

Sunday Punch (MGM) d.George Sidney: Dan Dailey, Jean Rogers, Guy Kibbee. Rogers finds herself in a boarding house full of boxers in entertaining programmer

Broadway (Universal) d. William Seiter: George Raft. Energetic remake of the studio's 1929 hit with Raft playing himself and recalling days as nightclub hoofer in the Roaring '20s

The Big Shot (Warner) d. Lewis Seiler: Chic Chandler, Humphrey Bogart. Bogie is three-time loser arrested for crime he did not commit. Like a collection of out-takes from '30s gangster cycle

Captains of the Clouds (Warner) d. Michael Curtiz: Alan Hale, Dennis Morgan, James Cagney. In his first Technicolor film, Cagney joins the Royal Canadian Air Force for a lark and becomes a hero

ADVENTURE

Gentleman Jim (Warner) d. Raoul Walsh: Errol Flynn. Perfect vehicle for Flynn as boxer James J Corbett. Ward Bond is John L Sullivan. One of the few films in which Flynn is really trying

Pittsburgh (Universal) d. Lewis Seiler: John Wayne, Marlene Dietrich, Randolph Scott. Scene set for customary Wayne-Scott brawl over Dietrich. Scott gets her this time

Reap the Wild Wind (Paramount) d. Cecil B De Mille: John Wayne. Rollicking yarn of 19th century wreckers. Real star is huge octopus which disposes of Wayne, unusually cast as a bad guy

Son of Fury (Fox) d. John Cromwell: Tyrone Power, Frances Farmer. Power is illegitimate son of nobleman sailing the seven seas and returning to claim his rightful inheritance in sprawling adventure

Arabian Nights (Universal) d. John Rawlins: Jon Hall, Maria Montez, Edgar Barrier, Leif Erickson. Kitsch goings-on in the desert in studio's first 3-colour Technicolor production

Beyond the Blue Horizon (Paramount) d. Alfred Santell: Richard Denning, Helen Gilbert, Dorothy Lamour, Jack Haley. Expedition sets out to prove jungle girl Lamour is lost heiress

Jungle Book (UA) d.Zoltan Korda: Sabu. Kipling tale of boy raised by wolves, directed with great brio by Korda, an expert practitioner of the cinema of Empire. Fine Miklos Rozsa score

Tarzan's New York Adventure (MGM) d.Richard Thorpe: Johnny Weissmuller. Tarzan is crammed into a business suit for visit to concrete jungle in search of kidnapped son

White Cargo (MGM) d.Richard Thorpe: Walter Pidgeon, Hedy Lamarr. Hedy is sultry Tondelayo, slinking around the plantation in her 'lurong', driving white men wild with desire

Tortilla Flat (MGM) d.Victor Fleming: John Qualen, Tim Holt, Spencer Tracy, John Garfield, Akim Tamiroff. Affectionate treatment of Steinbeck's novel of Monterey paisanos

The Black Swan (Fox) d.Henry King: Laird Cregar, Tyrone Power. Pirate king Power sails the Spanish Main in search of booty and Maureen O'Hara. Sterling support from Cregar, George Sanders

MELODRAMA

Mrs Miniver (MGM) d.William Wyler: Helmut Dantine, Greer Garson. Glossy Hollywood fantasy of life in wartime England. Absurd but affecting and 1942's most popular film – 7 Oscars including Best Actress

In This Our Life (Warner) d.John Huston: Bette Davis, Olivia de Havilland. Murky tale in which Bette ruins sister Olivia's life and her own. Watch out for bevy of stars in bar-room scene

The Gay Sisters (Warner) d.Irving Rapper: Nancy Coleman, Geraldine Fitzgerald, Barbara Stanwyck. Stanwyck marries George Brent for money. Byron Barr took the name of character he played – Gig Young

Moontide (Fox) d.Archie Mayo: Chester Gan, Jean Gabin, Ida Lupino. Gabin's warm masculinity in Hollywood debut lifts this gloomy tale of waterfront skullduggery

Crossroads (MGM) d.Jack Conway: Claire Trevor, William Powell, Hedy Lamarr, Basil Rathbone. Amnesiac Powell is innocent victim of cunning blackmail plot hatched by Rathbone. Set in pre-war Paris

The Vanishing Virginian (MGM) d.Frank · Borzage: Natalie Thompson, Spring Byington, Kathryn Grayson. Drama, comedy, romance mingle in well-observed tale of Southern family from 1913 to 1929

The Mystery of Marie Roget (Universal) d.Phil Rosen: Nell O'Day, Maria Montez, Edward Norris: Montez plans to murder sister O'Day but gets the chop herself in effective, low-budget Poe adaptation

The Loves of Edgar Allan Poe (Fox) d.Harry Lachman: John Shepperd, Linda Darnell. Highly romanticized account of the writer's brief, unhappy life skirts around the sordid details

Tales of Manhattan (Fox) d.Julien Duvivier: Roland Young, Marion Martin, Cesar Romero, Ginger Rogers, Henry Fonda. Portmanteau film linked by the changing ownership of a tailcoat

Keeper of the Flame (MGM) d.George Cukor: Katharine Hepburn. Reporter Spencer Tracy digs into sinister background of Hepburn's dead hero husband. Muffled anti-fascist tract

The Moon and Sixpence (UA) d.Albert Lewin: George Sanders, Elena Verdugo. Breakthrough for Sanders as Charles Strickland, the stockbroker turned artist in Maugham's pastiche of life of Gaugin

Journey for Margaret (MGM) d.W S Van Dyke: Margaret O'Brien. Heart-tugging O'Brien is the Blitz orphan adopted by Robert Young and Laraine Day. Van Dyke's last film

COMEDY

The Male Animal (Warner) d.Elliott Nugent: Henry Fonda, Olivia de Havilland, Jack Carson. Trouble for flustered academic Fonda, losing wife to old flame Carson and coming under fire from superior

The Magnificent Dope (Fox) d.Walter Lang: Henry Fonda, Lynn Bari. Super-salesman Don Ameche tries to turn helpless bumpkin Fonda into raging success. Recommended viewing for failures

To Be Or Not To Be (UA) d.Ernst Lubitsch: Jack Benny, Carole Lombard. Lombard's last film before death in plane crash. Brilliant black comedy involving theatrical troupe in wartime Poland

The Major and the Minor (Paramount)
d.Billy Wilder: Ginger Rogers. Ginger's
unconventional bid to avoid paying train
fare leads to romantic complications with
Ray Milland. Wilder's first

The Palm Beach Story (Paramount)
d.Preston Sturges: Claudette Colbert.
Claudette leaves husband Joel McCrea,
joins heiress Mary Astor and eccentric
brother Rudy Vallee, who slyly steals film

Life Begins at 8.30 (Fox) d.Irving Pichel:
Monty Woolley. Romance, comedy and
tears in tale of drunken actor Woolley and
crippled daughter Ida Lupino. Marvellous
scene with Woolley as tipsy Santa Claus

Rio Rita (MGM) d.S Sylvan Simon:
Lou Costello, Bud Abbott. A & C swamp co-
stars Kathryn Grayson and John Carroll in
glossy remake of 1929 RKO musical smash

My Favourite Blonde (Paramount)
d.Sidney Lanfield: Bob Hope, Madeleine
Carroll. Small-time vaudevillian Hope and his
performing penguin are co-opted by British
agent Carroll in flight from Nazis

Over My Dead Body (Fox) d.Malcolm St
Clair: Milton Berle. Ingenious romp with
thriller writer Berle volunteering to frame
himself for murder and then beat the rap

Larceny Inc (Warner) d.Lloyd Bacon:
Broderick Crawford, Edward G Robinson,
Jack Carson, Jane Wyman. Misfiring
gangster spoof brought Edward G
Robinson's contract with Warner to an end

Once Upon a Honeymoon (RKO) d.Leo
McCarey: Cary Grant, Ginger Rogers.
Misjudged comedy drama, set at beginning
of war, with reporter Grant rescuing Ginger
from her Nazi agent husband

Pardon My Sarong (Universal) d.Erle C
Kenton: Virginia Bruce, Lionel Atwill,
Robert Paige. Abbott and Costello on a
shark-infested desert island – Atwill one of
the sharks. Ink Spots sing 'Do I Worry?'

I Married a Witch (UA) d.René Clair: Veronica Lake, Fredric March. Reincarnated witch Lake wreaks vengeance on descendant of man who sent her to the stake (March) but falls in love with him

George Washington Slept Here (Warner) d.William Keighley: Percy Kilbride, Jack Benny, Ann Sheridan. Reluctant Benny is badgered by Sheridan into buying Pennsylvania farmhouse

My Sister Eileen (Columbia) d.Alexander Hall: Rosalind Russell, Janet Blair. Two naive sisters from Columbus, Ohio, move into a basement flat in New York's Greenwich Village

Gentleman at Heart (Fox) d.Ray McCarey: Cesar Romero, J Carrol Naish, Milton Berle, Rose Hobart. Wealthy bookie Romero acquires an art gallery and finds himself in the forgery business

Call out the Marines (RKO) d. Frank Ryan, William Hamilton: Victor McLaglen. Edmund Lowe. Knockabout attempt to revive the Flagg and Quirt characters from *What Price Glory?* (1926)

Ride 'Em Cowboy (Universal) d. Arthur Lubin: Bud Abbott, Lou Costello. A & C get work on a dude ranch. Ella Fitzgerald turns up to sing 'A Tisket A Tasket' and 'Rockin' 'n Reeling'

Roxie Hart (Fox) d.William Wellman: George Montgomery, Ginger Rogers, Adolphe Menjou. Ginger confesses to murder as publicity stunt, Menjou her shyster lawyer. Brilliant remake of *Chicago* (1928)

Seven Days Leave (RKO) d.Tim Whelan: Lucille Ball, Victor Mature. Diverting musical comedy in which Mature has a week to marry a girl he has never met (Ball) to scoop a $100,000 legacy

Road to Morocco (Paramount) d.David Butler: Bob Hope, Bing Crosby, Dorothy Lamour. Like Webster's Dictionary, the boys are Morocco-bound. Songs include 'Moonlight Becomes You'

Brooklyn Orchid (UA) d.Kurt Neumann: Joe Sawyer, Marjorie Woodworth, William Bendix. Sawyer and Bendix rescue beauty queen Woodworth from drowning. Then complications ensue in low-budget farce

A Yank at Eton (MGM) d.Norman Taurog: Mickey Rooney. Streetwise Mickey teamed with prissy Freddie Bartholomew in unashamed steal from *A Yank at Oxford* (1939)

The Tuttles of Tahiti (RKO) d.Charles Vidor: Florence Bates, Peggy Drake, Jon Hall, Charles Laughton. Amiable tale of Laughton's scapegrace family idling away their time in the South Seas

They All Kissed the Bride (Columbia) d.Alexander Hall: Roland Young, Joan Crawford, Melvyn Douglas, Ed Gargan. Crawford is hard-driving trucking magnate unfrozen by crusading journalist Douglas

The Talk of the Town (Columbia) d.George Stevens: Jean Arthur, Ronald Colman, Cary Grant. Colman is dry-as-dust law professor whose landlady (Arthur) is hiding a fugitive from justice (Grant)

Behind the Eight Ball (Universal) d.Edward F Cline: The Ritz Brothers. Chaotic musical-comedy involving murder and enemy spies in the Sunny Dunham Orchestra

WESTERNS

The Great Man's Lady (Paramount) d.William Wellman: Joel McCrea, Barbara Stanwyck. McCrea falls out with wife Stanwyck over the coming of the railroad in hand-me-down version of *Cimarron* (1931)

Bells of Capistrano (Republic) d.William Morgan: Virginia Grey, Gene Autry. Gene dealt with villain Morgan Conway and then hung up his holster for four years in the US Army

Deep in the Heart of Texas (Universal) d.Elmer Clifton. The first of seven Westerns co-starring Tex Ritter and Johnny Mack Brown. Tale of land-grabbing after the Civil War

Wild Bill Hickock Rides (Warner) d.Ray Enright: Cliff Clark, Bruce Cabot, Betty Brewer. Cabot in title role foils Ward Bond's plans to evict homesteaders. Constance Bennett is dance hall queen

The Omaha Trail (MGM) d.Edward Buzzell: James Craig, Pamela Blake, Edward Ellis. Craig helps to haul a new-fangled locomotive across the Old West, pausing to woo Blake and deal with Indians

Northwest Rangers (MGM) d.Joseph M Newman: William Lundigan. Lundigan tracks down boyhood pal in remake of 1934 Clark Gable/William Powell vehicle

The Spoilers (Universal) d.Ray Enright. Randolph Scott, Marlene Dietrich, John Wayne. Randolph Scott and John Wayne slug it out for the sultry Dietrich in rumbustious remake No. 4 of Rex Beach's novel

Shut My Big Mouth (Columbia) d.Charles Barton: Joe E Brown. Delicious Western spoof with Eastern dude Brown cleaning up town while dressed in drag for most of film

Apache Trail (MGM) d.Richard Thorpe: Ann Ayars, William Lundigan (r). Love and death come to a stagecoach station deep in the heart of Injun territory

ROMANCE

Casablanca (Warner) d.Michael Curtiz: Dooley Wilson, Humphrey Bogart, Ingrid Bergman. Time may go by, but it only serves to enhance this seamless example of the Hollywood machine at its smoothest

This Above All (Fox) d.Anatole Litvak: Tyrone Power, Joan Fontaine. Power fights the class war by deserting but WAAF Fontaine's love persuades him England's worth fighting for

Seven Sweethearts (MGM) d.Frank Borzage: Kathryn Grayson, Van Heflin, S Z 'Cuddles' Sakall. Sakall has seven lovely daughters, none of whom can marry until eldest one does

The Big Street (RKO) d.Irving Reis: Henry Fonda, Lucille Ball. Fonda is the stammering busboy who devotedly cares for vitriolic crippled singer Ball in sentimental version of Damon Runyon tale

Rings on Her Fingers (Fox) d.Rouben Mamoulian: Gene Tierney, Henry Fonda. Confidence tricksters Laird Cregar, Spring Byington and Tierney mistake the penniless Fonda for millionaire

We Were Dancing (MGM) d.Robert Z Leonard: Melvyn Douglas, Norma Shearer, Alan Mowbray. Fluffy romantic comedy has little more to do with original Coward playlet than title

Her Cardboard Lover (MGM) d.George Cukor: George Sanders, Norma Shearer, Robert Taylor. Limp comedy brought full stop to Norma's career. Not before time, some unkind souls might say

Now Voyager (Warner) d.Irving Rapper: Claude Rains, Bette Davis. Echt 'women's picture'. Dowdy spinster Davis is transformed by shrink Rains into chic recipient of Paul Henreid's lighted cigarettes

Meet the Stewarts (Columbia) d.Alfred E Green: William Holden, Tom Dugan, Ed Gargan, Frances Dee. Light-hearted domestic comedy about hard-up young newly-weds Holden and Dee

Girl Trouble (Fox) d.Harold Schuster: Don Ameche, Joan Bennett. Ameche rents apartment of society girl Bennett who pretends to be the maid

Random Harvest (MGM) d.Mervyn Le Roy: Greer Garson, Ronald Colman. Classic tearjerker in which amnesiac Colman contrives to marry Garson twice. Re-established Colman as major star

MUSICALS

My Favourite Spy (RKO) d.Tay Garnett: Kay Kyser, Jane Wyman, Robert Armstrong, Al Hill. Bandleader Kyser is chosen by Army Intelligence to infiltrate spy ring in nightclub. Proved Kyser was no comedian

Orchestra Wives (Fox) d.Archie Mayo: Lynn Bari, Cesar Romero, George Montgomery. High spot of limp musical drama comes when Glen Miller and his Orchestra play 'I've Got a Girl in Kalamazoo'

Panama Hattie (MGM) d.Norman Z McLeod: Red Skelton, Rags Ragland, Ben Blue, Ann Sothern. Cole Porter's hit falls apart in the studio's hands with Sothern in the role made famous by Ethel Merman

My Gal Sal (Fox) d. Irving Cummings: Victor Mature, Rita Hayworth. Turn-of-the century Technicolor extravaganza with Mature as Tin Pan Alley heart-throb Paul Dresser in love with fiery Broadway star Hayworth

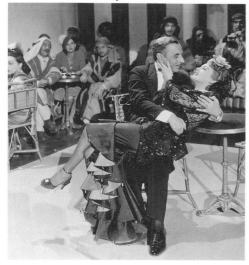

I Married an Angel (MGM) d. W S Van Dyke: Douglass Dumbrille, Jeanette MacDonald. Even Anita Loos' script failed to save MacDonald's final lacklustre outing with Nelson Eddy

Iceland (Fox) d. H Bruce Humberstone: Sonja Henie performs smoothly enough on the rink but falls flat on her face in vapid romance with Marine corporal John Payne

The Fleet's In (Paramount) d. Victor Schertzinger: William Holden, Leif Erickson, Dorothy Lamour. Brash slice of wartime escapism launched Betty Hutton, singing 'Build a Better Mousetrap'

Footlight Serenade (Fox) d. Gregory Ratoff: Betty Grable, Jane Wyman. Diverting backstage musical in which big-headed boxing champ makes a play for dancer Grable, who's married to actor John Payne

For Me and My Gal (MGM) d. Busby Berkeley: Judy Garland, Gene Kelly. Overly sentimental stroll down vaudeville's memory lane salvaged by magical rapport between Garland and Kelly in film debut

Cairo (MGM) d. W S Van Dyke: Jeanette MacDonald. Musical spoof on spy thrillers with MacDonald as opera singer turned torch singer who is suspected of being Nazi spy. A flop on all counts

Ship Ahoy (MGM) d. Edward Buzzell: Eleanor Powell. Flimsy shipboard spy comedy. Some machine-gun hoofing from Powell and sterling support of Bert Lahr, Red Skelton and Tommy Dorsey

Song of the Islands (Fox) d. Walter Lang: Betty Grable, Thomas Mitchell, Jack Oakie, George Barbier. Slim tale of plantation folk in the Pacific provides excuse to show off Grable's legs and Victor Mature's chest

Yankee Doodle Dandy (Warner) d. Michael Curtiz: Jeanne Cagney, James Cagney, Joan Leslie, Walter Huston. Cagney won Oscar for frenetic performance as showman George M Cohan in patriotic biopic

Springtime in the Rockies (Fox) d.Irving Cummings: Cesar Romero, Betty Grable. Shimmering Technicolor divertissement with Harry James and his band playing 'I Had the Craziest Dream'

Syncopation (RKO) d.William Dieterle: Bonita Granville, Todd Duncan. Granville and Jackie Cooper have two things in common – love of jazz and Walt Whitman. They should have stuck to Whitman

Laugh Your Blues Away (Columbia) d.Charles Barton: Jinx Falkenburg, Bert Gordon. A snobbish hostess hires two unemployed actors to entertain at a party. Her son and daughter fall in love with them

Star Spangled Rhythm (Paramount) d.George Marshall: Edward 'Rochester' Anderson, Katherine Durham. All the studio's stars, in a cheerful extravaganza. Songs by Johnny Mercer and Harold Arlen

Sing Your Worries Away (RKO) d.Edward Sutherland: Bert Lahr, Patsy Kelly. One-man show in which composer Lahr gets mixed up in a muddle of a million-dollar inheritance

Born to Sing (MGM) d.Edward Ludwig: Ben Carter, Virginia Weidler, Henry O'Neill. Resourceful Weidler saves her ex-con composing father from crooked music publisher – by putting on a show

You Were Never Lovelier (Columbia) d.William Seiter: Fred Astaire, Rita Hayworth. And indeed Rita never was as she danced 'I'm Old-Fashioned' with Fred on a romantically moonlit terrace. Stunning

Give Out Sisters (Universal) d.Edward F Cline: Dan Dailey, Grace McDonald, Donald O'Connor. Heiress McDonald's attempts to break into showbiz involve the Andrews Sisters posing as her elderly aunts

When Johnny Comes Marching Home (Universal) d.Charles Lamont: Donald O'Connor, Gloria Jean, Allan Jones. Singin' soldier Jones returns from the wars, falls for Jane Frazee

Holiday Inn (Paramount) d.Mark Sandrich: Marjorie Reynolds, Fred Astaire, Bing Crosby. Astaire dances, Bing sings Irving Berlin's 'White Christmas', so who cares about the corny plot?

Bambi (RKO) d.David D Hand. Disney adaptation of the novel by Felix Salten in which a young fawn grows up to be prince of the forest. Songs include 'Little April Shower'

Private Buckaroo (Universal) d.Edward F Cline: Corky Corcoran, Peggy Ryan, Donald O'Connor. The Andrews Sisters and Harry James put on a show. Best song 'Don't Sit under the Apple Tree'

Get Hep to Love (Universal) d.Charles Lamont: Gloria Jean, Donald O'Connor. Teenage Gloria runs away with the aim of becoming an opera star, gets to sing 'Drink to Me Only with Thine Eyes'

AMERICANA

Tennessee Johnson (MGM) d.William Dieterle: Lionel Barrymore, Van Heflin. Heflin in the title role in biopic of the Vice President who went to the White House after the assassination of Abraham Lincoln

The Magnificent Ambersons (RKO) d.Orson Welles: Tim Holt, Ray Collins, Agnes Moorehead. Adaptation of Booth Tarkington's family saga was mutilated by studio but survives as a masterpiece

The Remarkable Andrew (Paramount) d.Stuart Heisler: Brian Donlevy, Ellen Drew, William Holden. Ghost of former President helps book-keeper Holden fight small-town corruption. Whimsical nonsense

Andy Hardy's Double Life (MGM) d.George B Seitz: Mickey Rooney, Cecilia Parker. The studio tried out Esther Williams in this series entry – she looks a little big for Andy

Mrs Wiggs of the Cabbage Patch (Paramount) d.Norman Taurog: Carolyn Lee, Fay Bainter. Fourth time around for screen treatment of novel chronicling life of shanty town family

Blondie for Victory (Columbia) d.Frank Strayer: Arthur Lake, Penny Singleton. Scatterbrained Blondie lends her services to the Housewives of America in topical entry in long-running series

Pride of the Yankees (RKO) d.Sam Wood: Teresa Wright, Gary Cooper. Biopic of baseball star Lou Gehrig is quintessential film in the Cooper canon of shy, self-effacing heroes

HORROR

The Ghost of Frankenstein (Universal)
d.Erle C Kenton: Lon Chaney, Jr, Bela
Lugosi. Baron Frankenstein's second son
Cedric Hardwicke revives the big-booted
one but gives him Ygor's brain.

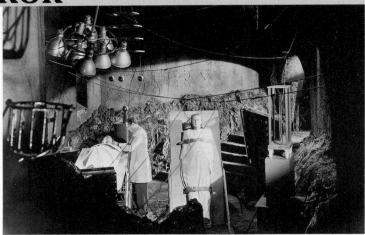

Frankenstein Meets the Wolf Man
(Universal) d.Roy William Neill: Lon Chaney,
Jr, Patric Knowles, Bela Lugosi. Lycanthrope
Chaney travels to Vasaria seeking cure
for his 'turns' but falls foul of the Monster

Dr Renault's Secret (Fox) d.Harry
Lachman: George Zucco, J Carrol Naish.
Zucco turns Naish into an apeman as part
of his experiments to speed up evolution.
Ingenious art direction by Nathan Juran

The Undying Monster (Fox) d.John
Brahm: John Howard, Heather Angel.
Moody werewolf on the moors spine tingler
relying heavily on suggestion. Anticipates
the Lewton RKO classics to come

The Night Monster (Universal) d.Ford
Beebe: Ralph Morgan. The demented
Morgan murders his way through the
doctors who crippled him. Bela Lugosi in
fine form as sinister butler

The Boogie Man Will Get You
(Columbia) d.Lew Landers: Boris Karloff,
Peter Lorre. Chaotic low-budget rip-off of
Arsenic and Old Lace. Karloff tries to create
electrical superman to help war effort

The Mummy's Tomb (Universal) d.Harold
Young: Lon Chaney, Jr. Elyse Knox. High
priest Turhan Bey brings the bandaged one
to US to settle accounts with archaeologist
Dick Foran. It all ends in tears

B MOVIES

Confessions of Boston Blackie
(Columbia) d.Edward Dmytryk: Chester
Morris. A murder has been committed at an
art auction and Blackie (Morris) finds
himself accused of the crime

**Sherlock Holmes and the Voice of
Terror** (Universal) d.John Rawlins: Basil
Rathbone, Evelyn Ankers, Nigel Bruce.
Holmes on the track of Nazi master spy
Thomas Gomez

Whistling in Dixie (MGM) d.S Sylvan
Simon: Ann Rutherford, Red Skelton.
Comedy-thriller sequel to *Whistling in the
Dark* with Skelton as the radio 'tec 'The
Fox' on track of buried treasure

The Falcon's Brother (RKO) d.Stanley
Logan: Tom Conway, George Sanders, Jane
Randolph. After three films as the debonair
sleuth, Sanders is bumped off to allow
real-life brother Conway to take over role

Maisie Gets Her Man (MGM) d.Roy Del
Ruth: Ann Sothern. Emancipated, heart of
gold chorine Sothern saves gullible
vaudevillian Red Skelton from the clutches
of a con artist

Kid Glove Killer (MGM) d.Fred
Zinnemann: Van Heflin, Marsha Hunt.
Zinnemann's feature debut and Heflin's first
starring role as wordly-wise criminologist
tracking down murderer Lee Bowman

One Dangerous Night (Columbia)
d.Michael Gordon: Warren William, Ann
Savage. The Lone Wolf (William) finds the
body of a murdered blackmailer and comes
under suspicion himself

Calling Dr Gillespie (MGM) d.Harold S
Bucquet: Phil Brown, Philip Dorn, Donna
Reed, Lionel Barrymore. Dorn plays Dutch
shrink working with Gillespie on case of
homicidal mania

Eyes in the Night (MGM) d.Fred
Zinnemann: Allen Jenkins, Horace McNally,
'Friday', Edward Arnold. Offbeat whodunnit
starring Arnold as a blind detective. Also
comeback film for Ann Harding

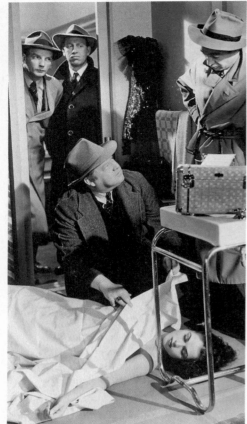

Quiet Please, Murder (Fox) d.John Larkin: Richard Denning, George Sanders. Detective Denning traps ingenious killer Sanders, whose sideline is faking priceless antiquarian books

Murder in the Big House (Warner) d.B Reeves Eason: Van Johnson, Ruth Ford. Fearless reporters Johnson and Faye Emerson blow the whistle on a murder ring in the state penitentiary

Grand Central Murder (MGM) d.S Sylvan Simon: Arthur Q Bryan, Sam Levene, Patricia Dane. Bitchy actress Dane is bumped off in a private car in station of title. Van Heflin arrives to investigate

Flight Lieutenant (Columbia) d.Sidney Salkow: Pat O'Brien, Warren Ashe. Air drama focussing on the consequences of a crash caused by a drunken pilot in which his colleague is killed

Careful Soft Shoulder (Fox) d.Oliver Garrett: Sheila Ryan, Aubrey Mather, Virginia Bruce. Bored socialite Bruce is tricked into spying for the Nazis. Underlines smart set's casual attitude to the war

Stand By All Networks (Columbia) d.Lew Landers: Mary Treen, John Beal. Beal is ace radio newscaster unmasking job lots of enemy agents between bulletins

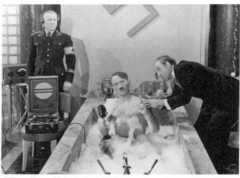

The Devil With Hitler (Roach) d.Gordon Douglas: Bobby Watson, Alan Mowbray. Weird burlesque with emissary of Satan arriving to make Adolf perform one good deed before he goes to Hell

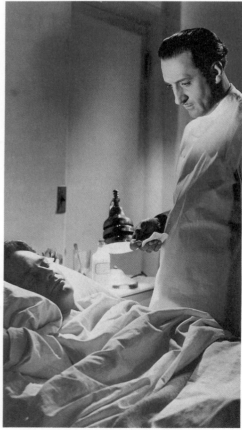

Little Tokyo USA (Fox) d.Otto Brower: Brenda Joyce, Preston Foster, Sen Yung, Melie Chang. Los Angeles cop Foster and newsgirl Joyce are framed on phoney murder rap by Japanese spy ring

The Invisible Agent (Universal) d.Edwin L Marin: Ilona Massey, Peter Lorre. Invisible agent Jon Hall outwits Axis spies. Massey primly averts her eyes when told he is naked as well as invisible

Fingers at the Window (MGM) d.Charles Lederer: Lew Ayres, Basil Rathbone. Rathbone effortlessly sinister as doctor perpetrating series of grisly hatchet murders by remote control

Counter Espionage (Columbia) d. Edward Dmytryk: Kurt Katch, Morton Lowry, Warren William. British Intelligence hire the Lone Wolf to break up spy ring out to steal plans of top-secret beam detector

Wrecking Crew (Paramount) d. Frank McDonald: Richard Arlen, Chester Morris. All-action Pine-Thomas fare with Arlen and Morris scrapping over Jean Parker. Exciting lives, these demolition men

The War Against Mrs Hadley (MGM) d. Harold S Bucquet: Fay Bainter, Jean Rogers, Halliwell Hobbes, Spring Byington. Bainter is the selfish woman trying to ignore the war. Mrs Miniver in reverse

Bombs Over Burma (PRC) d. Joseph H Lewis: Nedrick Young, Anna May Wong. Espionage caper on the Burma Road. Long stretches played without dialogue – perhaps wisely

Man's World (Columbia) d. Charles Barton: Frank Sully, Wynne Gibson, Edward Van Sloan, William Wright. Nurse Mona Jackson witnesses a murder, then gang boss ships her to mining town as a dance hostess

Personal Honour (Columbia) d. Charles Barton: Tom Brown, Jean Parker, Paul Herbert. Surly Tom Brown joins the Navy to win Jean Parker but redeems himself by saving rival's life

Busses Roar (Warner) d. D Ross Lederman: Richard Travis, Julie Bishop. A saboteur's bomb is placed on a bus timed to go off in the middle of an oil field. The passengers prove heroic

The Panther's Claw (PRC) d. William Beaudine: Sidney Blackmer (c). Serviceable screen revival of Anthony Abbott's sleuth Thatcher Colt, played with aplomb by Blackmer

Pacific Rendezvous (MGM) d. George Sidney: Lee Bowman, Milburn Stone. Shrill spy thriller with Naval Intelligence man Bowman using his decoding skills to round up a gang of saboteurs

Manila Calling (Fox) d. Herbert I Leeds: Lloyd Nolan, Carole Landis, Martin Kosleck, Ralph Byrd, Harold Huber. Nolan forms stay-behind guerrilla group in Mindanao after Japanese invasion

Jackass Mail (MGM) d.Norman Z McLeod: Marjorie Main (c). Mixture of slugging sentiment and comedy with Main as hardbitten saloon bar queen and Wallace Beery as wily old reprobate

Young America (Fox) d.Louis King: Lynne Roberts, Robert Cornell, Irving Bacon. Juvenile romance with spoilt city girl Jane Withers learning to make out with the hicks of Button Willow Valley

The Night Before the Divorce (Fox) d.Robert Siodmak: Lynn Bari, Joseph Allen, Jr. A murder comes to the rescue of Allen and Bari's tottering marriage in brisk comedy-thriller

Lucky Legs (Columbia) d.Charles Barton: Jinx Falkenburg (c). Falkenburg's legs are about the only thing worth looking at in dimwitted comedy built around an embezzler's will

Tish (MGM) d.S Sylvan Simon: Guy Kibbee, Marjorie Main, Zasu Pitts, Aline MacMahon. Three old maids adopt an orphan with comic consequences. Adapted from Mary Rinehart's best-sellers

The Mad Martindales (Fox) d.Alfred Werker: Marjorie Weaver, Alan Mowbray. Turn of the century family comedy with Jane Withers trying to save father Mowbray from madcap business schemes

It Happened in Flatbush (Fox) d.Ray McCarey: Carole Landis, Lloyd Nolan, James Burke. Lively little baseball yarn with Nolan taking over team in mid-season and romancing its beautiful owner Landis

Mexican Spitfire's Elephant (RKO) d.Leslie Goodwins: Arnold Kent, Lupe Velez. The cut-rate Carmen Miranda gets in a twist over elephant figurine containing stolen gem. Sterling support from Leon Errol

The Affairs of Martha (MGM) d.Jules Dassin: Marsha Hunt, Barry Nelson, Richard Carlson. Family maid Hunt marries the boss's son and then writes scandalous book about her life

Cadet Girl (Fox) d.Ray McCarey: Carole Landis, George Montgomery. West Point man Montgomery falls for torch singer Landis and puts his budding military career at risk

The Bashful Bachelor (RKO) d.Malcolm St Clair: Norris Goff, Chester Lauck. Small-town comedy in which two elderly store owners invest in a race horse. Zasu Pitts twitters away in small part

Perils of Nyoka (Republic) d.William Witney: Kay Aldridge (c). Desert-set serial with Lorna Gray in excellent form as the evil Vultura whose pet is Satan the gorilla

Spy Smasher (Republic) d.William Witney: Kane Richmond, Frank Corsaro. Freelance agent Richmond rings down the curtain on The Mask's counterfeiting ring in hard-hitting serial

BRITISH & FOREIGN

Secret Mission (Excelsior) d.Harold French: Brefni O'Rourke, Nancy Price, James Mason, Hugh Williams, Roland Culver, Carla Lehmann. Agents Williams and Culver penetrate a German HQ

In Which We Serve (Two Cities) d.Noel Coward, David Lean: Noel Coward (l). Coward also wrote the story of the destroyer *Torrin*, told through the memories of her crew. He modelled his own role on Mountbatten

The Day Will Dawn (Niskos) d.Harold French: Finlay Currie, Deborah Kerr, Hugh Williams. Devil-may-care racing journalist Williams guides British bombers into a raid on U-boat base in Norway

The Foreman Went to France (Ealing) d.Charles Frend: Clifford Evans, Tommy Trinder. Civilian Evans, stalwart Tommies and American Constance Cummings save vital British machinery as France collapses

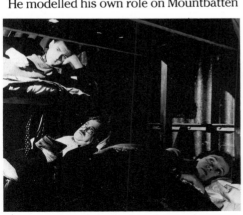

Salute John Citizen (British National) d.Maurice Elvey: Eric Micklewood, Mabel Constanduros, Edward Rigby. Modest family saga of the Buntings coping with the Blitz and bereavement

Unpublished Story (Two Cities) d.Harold French: Richard Greene. War correspondent Greene returns from Dunkirk and exposes a peace organization as a front for the inevitable Axis spy ring

The Next of Kin (Ealing) d.Thorold Dickinson: Nova Pilbeam, Geoffrey Hibbert. Stark warning against wartime complacency as loose tongues fatally compromise a commando raid on France

Let the People Sing (British National)
d.John Baxter: Fred Emney, Alastair Sim,
Edward Rigby. A mixed bunch of people
join forces to save a village hall from
developers. Emney steals the film.

The Goose Steps Out (Ealing) d.Will Hay
Basil Dearden: Will Hay (c). Shabby British
schoolmaster Hay is smuggled into Nazi
academy for spies, posing as his German
double. Hilarious

Coastal Command (Crown Film Unit)
d.Jack Holmes. Documentary closely
modelled on *Target for Tonight* (1941)
follows a Sunderland flying boat on
operations. Score by Vaughan Williams

Sabotage at Sea (British National)
d.Leslie Hiscott: Margaretta Scott, Martita
Hunt, Jane Carr, Felix Aylmer. Murder and
sabotage on wartime merchantman. Comedy
provided by Wally Patch, Ronald Shiner

The Young Mr Pitt (Twentieth Century)
d.Carol Reed: John Mills, Robert Donat.
Creaking historical drama aims at drawing
parallel between Pitt's fight against
Napoleon and Churchill's against Hitler

Les Visiteurs du Soir (France) d.Marcel
Carné: Arletty. Two emissaries of the Devil
arrive to cause mischief at a medieval feast
in oblique allegory on the Occupation.
Intermittently haunting

Ossessione (Italy) d.Luchino Visconti:
Massimo Girotti, Clara Calamai.
Smouldering melodrama based on 'The
Postman Always Rings Twice' was signpost
to the postwar neo-realist Italian films

The First of the Few (GFD) d.Leslie
Howard: David Niven. Howard directs and
stars in romanticized biopic of the man
who designed the Spitfire. Niven plays his
test pilot

Blossoming Port (Japan) d.Keisuke
Kinoshita. Two con-men deceive an island
people into backing a bogus shipyard, but
the simple islanders turn them into
honest men

L'Honorable Catherine (France)
d.Marcel L'Herbier: Edwige Feuillère (1).
Smoothly crafted comedy showcase for the
talents honed by Edwige Feuillère at
France's distinguished Comédie Française

1943

During the course of 1942 the scales had tipped against the Axis powers. The Battles of Midway and the Coral Sea had brought an end to Japanese expansion in the Pacific. In North Africa Rommel was turned back from the gates of Cairo in the second Battle of El Alamein. In Russia a German army was encircled in the snows of Stalingrad. In 1943 the number of Hollywood films dealing directly and indirectly with the war reached a peak.

Among the most successful were *Guadalcanal Diary*, *Destination Tokyo*, *Cry Havoc*, *Immortal Sergeant*, *The Cross of Lorraine*, *A Guy Named Joe* and *Hitler's Children*. *This is the Army*, Irving Berlin's tribute to the US fighting man, was a big hit for Warner. *The More the Merrier* was a delightful comedy inspired by the wartime housing shortage in Washington. Sherlock Holmes, Tarzan and The East Side Kids were all thrown into the celluloid battle against Nazi spies and saboteurs.

Keeping the troops happy was Betty Grable, whose million-dollar legs had carried her into the box office Top Ten in 1942 and kept her there alongside Greer Garson (the only other female entry) in 1943. The other money-spinners were Bob Hope, Bing Crosby, Abbott and Costello, Gary Cooper, Humphrey Bogart, James Cagney, Mickey Rooney and Clark Gable. It was Gable's twelfth successive appearance in the Top Ten, but now the sequence was interrupted by his departure for war service with the US Army.

Casablanca won the Best Picture Award and a Best Director Oscar for Michael Curtiz. Paul Lukas was voted Best Actor for his performance in Lillian Hellman's *Watch on the Rhine*. Jennifer Jones carried off the Best Actress Award as the teenage visionary of *Song of Bernadette*. The film itself won awards for Cinematography, Art Direction and Music Score. Katina Paxinou gained a well-deserved Best Supporting Actress Award as Pilar in *For Whom the Bell Tolls*, while Charles Coburn was chosen as Best Supporting Actor for his performance in *The More the Merrier*.

Two notable westerns were released in 1943. William Wellman's *The Ox-Bow Incident* was a bleak indictment of lynch law which succeeded in making a virtue of the studio interiors on which most of it was shot. Howard Hughes'

long-delayed *The Outlaw* was most emphatically built around Jane Russell's principal assets.

Death took veteran actor Hobart Bosworth, and Charles Ray, a sad and forgotten figure who had once been silent cinema's favourite 'country boy' star. Conrad Veidt died of a heart attack shortly after completing *Above Suspicion*. Robert Mitchum got his foot on the bottom rung of the Hollywood ladder, as a heavy in Hopalong Cassidy movies. Other young hopefuls included Dane Clark, Jeanne Crain, Rhonda Fleming, Kim Hunter, Richard Jaeckel, Gail Russell and Dorothy McGuire.

In Britain the turn of the tide against the Axis enabled film makers to anticipate the end of the war. Significantly, Alberto Cavalcanti's *Went the Day Well?* is framed between a prologue and epilogue which are delivered *after* the war is over. Documentary film making reached a peak with Humphrey Jennings' *Fires Were Started*, and its influence could be seen in such films as *San Demetrio, London* and Launder and Gilliat's *Millions Like Us*, a well-observed populist epic set in an aircraft factory. Paddling resolutely against the populist tide was Michael Powell's *The Life and Death of Colonel Blimp*. Savaged on its release as a celebration of everything that was reactionary in British society, it can now be seen as one of the great British films of the war years, informed with all the idiosyncratic romanticism of Powell and his long-time collaborator, screenwriter Emeric Pressburger.

Sadly, *My Learned Friend* marked the end of the film career of Will Hay, one of the giants of British screen comedy. Leslie Howard, who had become one of Britain's busiest wartime producer/directors, was killed when the 'plane in which he was flying was shot down over the Atlantic.

Wartime cinema audiences in Britain reached an all-time high. Replying to a questionnaire sent to him by the Wartime Social Survey, a young coal miner boasted that in 1943 he had seen 382 films. A surfeit of war subjects prompted a desire for pure escapism, which was answered by Gainsborough's *The Man in Grey*, a lurid Regency melodrama which established James Mason as British cinema's No 1 sex symbol.

ACTION

Sahara (Columbia) d. Zoltan Korda: Humphrey Bogart. American sergeant Bogie and assorted Tommies defend desert oasis from a battalion of thirsty Germans. Owes a lot to Ealing's *Nine Men* (1943)

Five Graves to Cairo (Paramount) d. Billy Wilder: Anne Baxter, Erich von Stroheim. British agent Franchot Tone is after the secret of Rommel's vital supply dumps. Von Stroheim superb as the Desert Fox

Salute to the Marines (MGM) d. S Sylvan Simon: Keye Luke, Wallace Beery. Japanese bombs bounce off Beery as two-fisted top sergeant coming out of retirement when the Philippines are invaded

Gung Ho! (Universal) d. Ray Enright: Randolph Scott. Bonehead, ultra-jingoistic actioner makes *The Green Berets* look like a Pacifist tract. Based on the real-life Makin Island raid of 17 August 1942

China (Paramount) d. John Farrow: William Bendix, Alan Ladd, Loretta Young. Mercenary oil man Ladd is persuaded by Young to join Chinese guerrillas fighting against the Japanese

Bombardier (RKO) d. Richard Wallace: Pat O'Brien, Randolph Scott. Bombardier O'Brien and pilot Scott tangle over Anne Shirley before Scott goes out with a big bang over Tokyo

Edge of Darkness (Warner) d. Lewis Milestone: Ann Sheridan, Tom Fadden, Errol Flynn. Flynn leads a revolt against the Nazis by Norwegian fishing folk. Filmed at the height of his rape scandal

Action in the North Atlantic (Warner) d. Lloyd Bacon: Humphrey Bogart, Raymond Massey. A Liberty ship is separated from its convoy and then plays cat and mouse with a U-boat

Air Force (Warner) d. Howard Hawks: John Garfield, Harry Carey, George Tobias. 'Fried Jap coming down' is famous Tobias quip in realistic tale of B-17 bomber *Mary Ann* and her crew

Destination Tokyo (Warner) d. Delmer Daves: Cary Grant, John Garfield (c). Captain Cary Grant navigates his submarine *Copperfin* right into Tokyo Bay. Garfield excellent as cocky crewman

Immortal Sergeant (Fox) d. John M Stahl: Henry Fonda. Tough old sergeant Thomas Mitchell gives dithering corporal Fonda the backbone to lead his comrades out of tight spot in Libyan desert

Above Suspicion (MGM) d. Richard Thorpe: Conrad Veidt, Joan Crawford, Fred MacMurray. Honeymooners Fred and Joan spy for Britain in 1939 Germany. Crawford's last at MGM and Veidt's last anywhere

Bataan (MGM) d. Tay Garnett: Lloyd Nolan, Robert Taylor. Gritty drama of American and Filippino troops' sacrificial rearguard action against the Japanese after the fall of Mindanao

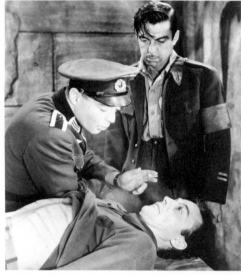

The Cross of Lorraine (MGM) d. Tay Garnett: Peter Lorre, Gene Kelly, Richard Whorf. Gutsy Resistance drama with Lorre outstanding as sadistic prison guard making life hell for everyone

Guadalcanal Diary (Fox) d. Lewis Seiler: Richard Jaeckel, Preston Foster, Lloyd Nolan. Painstaking adaptation of Richard Tregaskis' account of the part played by the Marines in the retaking of the Solomons

Bomber's Moon (Fox) d. Charles Fuhr: Walter Kingsford, Annabella, George Montgomery. Deliriously bad espionage adventure. No wonder real directors Ludwig and Schuster used a pseudonym

Hangmen Also Die (UA) d. Fritz Lang: Anna Lee, Brian Donlevy. Brecht-scripted account of the assassination of Heydrich seems trivial when compared to the reality of occupied Czechoslovakia

Behind the Rising Sun (RKO) d. Edward Dmytryk: Robert Ryan. Japanese-American Tom Neal volunteers to fight in Sino-Japanese war but is horrified by the brutality of his Japanese comrades

Assignment in Brittany (MGM) d.Jack Conway: Jean-Pierre Aumont, George Coulouris. Hollywood debut for Aumont and Signe Hasso in tale of Free French officer on undercover mission in France

Chetniks (Fox) d.Louis King: Anna Sten, Philip Dorn, Martin Kosleck. Tribute to Yugoslav guerrillas led by General Mihailovic. Dorn played the general, later liquidated by Tito

The Moon is Down (Fox) d.Irving Pichel: Dorris Bowden. Drama of occupied Norwegian town. Cedric Hardwicke, as German officer, gives fine portrayal of civilized man in uncivilized situation

The North Star (RKO) d.Lewis Milestone: Anne Baxter, Farley Granger. The German invasion of Soviet Union seen through the eyes of a small Russian village. Written by Lillian Hellman, Granger's screen debut

Tonight We Raid Calais (Fox) d.John Brahm: Lee J Cobb, Annabella. Slapdash effort with British Intelligence officer John Sutton pinpointing vital German armaments factory for RAF bombers

For Whom the Bell Tolls (Paramount) d.Sam Wood: Gary Cooper, Ingrid Bergman, Katina Paxinou. Adventurer Cooper romances guerrilla Bergman in Hemingway version of Spanish Civil War

ADVENTURE

Background to Danger (Warner) d.Raoul Walsh: George Raft. Eric Ambler thriller set in Turkey emerges as failed *Casablanca* lookalike. Sydney Greenstreet provides villainous relief

Journey into Fear (RKO) d.Norman Foster: Everett Sloane, Dolores Del Rio, Joseph Cotten. Cotten is pursued by Gestapo through the Levant in patchy Orson Welles adaptation of Eric Ambler novel

White Savage (Universal) d.Arthur Lubin: Maria Montez, Sabu. Jon Hall delivers immortal line 'Kaloe, you don't need Vitamin A' after smothering Montez with kisses. The earthquake's not bad either

Northern Pursuit (Warner) d.Raoul Walsh: Errol Flynn. Canadian Mountie Flynn infiltrates group of saboteurs. Can you spot his sardonic reference to recent rape scandal?

Tarzan Triumphs (RKO) d.William Thiele: Johnny Sheffield, Frances Gifford, Johnny Weissmuller. Tarzan routs a band of German paratroopers who descend on the jungle. Gifford is white princess Zandra

Tarzan's Desert Mystery (RKO) d.William Thiele: Johnny Weissmuller. In quick succession Tarzan encounters an American chorus girl, Nazi agents, Arab sheiks, prehistoric monsters and giant spiders

Cobra Woman (Universal) d.Robert Siodmak: Jon Hall, Sabu, Maria Montez, Lon Chaney, Jr. Camp classic in which La Montez essays the dual role of native innocent and her evil high priestess sister

MELODRAMA

Crash Dive (Fox) d.Archie Mayo: Tyrone Power, Dana Andrews. Tense submarine movie is undercut by the male leads' formula rivalry over girl – this time Anne Baxter

This Land Is Mine (RKO) d.Jean Renoir: Charles Laughton, Maureen O'Hara, John Donat. Occupation drama with Laughton as cowardly mother-fixated teacher who finally speaks out when tried for murder

Pilot No 5 (MGM) d.George Sidney: Franchot Tone, Marsha Hunt, Gene Kelly. Flashback time as Tone is chosen to fly suicide mission. Once he is airborne his comrades discuss his chequered life

So Proudly We Hail (Paramount) d.Mark Sandrich: Veronica Lake, Claudette Colbert. Claudette is emotional sheet anchor in tale of small band of nurses on the island fortress of Corregidor

Cry Havoc (MGM) d.Richard Thorpe: Ann Sothern. All-female cast emote furiously as nurses trapped in a jungle dug-out in the Philippines. Never quite struggles free from its stage origins

Watch on the Rhine (Warner) d.Herman Shumlin: Paul Lukas, Bette Davis. Lukas repeats stage role of anti-Nazi resistance leader in Dashiell Hammett adaptation of Lilian Hellman's play

The Fallen Sparrow (RKO) d. Richard Wallace: Martha O'Driscoll, John Garfield. Spanish Civil War veteran Garfield is dogged by German agent Maureen O'Hara after he returns to America

A Guy Named Joe (MGM) d. Victor Fleming: Irene Dunne, Spencer Tracy, Ward Bond. Tracy is dead fighter pilot sent back to Earth to guide young airman Van Johnson through the pitfalls of war

Flesh and Fantasy (Universal) d. Julien Duvivier: Charles Boyer, Barbara Stanwyck. A trio of macabre short stories. In the third segment Boyer plays a circus aerialist who dreams that he will fall

Lassie Come Home (MGM) d. Fred Wilcox: Roddy McDowall. Poverty-stricken family sell the noble canine to the Duke of Rudling. Lassie, McDowall and small Elizabeth Taylor tug at the heart strings

Shadow of a Doubt (Universal) d. Alfred Hitchcock: Teresa Wright, Joseph Cotten. Americana and murder as small-town girl Wright suspects beloved Uncle Charley (Cotten) is 'Merry Widow' killer

Lady of Burlesque (UA) d. William Wellman: Barbara Stanwyck. Snappy adaptation of Gypsy Rose Lee's 'G-String Murders' with homicidal maniac working his way through the chorus line broads

Forever and a Day (RKO) d. (among others) Frank Lloyd, Herbert Wilcox, René Clair: Ray Milland, Anna Neagle, Dame May Whitty. Parade of stars in history of a London House

The Hard Way (Warner) d. Vincent Sherman: Dennis Morgan, Ida Lupino, Joan Leslie. Lupino's driving ambition to turn sister Leslie into a star leads only to tears. Gladys George wonderful in small part

Happy Land (Fox) d. Irving Pichel: Don Ameche (r). Tearjerker in which grandfather's ghost (Harry Carey) returns to comfort family bereaved by war

Old Acquaintance (Warner) d. Vincent Sherman: Miriam Hopkins, Bette Davis. Hopkins gets the bitchy role in John Van Druten's story of two sparring writers. Sparks flew off the set as well

COMEDY

What a Woman (Columbia) d.Irving Cummings: Rosalind Russell, Brian Aherne. Russell is the hustling literary agent with an eye on Hollywood, Aherne the laid-back writer profiling her career

Young and Willing (UA) d.Edward H. Griffith: Barbara Britton, Susan Hayward. Six aspiring young actors lead producer Robert Benchley a merry dance in sprightly adaptation of stage success

Crazy House (Universal) d.Edward F Cline: Cass Daley, Ole Olsen, Billy Gilbert, Chic Johnson (r). Gag-a-minute romp with O and J playing a couple of comics on the make in Tinsel Town

They Got Me Covered (RKO) d.David Butler: Dorothy Lamour, Bob Hope. Witless newsman Hope goes after Nazi agents, is vamped, doped, fooled into marrying burlesque queen Gloria the Glow Girl

Claudia (Fox) d.Edmund Goulding: Dorothy McGuire, Robert Young. Moving tale of impulsive child-like wife adapted from Rose Franken's successful play. McGuire delightful in screen debut

The Heavenly Body (MGM) d.Alexander Hall: William Powell, Hedy Lamarr. Sophisticated Powell as distinguished astronomer given food for thought by wife Lamarr's interest in astrology

Slightly Dangerous (MGM) d.Wesley Ruggles: Lana Turner, Robert Young. Working girl Lana fakes amnesia and claims to be a millionaire's long-lost daughter in snappily handled farce

Holy Matrimony (Fox) d.John M. Stahl: Gracie Fields, Monty Woolley. Artist Woolley fakes his own death and marries widow Gracie in homely adaptation of Arnold Bennett's romantic comedy

Hi Diddle Diddle (UA) d.Andrew L Stone: Martha Scott, Adolphe Menjou, Pola Negri. Rakish Menjou is well matched by silent star Negri in feverish comedy of young lovers, con-artist parents

It Ain't Hay (Universal) d.Erle C Kenton: Lou Costello, Bud Abbott. And it ain't very funny either as A & C mug their way through remake of Damon Runyon tale first filmed as *Princess O'Hara* (1935)

Arsenic and Old Lace (Warner) d.Frank Capra: Cary Grant. Cary discovers a corpse in the window seat and over-acts outrageously in exuberant adaptation of Joseph Kesselring's black comedy

The Heat's On (Columbia) d.Gregory Ratoff: Mae West, William Gaxton. Mae only did this film to save Ratoff from bankruptcy but even she can't salvage this terrible musical comedy

A Night to Remember (Columbia) d.Mitchell Leisen: Brian Aherne, Loretta Young. Wisecracking comedy-thriller with Young and crime writer Aherne discovering a body in their apartment

DuBarry Was a Lady (MGM) d.Roy Del Ruth: Red Skelton, Lucille Ball. Hat check boy Skelton drinks a Mickey Finn and dreams he is Louis XV in glossy treatment of Cole Porter musical comedy

The Amazing Mrs Holliday (Universal) d.Bruce Manning: Deanna Durbin. Sentimental tale with Durbin posing as Harry Davenport's widow to save Chinese war orphans from deportation

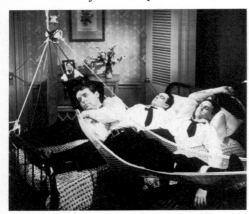

Sailor's Holiday (Columbia) d.William Berke: Arthur Lake, Bob Haymes, Lewis Wilson. Sailor 'Marblehead' Tompkins (Lake) is on leave in Hollywood. His one ambition is to kiss Rita Hayworth

Rationing (MGM) d.Willis Goldbeck: Wallace Beery, Dorothy Morris, Marjorie Main. Routine Beery vehicle casts him as harassed shopkeeper tangled up in wartime red tape

Rookies in Burma (RKO) d.Leslie Goodwins: Alan Carney, Claire Carleton, Joan Barclay, Wally Brown. Wally and Al escape from the Japanese and blunder through the jungle with two showgirls

The Man from Down Under (MGM) d. Robert Z Leonard: Charles Laughton, Binnie Barnes, Luis Alberni. Laughton miscast in Wallace Beery-type role in rambling Australian drama

Never a Dull Moment (Universal) d. Edward Lilley: The Ritz Brothers. The Brothers pose as mobsters in their nightclub act and then get mixed up in a jewel robbery

The More the Merrier (Columbia) d. George Stevens: Joel McCrea, Jean Arthur. The wartime housing shortage sparks romance between Joel and Jean. Doughty support from Charles Coburn

Mr Lucky (RKO) d. H C Potter: Laraine Day, Gladys Cooper, Cary Grant. Mobster Grant aims to cheat American War Relief Society to launch gambling ship, but is reformed by the lovely Ms Day

Princess O'Rourke (Warner) d. Norman Krasna: Jack Carson, Jane Wyman, Robert Cummings. Olivia de Havilland is the heir to a European throne who falls for pilot Bob Cummings and causes a diplomatic furore

The Meanest Man in the World (Fox) d. Sidney Lanfield: Jack Benny, Edward 'Rochester' Anderson. Jack's reputation as ambulance-chasing lawyer nearly torpedoes romance with Priscilla Lane

Johnny Come Lately (UA) d. William K Howard: James Cagney, Margaret Hamilton. Cagney is the scruffy, heart-of-gold newspaperman fighting corruption in small turn-of-the-century town

Margin for Error (Fox) d. Otto Preminger: Joan Bennett, Otto Preminger. Odd comedy drama, adapted from stage hit, in which Jewish cop Milton Berle has to guard overbearing German diplomat Preminger

Young Ideas (MGM) d. Jules Dassin: Susan Peters, Mary Astor, Elliott Reid. Comedy with campus background was developed from a film script sent in, unsolicited, by college boy William Noble

WESTERNS

A Woman of the Town (UA) d.George Archainbaud: Claire Trevor, Albert Dekker. Trevor appears to be more of a welfare worker than saloon bar queen in turgid tale of Dodge City. Dekker plays Bat Masterson

The Outlaw (Howard Hughes) d.Howard Hughes, Howard Hawks: Thomas Mitchell, Walter Huston, Jane Russell, Jack Buetel. Buetel's Billy the Kid fights with Huston's Doc Holliday over busty Russell

Dawn on the Great Divide (Mon) d.Howard Bretherton: Rex Bell, Buck Jones (c), Raymond Hatton (r). This entry in the Rough Riders series was released after Jones' death at the end of 1942

Klondike Kate (Columbia) d.William Castle: Ann Savage. Shrewish Savage co-stars with regular partner Tom Neal in yarn of the rootin' tootin' shootin' Klondike of the 90s

The Ox-Bow Incident (Fox) d.William Wellman: Paul Hurst , Henry Fonda, Henry Morgan (r). Bleak expressionistic anti-heroic Western, in which three innocent cowboys are lynched for rustling

Calling Wild Bill Elliott (Republic) d.Spencer Bennet: Bill Elliott, Anne Jeffreys. Elliott's first outing at Republic also features George Hayes as somewhat heavygoing comic relief

The Kansan (UA) d.George Archainbaud: Richard Dix. Dix is the roaming cowboy who settles in a small town, rids it of outlaws and then turns his attentions to big, bad Albert Dekker

King of the Cowboys (Republic) d.Joseph Kane: Roy Rogers, Peggy Moran. Rogers is the rodeoing government agent on the track of Nazi saboteurs led by Gerald Mohr in topical series entry

Lone Star Trail (Universal) d.Ray Taylor: Johnny Mack Brown (l), Robert Mitchum (cr). Framed for robbery, Mack Brown sets out to find the real villains. Tremendous fight with Mitchum

The Drifter (PRC) d.Sam Newfield: Carol Parker, Buster Crabbe. Buster leads schizophrenic existence as Robin Hood of the Range and bank robber trading on reputation of his other half

Hoppy Serves a Writ (UA) d. George Archainbaud: Victor Jory, William Boyd. The last Cassidy series film to be based on an original story by Clarence Mulford. Also first to feature Mitchum in a big part

Desperadoes (Columbia) d. Charles Vidor: Bernard Nedell, Randolph Scott, Raymond Walburn. Outlaw Glenn Ford decides to go straight and joins forces with lawman Scott to clean up wide-open town

Arizona Trail (Universal) d. Vernon Keays: Tex Ritter, Fuzzy Knight. Tex puts aside his differences with stepbrother Dennis Moore to help Orville Alderson defend his ranch from landgrabbers

ROMANCE

A Lady Takes a Chance (RKO) d. William Seiter: John Wayne, Jean Arthur. Rodeo rider Wayne introduces bored Easterner Arthur to the 'real west', whereupon she falls in love

Hers to Hold (Universal) d. Frank Ryan: Joseph Cotten, Deanna Durbin. Deanna gets a job in an aircraft factory to be near pilot Cotten. This does not prevent her singing several songs

His Butler's Sister (Universal) d. Frank Borzage: Deanna Durbin, Franchot Tone, Evelyn Ankers. Ambitious young singer Durbin is employed as composer Tone's maid. Many complications ensue

Heaven Can Wait (Fox) d. Ernst Lubitsch: Don Ameche, Gene Tierney. Sentimental romantic fantasy about flippant charmer Ameche being given a reprieve from Hell by Laird Cregar's Devil

Tender Comrade (RKO) d. Edward Dmytryk: Robert Ryan, Ginger Rogers. Plucky Ginger makes do while husband Ryan is away on war service, then faces up to bereavement after his death

The Constant Nymph (Warner) d.Edmund Goulding: Charles Boyer, Joan Fontaine. Boyer is the unfulfilled composer turned music tutor with whom Joan Fontaine falls tragically in love

My Friend Flicka (Fox) d.Harold Schuster: Preston Foster, Roddy McDowall, Rita Johnson. Roddy's devotion to an unmanageable horse is mercilessly milked for sentiment

Song of Russia (MGM) d.Gregory Ratoff: Robert Taylor, Susan Peters. Gallant attempt to give the Miniver treatment to Soviet Russia with conductor Taylor falling for musician Peters

MUSICALS

The Desert Song (Warner) d.Robert Florey: Irene Manning, Dennis Morgan. Sigmund Romberg's operetta updated to 1939 with American Dennis Morgan helping the Riffs against oppressive Germans

Thank Your Lucky Stars (Warner) d.David Butler: Olivia de Havilland, George Tobias, Ida Lupino. Flimsy story climaxes with all-star charity show. Low point is John Garfield singing 'Blues in the Night'

Stormy Weather (Fox) d.Andrew L Stone: Cab Calloway, Bill Robinson. Romance between Robinson and Lena Horne holds together parade of black stars. Lena unforgettable singing title song

Stage Door Canteen (UA) d.Frank Borzage: Franklin Pangborn, Johnny Weissmuller. Star-studded tribute to the American Theatre Wing includes only screen appearance of Katherine Cornell

Thousands Cheer (MGM) d.George Sidney: Gene Kelly. Gene performs the enchanting 'Mop Dance' in MGM's wartime showcase with 'more stars than there are in the heavens'

Sweet Rosie O'Grady (Fox) d.Irving Cummings: Betty Grable. Technicolor extravaganza set in the 1880s with musical comedy star Grable tangling romantically with newsman Robert Young

This Is the Army (Warner) d.Michael Curtiz. All-stops-out flagwaver is Irving Berlin's musical tribute to the American soldier. Berlin appears in 'Oh How I Hate to Get Up in the Morning' routine

Wintertime (Fox) d.John Brahm: Carole Landis, Cesar Romero. Last Sonja Henie vehicle for Fox in which the skating star comes to the rescue of a bankrupt winter resort. Missable

Something to Shout About (Columbia) d.Gregory Ratoff: Jack Oakie, Veda Ann Borg, William Gaxton, Janet Blair, Don Ameche. So-so backstage fare. Screen debut of Tula Finklea, who became Cyd Charisse

The Sky's the Limit (RKO) d.Edward H Griffith: Fred Astaire, Joan Leslie. Fred is incognito Flying Tigers hero who falls for Leslie. Features 'One For My Baby, (And One More For the Road)'

Cabin in the Sky (MGM) d.Vincente Minnelli: Edward 'Rochester' Anderson, Ethel Waters, Kenneth Spencer. Musical fable filled with racial stereotypes but saved by marvellous score

Higher and Higher (RKO) d.Tim Whelan: Michele Morgan, Frank Sinatra. Scullery maid Morgan is transformed into debutante the better to catch the eye of personable Frank, but she finally plumps for Jack Haley

Hit the Ice (Universal) d.Charles Lamont: Lou Costello, Cornelia Campbell. Abbott and Costello are a couple of press photographers who are mistaken for bank robbers. Plenty of songs

The Gang's All Here (Fox) d.Busby Berkeley. Banana time for Carmen Miranda singing 'The Lady with the Tutti Frutti Hat'. Berkeley's first movie in colour and his only film with Alice Faye

I Dood It (MGM) d.Vincente Minnelli: Eleanor Powell. Eleanor marries Red Skelton on the rebound but everything works out fine in remake of Buster Keaton's silent comedy *Spite Marriage* (1929)

Hello, Frisco, Hello (Fox) d.H Bruce
Humberstone: June Havoc, Jack Oakie.
Opulent Fox style bolsters slim tale of Alice
Faye's rise from saloon singer to box office
sensation. Features 'You'll Never Know'.

Best Foot Forward (MGM) d.Edward
Buzzell: Lucille Ball, Tommy Dix. George
Abbot's Broadway smash with Dix asking
film star Ball to be his date at military
school dance

Dixie (Paramount) d.Edward Sutherland:
Bing Crosby. Bing strolls amiably through
biopic of Daniel Decator Emmett of the
'Virginia Minstrels'. Dorothy Lamour
provides the decoration

Coney Island (Fox) d.Walter Lang: Phil
Silvers, George Montgomery, Betty Grable.
Saloon entertainer Grable promoted by
carnival men Montgomery, Cesar Romero.
Remade as *Wabash Avenue* (1950)

Broadway Rhythm (MGM) d.Roy Del
Ruth: Lena Horne. Lena sings 'Brazilian
Boogie' in anodyne adaptation of Jerome
Kern-Oscar Hammerstein II stage show
Very Warm for May

Girl Crazy (MGM) d.Norman Taurog: Judy
Garland, Mickey Rooney. Mickey and Judy's
eighth film together was remake of 1932
RKO hit. Beguiling George and Ira Gershwin
score

Presenting Lily Mars (MGM) d.Norman
Taurog: Judy Garland. Judy is small-town
girl finding fame on Broadway, romancing
producer Van Heflin on the way. Also
features Tommy Dorsey Orchestra

Reveille with Beverley (Columbia)
d.Charles Barton: Ann Miller, Tim Ryan.
Miller is disc jockey running early morning
wake-up programme on army base. Frank
Sinatra sings 'Night and Day'

Riding High (Paramount) d.George Marshall: Victor Moore, Dick Powell, Dorothy Lamour. Lamour is burlesque queen who returns to Arizona to find father Moore's silver mine on the skids

Moonlight in Vermont (Universal) d.Edward Lilley: Betty McCabe, Ray Malone, Vivian Austin. Newcomer Malone partners Gloria Jean in putting on barnyard revue after she has to leave drama school

Always a Bridesmaid (Universal) d.Erle C Kenton: Billy Gilbert, The Andrews Sisters, Charles Butterworth. Tenuous plot has 'tec Patric Knowles joining lonely hearts agency in order to trap a nightclub swindler

Happy Go Lucky (Paramount) d.Curtis Bernhardt: Mary Martin, Rudy Vallee, Dick Powell. Cigarette girl Martin angles for millionaire Vallee, and winds up with beachcomber Powell

Hit Parade of 1943 (Republic) d.Albert S Rogell: Susan Hayward, John Carroll. Peppy Hayward ghosts the songs written by played-out tunesmith Carroll in pleasant musical romance

Let's Face It (Paramount) d.Sidney Lanfield: Betty Hutton, Bob Hope. Loud, vulgar comedy with Hope one of three soldiers hired by suspicious wives to make philandering husbands jealous

Johnny Doughboy (Republic) d.John H Auer: Jane Withers (c). Valiant attempt to give the glamour treatment to child star Withers, who enjoys gawky romance with middle-aged playwright Henry Wilcoxon

The Sultan's Daughter (Mon) d.Arthur Dreifuss: Gene Stutenroth, Jack LaRue, Charles Butterworth, Fortunio Bonanova, Ann Corio. Poverty row road movie. Corio mixed up with vaudevillians, Nazi spies

BIOPICS

The Adventures of Mark Twain (Warner) d.Irving Rapper: Alexis Smith, Fredric March. Platitudinous canter through Twain's crowded life gives little flavour of his own peculiar genius

Madame Curie (MGM) d.Mervyn Le Roy: Greer Garson, Walter Pidgeon. The film in which Greer discovers radium is given the *Random Harvest* treatment but fails to flicker into life

The Song of Bernadette (Fox) d.Henry King: Jennifer Jones, Anne Revere. Meandering, sentimental version of the founding of the famous grotto at Lourdes. Won best actress Oscar for Jones

Mission to Moscow (Warner) d.Michael Curtiz: Ann Harding (l), Walter Huston. Skilfully directed pro-Russian tub-thumper based on memoirs of Ambassador Joseph E Davies

Flight for Freedom (RKO) d.Lothar Mendes: Herbert Marshall, Fred MacMurray, Rosalind Russell. Highly fictionalized biography of 'Lady Lindbergh' Amelia Earhart never really takes off

Jack London (UA) d.Alfred Santell: Michael O'Shea. London's stint as war correspondent in Russo-Japanese war is given World War II propaganda twist in lively, action-filled biopic

HORROR

I Walked with a Zombie (RKO) d.Jacques Tourneur: Christine Gordon, Frances Dee, Darby Jones. Jane Eyre transposed to the West Indies in tale of Voodoo possession. Brilliant art direction by Albert D'Agostino

The Ghost Ship (RKO) d.Mark Robson: Richard Dix (r). One of Dix's best performances as psychopathic sea captain murdering his way through the crew, also his last film at RKO

Cat People (RKO) d.Jacques Tourneur:
Simone Simon. Simon in the grip of an
ancient panther curse in the first of
producer Val Lewton's small masterpieces
of mood and suggestion

The Seventh Victim (RKO) d.Mark
Robson: Erford Gage, Kim Hunter. Innocent
Hunter stumbles on a coven of Satan
worshippers in her hunt for missing sister
Jean Brooks. Moody B masterpiece

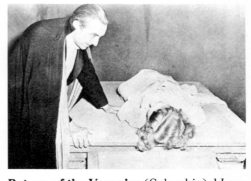

The Ape Man (PRC) d.William Beaudine:
Bela Lugosi. Bela kills to obtain spinal fluid,
the only antidote to the simian side to his
nature. Rockbottom horror played for all
it's worth – about four dollars

Return of the Vampire (Columbia) d.Lew
Landers: Bela Lugosi. Bela, looking rather
the worse for wear, is a Rumanian vampire
revived in the London Blitz by a German
bomb's near-miss on his grave

The Phantom of the Opera (Universal)
d.Arthur Lubin: Claude Rains, Susanna
Foster. Rains is stranded in Lon Chaney
role as the studio turns the horror classic
into an ersatz musical

The Leopard Man (RKO) d.Jacques
Tourneur: James Bell, Jean Brooks. A series
of strange murders is committed in a New
Mexico town. As with all Lewton-produced
films, full of visual felicities

The Mad Doctor of Market Street
(Universal) d.Joseph H Lewis: Una Merkel.
Lewis adds characteristic flourishes to tale
of evil South Seas doctor Lionel Atwill and
his strange hypnotic power

Son of Dracula (Universal) d.Robert
Siodmak: Frank Craven, Lon Chaney, Jr.
Chaney is the rather overweight and
anagramatically named Count Alucard.
Superb special effects from John P Fulton

B MOVIES

Hitler's Children (RKO) d.Edward Dmytryk: Bonita Granville, Kent Smith, Tim Holt. Bonita finds herself in a Nazi sterilisation programme in exploitation film which cleaned up at the box-office

The Strange Death of Adolf Hitler (Universal) d.James Hogan: Ludwig Donath. Lurid exploitation melodrama in which Donath impersonates Hitler and is shot by wife Gale Sondergaard for his pains

Hitler's Madman (MGM) d.Douglas Sirk: Patricia Morison, Alan Curtis. John Carradine hams it up as Reinhard Heydrich in independent cheapie sold by producer Seymour Nebenzal to MGM

Gangway for Tomorrow (RKO) d.John H Auer: Margo. Flashback drama telling the different tales of five war workers as they ride to the factory in a car owned by Charles Arnt

Corregidor (PRC) d.William Nigh. The action is eked out with miles of stock footage while Donald Woods tangles with Otto Kruger over Elissa Landi as the Japanese close in

We've Never Been Licked (Universal) d.John Rawlins: Noah Beery, Jr, Richard Quine. Feeble war training melodrama with Quine suspected of pro-Japanese sympathies

Paris after Dark (Fox) d.Leonide Moguy: Brenda Marshall, George Sanders, Gene Gary. Sanders is French doctor working for Resistance in film directed by Frenchman who escaped his country in 1940

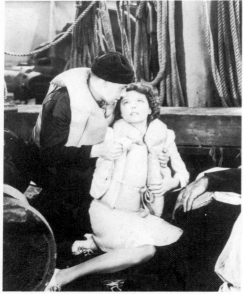

The Navy Comes Through (RKO) d.Edward Sutherland: George Murphy, Jane Wyatt. Rusty old freighter gets the better of half the Kriegsmarine and Luftwaffe in enjoyably improbable Atlantic convoy drama

They Came to Blow Up America (Fox) d.Edward Ludwig: Poldy Dur, George Sanders. Smooth Sanders is double agent, Ward Bond an FBI man and Anna Sten femme fatale in brisk espionage thriller

Appointment in Berlin (Columbia) d.Alfred E Green: Marguerite Chapman, George Sanders, Onslow Stevens. Busy Sanders turns up in the German capital as ex-RAF man turned spy

Calling Dr Death (Universal) d.Reginald LeBorg: Patricia Morison. Lon Chaney, Jr, stars in murder mystery marking first of spine chillers derived from radio's 'Inner Sanctum' broadcasts

No Place for a Lady (Columbia) d.James Hogan: Margaret Lindsay, William Gargan. Zippy detective drama enlived with some occult touches. Jerome Cowan appears as highly improbable nightclub singer

The Mystery of the 13th Guest (Mon) d.William Beaudine: Dick Purcell. Muddled thriller enlivened by several electrocutions. Leaves enough loose ends to tie up entire cast

Murder in Times Square (Columbia) d.Lew Landers: Marguerite Chapman, Edmund Lowe, Veda Ann Borg. Lowe's bombastic playwright is dig at Orson Welles in tale of rattlesnake-venom killer

Seven Miles from Alcatraz (RKO) d.Edward Dmytryk: Erford Gage, George Cleveland, Bonita Granville. Escaped convicts James Craig, Frank Jenks fetch up on lighthouse full of Nazi spies

Whispering Footsteps (Republic) d.Howard Bretherton: John Hubbard, Rita Quigley. Fear stalks the streets of a small American town and clean-cut young clerk John Hubbard is suspected of murder

Passport to Suez (Columbia) d.Andre de Toth: Eric Blore, Warren William. The Lone Wolf sorts out a spy ring in Alexandria in passable B version of *Casablanca*.William's last appearance as Michael Lanyard

Cosmo Jones in the Crime Smasher (Mon) d.James Tinling: Frank Graham, Richard Cromwell, Mantan Moreland, Edgar Kennedy. Graham repeats his CBS radio role as the correspondence-school sleuth

Crime Doctor (Columbia) d.Michael Gordon: Ray Collins, Warner Baxter. First in thriller series based on Max Marcin radio programme with Warner Baxter as criminal turned psychologist Dr Robert Ordway

The Falcon and the Co-Eds (RKO) d.William Clemens: Jean Brooks, Tom Conway. Ladies' man Conway is in his element unravelling a murder in a girls seminary

After Midnight with Boston Blackie
(Columbia) d.Lew Landers: Chester Morris,
George E Stone, Ann Savage. Blackie is
once again on the lam from the cops, suspected of ex-con Walter Baldwin's murder

**Sherlock Holmes and the Secret
Weapon** (Universal) d.Roy William Neill:
Nigel Bruce, Basil Rathbone. Three
murders in a convalescent home – always
when the clock strikes 13!

Two Senoritas from Chicago (Columbia)
d.Frank Woodruff: Ann Savage, Joan Davis,
Jinx Falkenburg. Flimsy comedy-musical
with chambermaid Davis selling a play she
discovers in the hotel waste bin

Crime Doctor's Strangest Case
(Columbia) d.Eugene Forde : Warner Baxter,
Rose Hobart, Reginald Denny, Jerome
Cowan, Gloria Dickson. Baxter clears man
accused of murdering his former employer

He Hired the Boss (Fox) d.Thomas Z
Loring: Stuart Erwin. Timid clerk Erwin
takes over the company he works for and
fires the boss (Thurston Hall), but finds it
all too much for him

Government Girl (RKO) d.Dudley Nichols:
Sonny Tufts, Olivia de Havilland. Dismal
rip-off of *The More the Merrier*, made under
protest by de Havilland and containing her
worst performance, deserves the B tag

Power of the Press (Columbia) d.Lew
Landers: Guy Kibbee, Gloria Dickson,
Douglas Leavitt. Fearless newspeople
expose nasty proprietor Otto Kruger as
murdering traitor

Swing Fever (MGM) d.Tim Whelan:
William Gargan, Kay Kyser, Curt Bois. Kyser
is a musician with a gift for hypnosis, which
he seems to have used on everyone
connected with the film

Mister Big (Universal) d.Charles Lamont:
Elyse Knox, Gloria Jean. Snappy little
programmer about college kids turning
their drama school's annual show into a
swinging revue

So's Your Uncle (Universal) d.Jean
Yarbrough: Billie Burke, Donald Woods,
Elyse Knox. Woods makes up as his elderly
uncle to avoid his creditors but finds Billie
Burke falling for him in comedy of errors

Ghosts on the Loose (Mon) d. William Beaudine: East Side Kids, Ava Gardner, Rick Vallin. Ava was Mrs Mickey Rooney when she helped the kids unmask Nazi agent Bela Lugosi. Carl Foreman wrote the script

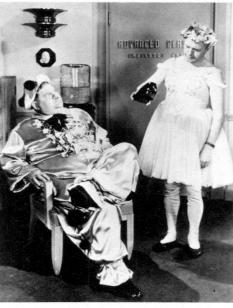

Dancing Masters (Fox) d. Malcolm St Clair: Oliver Hardy, Stan Laurel. Sad stuff from L & H as they are evicted from their dancing school and set about helping young inventor friend Robert Bailey

Ladies Day (RKO) d. Leslie Goodwins: Lupe Velez. Shriek-a-minute Lupe puts baseball star Eddie Albert right off his stroke in witless romantic comedy. He can't play when he's in love

Good Morning Judge (Universal) d. Jean Yarbrough: Dennis O'Keefe, Louise Allbritton (c). Music publisher O'Keefe slips Allbritton a Mickey Finn after realizing she's the lawyer suing him for plagiarism

Follow the Band (Universal) d. Jean Yarbrough: Anne Rooney, Eddie Quillan. Farmboy's expertise on the trombone provides slender excuse for a parade of nightclub floorshow numbers

Air Raid Wardens (MGM) d. Edward Sedgwick: Oliver Hardy, Stan Laurel, Edgar Kennedy. Rejected by the US Army, Navy and Air Force, Stan and Ollie become wardens and save a factory from sabotage

Jitterbugs (Fox) d. Malcolm St Clair: Stan Laurel, Oliver Hardy. L & H don a variety of disguises to help Vivian Blaine regain money from some swindlers. Amusing riverboat climax

Lost Angel (MGM) d. Roy Rowland: Margaret O'Brien, Keenan Wynn. Carefully crafted B+ vehicle for O'Brien as small genius taught the joys of childhood by reporter James Craig

Cinderella Swings It (RKO) d. Christy Cabanne: Willie Best, Gloria Warren, Leonid Kinsky. Would-be opera singer Warren is persuaded to 'swing it' in last of 'Scattergood Baines' series

She Has What it Takes (Columbia) d. Charles Barton: Tom Neal, Ann Evers, Jinx Falkenburg. Ambitious young actress Falkenburg pretends to be the daughter of famous recently deceased star

Campus Rhythm (Mon) d. Arthur Dreifuss: Claudia Drake, Robert Lowery, Gale Storm. Singer Gale Storm enrols at a college under an assumed name in routine campus-bound second feature

Sarong Girl (Mon) d.Arthur Dreifuss: Bill Henry, Ann Corio, Damian O'Flynn. Corio is Dixie Barlow, an exotic dancer out on bail after a police raid closes down the burlesque show in which she is appearing

Petticoat Larceny (RKO) d.Ben Holmes: Tom Kennedy, Joan Carroll, Vince Bartlett, Jimmy Conlin. Seeking colour for her broadcast scripts, little Joan runs away and falls in with some kind-hearted crooks

Footlight Glamour (Columbia) d.Frank Strayer: Jonathan Hale, Penny Singleton, Arthur Lake, Rafael Storm, Ann Savage. More chaos with Blondie, Dagwood and the Bumstead brood in routine series entry

Gildersleeve on Broadway (RKO) d.Gordon Douglas: Ann Doran, Harold Peary. Madcap comedy series spun off from popular radio show with portly Peary in the title role. Strictly kids' stuff

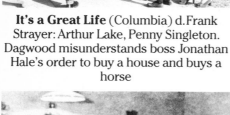

It's a Great Life (Columbia) d.Frank Strayer: Arthur Lake, Penny Singleton. Dagwood misunderstands boss Jonathan Hale's order to buy a house and buys a horse

Swing Shift Maisie (MGM) d.Norman Z McLeod: Ann Sothern, James Craig. Maisie dons overalls for the war effort and goes into a tailspin over handsome young test pilot James Craig

The Phantom (Columbia) d.B Reeves Eason: Tom Tyler. With the help of a four-footed pal Devil, Tyler foils villains in their search for the treasure of the lost city of Zoloz. Zippy serial

Batman (Columbia) d.Lambert Hillyer: Douglas Croft, J Carrol Naish, Lewis Wilson. Evil Dr Daka is out to steal America's radium for the Axis powers using his zombie army

Captain America (Republic) d.John English, Elmer Clifton: George J Lewis, David Sharpe, Dick Purcell. Republic's most expensive serial crammed with the Lydecker brothers' best special effects

BRITISH & FOREIGN

Adventures of Tartu (MGM) d.Harold S Bucquet: Glynis Johns, Robert Donat. Fanciful thriller set in Czechoslovakia with British Officer Donat posing as Rumanian diplomat to blow up poison-gas plant

Undercover (Ealing) d.Sergei Nolbandov: Mary Morris, Michael Wilding. Phoney tale of Yugoslavian partisans was shot in the mountains of Wales. One of Ealing's unhappier wartime efforts

We Dive at Dawn (Gainsborough) d.Anthony Asquith: John Mills, Norman Williams, Eric Portman, Jack Watling. Submarine thriller works up fine head of tension as it stalks German battleship

Nine Men (Ealing) d.Harry Watt: John Varley, Jack Lambert. Watt used all his documentary skills in gripping tale of group of Tommies cut off in the desert and besieged by the enemy

San Demetrio, London (Ealing) d.Charles Frend: Frederick Piper, Robert Beatty (extreme right). Understated, heroic tale of seamen who abandon blazing tanker, reboard her and sail her back to the Clyde

Fires Were Started (Crown Film Unit) d.Humphrey Jennings. Poetic documentary tribute to the work of the Auxiliary Fire Service during the London Blitz. One of the finest documentaries of the war

The Silent Village (Crown Film Unit) d.Humphrey Jennings. The reconstruction of the tragedy of Lidice is re-enacted by a similar community, the Welsh mining village of Cwmgiedd

The Bells Go Down (Ealing) d.Basil Dearden: Philip Friend, Tommy Trinder, Mervyn Johns, William Hartnell. Energetic study of assorted members of an auxiliary fire crew carefully avoids heroic clichés

Desert Victory (Army, Air Force Film Units) d.Roy Boulting. Skilfully compiled documentary charts the desert war from the first battle of El Alamein to the triumphant entry into Tripoli

They Met in the Dark (Independent) d.Carl Lamac: James Mason, Joyce Howard, Edward Rigby. Discredited naval officer Mason and Canadian girl Howard uncover a spy ring in a seedy theatrical agency

The Demi-Paradise (Two Cities)
d.Anthony Asquith: Margaret Rutherford.
Tribute to Russians is national ego
massage as Soviet engineer Laurence
Olivier adapts to British way of life

Went the Day Well? (Ealing) d.Alberto
Cavalcanti: Valerie Taylor, Leslie Banks. A
sleepy English village is taken over by
German paratroops disguised as British
soldiers on exercise

Happidrome (MGM) d.Phil Brandon:
Robbie Vincent, Harry Korris. Film version
of radio programme of same name. Korris
in splendid form as a seedy, chiselling
impresario, in the manner of W C Fields

The Life and Death of Colonel Blimp
(Archers) d.Michael Powell: Vincent
Holman, Roger Livesey. Densely layered
national epic following a military man from
impetuous youth to blustering old age

It's That Man Again (Gainsborough)
d.Walter Forde: Tommy Handley, Horace
Percival. Handley is accident-prone mayor
of Foaming-at-the-Mouth in scrappy screen
version of classic radio show

Millions Like Us (Gainsborough) d.Frank
Launder and Sidney Gilliat: Patricia Roc,
Megs Jenkins. Intensely moving populist
drama built around the lives of a group of
young women working in an aircraft factory

The Man in Grey (Gainsborough) d.Leslie
Arliss: Margaret Lockwood, James Mason.
Preposterous Regency melodrama,
mounted with delirious conviction,
established Mason as snarling sex symbol

My Learned Friend (Ealing) d.Will Hay,
Basil Dearden: Claude Hulbert, Will Hay,
Mervyn Johns. Hay's last film is black
comedy with madman Johns murdering his
way towards Will and Claude

Bell-Bottom George (Columbia) d.Marcel
Varnel: George Formby. George
masquerades as a sailor, uncovers nest of
German spies, thrashes his ukelele – all the
usual stuff for Formby fans

The Gentle Sex (Two Cities) d.Leslie
Howard: Lilli Palmer, Joyce Howard. Lilli
Palmer is outstanding in drama of seven
ATS girls told in restrained, documentary
style and adroitly directed by Howard

1944

The war was drawing to a close, but the demands it had made on personnel were felt in all the studios. Among the many stars drawn into the war effort were Captain Clark Gable USAAF, Major James Stewart USAAF, Lieutenant Douglas Fairbanks, Jr, Lieutenant Commander Robert Montgomery, Lieutenant Richard Barthelmess, Lieutenant Robert Taylor and Lieutenant Robert Stack – all of the US Navy. After completing *National Velvet*, Mickey Rooney went into the Army, finishing the war as a corporal.

In Britain David Niven went into the Commandos, while Laurence Olivier and Ralph Richardson joined the Navy. Marlene Dietrich threw herself into a long and gruelling series of tours entertaining troops overseas. Al Jolson won an entirely new audience singing to troops in the principal theatres of war.

The cinema boom continued unabated, with MGM recording profits of $14.5 million on a record gross of $166 million. Paramount cleaned up with a huge hit, *Going My Way*, which both the Academy and the New York Critics voted the year's best film. Its star Bing Crosby picked up the Best Actor Award as the singing priest Father O'Malley. Barry Fitzgerald won the Best Supporting Actor Oscar for his performance as Crosby's prickly colleague. Director Leo McCarey completed the triumph by carrying away the Best Director Award.

Going My Way was the most notable of a cycle of movies which boasted strong religious themes. Fox got the message and, following Gregory Peck's debut in *Days of Glory*, cast their new young star as the missionary-priest

hero of *The Keys of the Kingdom*. Other new faces of 1944 were Lauren Bacall, making a memorable debut opposite Humphrey Bogart in *To Have and Have Not*, Charles Korvin, Faye Emerson and cheerful, open-faced Bill Williams, Ann Blyth, Judy Holliday, Jane Powell, Zachary Scott and Audrey Totter. Silent star Harry Langdon died completely forgotten.

Among the war films released in the year were DeMille's *The Story of Dr Wassell*, *The Purple Heart* and *Thirty Seconds over Tokyo*. Closer to home, *See Here, Private Hargrove* explored the more humorous aspects of army life. Other outstanding films of the year included *Double Indemnity*, *Laura*, *Meet Me in St Louis* – with Judy Garland at her most captivating – and *Gaslight*, which won Ingrid Bergman the Best Actress Oscar. The Best Supporting Actress Award went to Ethel Barrymore for her performance in Clifford Odets' gloomy low-life drama *None but the Lonely Heart*.

In Britain, Gainsborough continued to plunder the rich seam of costume melodrama which the studio had unearthed with *The Man in Grey*. *Fanny by Gaslight* and *Madonna of the Seven Moons* were big successes, the latter elevating Stewart Granger to the front rank of British stars. Gainsborough also produced Sidney Gilliat's *Waterloo Road*, a contemporary drama which looked forward to the 'social realism' of the late 1950s. Laurence Olivier's *Henry V* struck a note appropriate for the victory which now clearly lay ahead, winning its director/star a new York Critics Award and a special Oscar.

ACTION

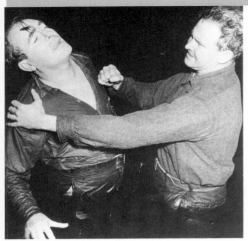

Secret Command (Columbia) d.Edward Sutherland: Pat O'Brien, Barton MacLane. Agent O'Brien is sent on an undercover mission to smash a sabotage ring operating in a shipyard. Carole Landis co-stars

The Imposter (Universal) d.Julien Duvivier: Jean Gabin. Criminal Gabin is saved from the guillotine by Nazi air raid, joins the Free French and becomes a hero. Ellen Drew is the love interest

The Purple Heart (Fox) d.Lewis Milestone: Dana Andrews, Farley Granger, Sam Levene, John Craven, Richard Loo. Reconstruction of the fate at Japanese hands of some of the first Americans to bomb Tokyo

To Have and Have Not (Warner) d.Howard Hawks: Dan Seymour, Lauren Bacall, Humphrey Bogart. Bogart as Hemingway's gun-running hero and Bacall there to tell him 'Put your lips together and blow'

The Master Race (RKO) d.Herbert Biberman: George Coulouris. Posing as a Belgian patriot, diehard Nazi Coulouris attempts to spread disaffection in town awaiting liberation

Thirty Seconds over Tokyo (MGM) d.Mervyn Le Roy: Spencer Tracy. Technically proficient, heroic presentation of first American bombing raid on Japan. Tracy plays General Doolittle

Lifeboat (Fox) d.Alfred Hitchcock: John Hodiak, Mary Anderson, Hume Cronyn, Henry Hull, Tallulah Bankhead. Tallulah steals the show, damp but unaltered. Hitchcock turns up in a newspaper

The Black Parachute (Columbia) d.Lew Landers: Ivan Triesault, Jonathan Hale, Larry Parks. Parks is the secret agent, Triesault the Nazi officer and Hale king of occupied country in Resistance melodrama

None Shall Escape (Columbia) d.Andre de Toth: Henry Travers, Dorothy Morris, Marsha Hunt. Nazi general Alexander Knox is arraigned before an international war-guilt court in Poland, the scene of his crimes

Mr Winkle Goes to War (Columbia) d.Alfred E Green: Robert Armstrong, Edward G Robinson. Henpecked, middle-aged Robinson is accidentally drafted and, predictably, winds up a hero

Sergeant Mike (Columbia) d.Henry Levin: Larry Parks. Parks is transferred from a machine gun unit to the 'K.9' Corps and put in charge of Mike, a dog being trained for war

Passage to Marseilles (Warner) d.Michael Curtiz: Humphrey Bogart, Helmut Dantine, Billy Roy, George Tobias. Complex flash-back drama of escaped Devil's Island convict Bogart joining Bomber Command

Passport to Destiny (RKO) d.Ray McCarey: Elsa Lanchester. Pop-eyed Cockney charlady Lanchester marches off to Berlin to assassinate Hitler. Glorious nonsense

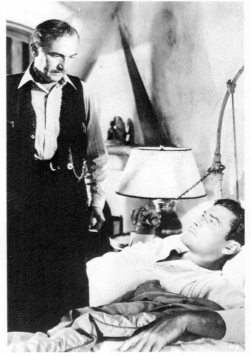

The Seventh Cross (MGM) d.Fred Zinnemann: Spencer Tracy. Creditable attempt to show not all Germans are bad as escaped concentration camp prisoner is helped by sympathetic countrymen

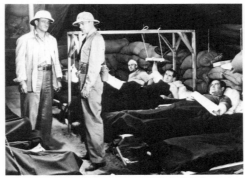

Fighting Seabees (Republic) d.Edward Ludwig: John Wayne (l). Big John is the hotheaded leader of a bunch of engineers in the Pacific war. He blows up an oil tank, himself and several divisions of Japanese

Uncertain Glory (Warner) d.Raoul Walsh: Paul Lukas, Errol Flynn. Condemned to the guillotine, Frenchman Flynn escapes and, with the help of Lukas and Jean Sullivan, becomes Resistance hero

Wing and a Prayer (Fox) d.Henry Hathaway: Dana Andrews, Don Ameche. The story of an aircraft carrier and a new group of pilots' introduction to the realities of combat

Storm over Lisbon (Republic) d.George Sherman: Erich von Stroheim, Vera Hruba Ralston, Eduardo Ciannelli. German agent von Stroheim is after vital film strip held by American reporter Richard Arlen

Tampico (Fox) d.Lothar Mendes: Victor McLaglen, Lynn Bari, Edward G Robinson. Tanker captain Robinson marries Bari after picking her up from a torpedoed ship. But she comes under suspicion of spying

First Comes Courage (Columbia) d.Dorothy Arzner: Merle Oberon, Carl Esmond. Norwegian patriot Oberon poses as collaborator to gain information for Resistance

Till We Meet Again (Paramount) d.Frank Borzage: Ray Milland, Vladimir Sokoloff, Barbara Britton. Plucky nun Britton shepherds downed pilot Milland back to the Allied lines

Days of Glory (RKO) d.Jacques Tourneur: Lowell Gilmour, Gregory Peck, Tamara Toumanova. Newcomers Peck and Toumanova are Russian partisans romancing and fighting Germans

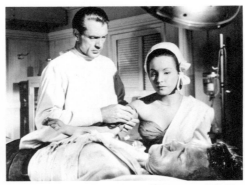

The Story of Dr Wassell (Paramount) d.Cecil B DeMille: Gary Cooper, Carol Thurston, Dennis O'Keefe. Sluggish account of dedicated Navy doctor slips well below par for Cooper and DeMille

The Conspirators (Warner) d.Jean Negulesco: Victor Francen, Peter Lorre, Hedy Lamarr, Sydney Greenstreet. Echoes of *Casablanca* in smoothly handled tale of spies and femmes fatales in neutral Lisbon

Experiment Perilous (RKO) d.Jacques Tourneur: Hedy Lamarr, George Brent. Muted reprise of *Gaslight* with Paul Lukas terrorizing wife Hedy to the brink of insanity

The Hitler Gang (Paramount) d.John Farrow: Robert Watson, Martin Kosleck. Documentary-tinged examination of Hitler's rise to power – a kind of March of Time treatment of the Fuehrer's private life

The Ministry of Fear (Paramount) d.Fritz Lang: Ray Milland. Graham Greene's psychological drama gutted to provide smooth, atmospheric espionage thriller with Milland pursued by Nazi spy ring

Murder My Sweet (RKO) d.Edward Dmytryk: Dick Powell (l). Song-and-dance man Powell switches to unshaven hardboiled hero as Philip Marlowe in best of all the Chandler film adaptations

The Thin Man Goes Home (MGM) d.Richard Thorpe: William Powell. A local painter is shot dead on Nick and Nora's doorstep, plunging them into a plot to sabotage a nearby war factory

Roger Touhy, Gangster (Fox) d.Robert Florey: Lois Andrews, Victor McLaglen, Preston Foster. Foster is Touhy, one of Al Capone's henchmen, in taut thriller made with FBI co-operation

Secrets of Scotland Yard (Republic) d.George Blair: Edgar Barrier, Stephanie Bachelor. Dark doings in the British War Office's cypher room. C Aubrey Smith lumbers to the rescue

Crime by Night (Warner) d.William Clemens: Faye Emerson, Cy Kendall, Charles Wilson, Jane Wyman, Jerome Cowan. Cowan's last starring role as a vacationing gumshoe finding a body

ADVENTURE

Frenchman's Creek (Paramount) d.Mitchell Leisen: Dennis Green, Joan Fontaine. Joan is romanced by dashing pirate Arturo de Cordova in handsome Daphne du Maurier adaptation

Kismet (MGM) d.William Dieterle: Ronald Colman, Marlene Dietrich. Encased in gold body paint, Marlene treated this bloated Arabian Nights extravaganza with her customary monumental cool

Gypsy Wildcat (Universal) d.Roy William Neill: Maria Montez, Jon Hall. More exotic rubbish from Montez, joining forces with Hall to give lecherous, murdering aristocrat Douglass Dumbrille his just desserts

Mademoiselle Fifi (RKO) d.Robert Wise: Edmund Glover, Simone Simon, John Emery. 'Mademoiselle' of title is not Simon but brutal German officer who meets death at her hands in Franco-Prussian War

Summer Storm (UA) d.Douglas Sirk: Linda Darnell, George Sanders. Darnell is the femme fatale who brings misery to all those involved with her in Hollywood kitsch Chekov adaptation

Barbary Coast Gent (MGM) d.Roy Del Ruth: Binnie Barnes, Frances Rafferty, Bruce Kellogg, Wallace Beery. Tailor-made Beery vehicle with the old reprobate falling in and out of trouble in 1870s San Francisco

MELODRAMA

I Love a Soldier (Paramount) d.Mark Sandrich: Sonny Tufts, Paulette Goddard, Mary Treen. Paulette believes that wartime marriages are too risky, until she meets lonely soldier Sonny

Keep Your Powder Dry (MGM) d.Edward Buzzell: Lana Turner, Laraine Day. Lana and Laraine spend most of the time at each other's throats in war training drama, but love of the Service unites them by the end

And Now Tomorrow (Paramount) d.Irving Pichel: Alan Ladd, Cecil Kellaway, Loretta Young. Frozen-faced Ladd is the ear specialist who cures Young of her deafness and wins her hand

The Impatient Years (Columbia) d.Irving Cummings: Lee Bowman, Charles Coburn, Jean Arthur. Wartime separation and problems of readjustment threaten to undermine Arthur and Bowman's marriage

Mrs Parkington (MGM) d.Tay Garnett: Greer Garson, Walter Pidgeon. Greer progresses from boarding-house slavey to matriarch of a family poisoned by wealth. Pidgeon her philandering husband

Ladies Courageous (Universal) d.John Rawlins: Geraldine Fitzgerald, Loretta Young. Personal problems loom larger than the aircraft in tribute to the Women's Auxiliary Ferrying Squadron

Double Indemnity (Paramount) d.Billy Wilder: Barbara Stanwyck, Fred MacMurray. Stanwyck superb as the double-crossing blonde wife, sinuously exploiting MacMurray's moral inertia

Dark Waters (UA) d.Andre de Toth: John Qualen, Merle Oberon. Strange goings-on down on the old plantation as seemingly friendly Thomas Mitchell sets out to drive new arrival Oberon insane

Christmas Holiday (Universal) d.Robert Siodmak: Richard Whorf, Gene Kelly, Deanna Durbin. Painful attempt to ease Durbin into adulthood playing nightclub singer wife of petty hoodlum Gene Kelly

The Woman in the Window (RKO) d.Fritz Lang: Joan Bennett. Sultry Joan mesmerizes family man Edward G Robinson and with the aid of Dan Duryea slowly picks him apart at the seams in classic film noir

The Phantom Lady (Universal) d.Robert Siodmak: Ella Raines, Thomas Gomez. Raines and detective Thomas Gomez search for a missing witness to clear Alan Curtis of charge of murdering his wife

Address Unknown (Columbia) d.William Cameron Menzies: Frank Reicher, Paul Lukas. Lukas as art gallery owner returning to his native Germany and making harrowing compromises with Nazism

Tomorrow the World (UA) d.Leslie Fenton: Fredric March, Joan Carroll, Agnes Moorehead. Small-town academic March takes in orphaned German nephew (Skippy Homeier) who turns out to be a little Nazi beast

Gaslight (MGM) d.George Cukor: Ingrid Bergman, Charles Boyer, Joseph Cotten. Bergman won Oscar for agony she endures at hands of husband Boyer's finely calculated sadism

Between Two Worlds (Warner) d.Edward A Blatt: Paul Henreid, Eleanor Parker, George Tobias. Remake of *Outward Bound* (1930) in which a fog-bound passenger ship sails to the other world

None But the Lonely Heart (RKO) d.Clifford Odets: Cary Grant, Barry Fitzgerald. Turgid drama of London low life, with Grant as petty crook Ernie Mott, a nod to former self, Archie Leach

The Climax (Universal) d.George Waggner: Susanna Foster, Boris Karloff. Boris tries to hypnotize singer Foster out of recreating opera role made famous by a diva he murdered ten years before

Dragon Seed (MGM) d.Jack Conway, Harold S Bucquet: Katharine Hepburn, Turhan Bey. Hepburn is at her most resistibly coltish as Jade, the young Chinese peasant caught up in the war with Japan

Laura (Fox) d.Otto Preminger: Vincent Price, Judith Anderson, Gene Tierney, Clifton Webb. Tierney's portrait casts a spell over detective Dana Andrews. Webb is the feline Waldo Lydecker

The Mask of Dimitrios (Warner) d.Jean Negulesco: Sydney Greenstreet, Peter Lorre. Greenstreet and Lorre bring their double act as the Laurel and Hardy of the thriller to adaptation of Eric Ambler novel

The Keys of the Kingdom (Fox) d.Harold Young: Vincent Price, Gregory Peck. Peck's first major film putting his immaculately chiselled features to good use as the missionary working in China

COMEDY

The Canterville Ghost (MGM) d.Jules Dassin: Charles Laughton, Margaret O'Brien, Robert Young, William Gargan. Upstaging maestros Laughton and O'Brien star in comedy of GIs billeted in haunted castle

Nothing But Trouble (MGM) d.Sam Taylor: Stan Laurel, Oliver Hardy. L & H as a muddling chef and butler meet the young king of a government in exile in their last film at MGM

Casanova Brown (RKO) d.Sam Wood: Patricia Collinge, Teresa Wright, Gary Cooper. Cooper divorces wife Wright and is preparing to remarry when he discovers she's pregnant

The Great Moment (Paramount) d.Preston Sturges: Joel McCrea, Betty Field, William Demarest. Sturges peps up story of the dentist who discovered anaesthetic effect of ether with undigested slabs of comedy

The Big Noise (Fox) d.Malcolm St. Clair: Stan Laurel, Oliver Hardy. L & H guard a newly invented bomb. Mishaps include flight over a target range in radio-directed 'plane

Together Again (Columbia) d.Charles Vidor: Irene Dunne, Charles Coburn, Charles Boyer. Suave sculptor Boyer pursues local politician Dunne while deftly fending off her daughter Mona Freeman

In Society (Universal) d.Jean Yarbrough: Lou Costello, Bud Abbott (r). Hamfisted plumbers A & C are accidentally invited to spend a weekend with the smart set. Arthur Treacher appears in usual butler role

The Princess and the Pirate (RKO) d.David Butler: Bob Hope, Virginia Mayo. Bob saves Virginia from pirate king The Hook (Victor McLaglen) then mugs his way through swashbuckling spoof

Rainbow Island (Paramount) d.Ralph Murphy: Barry Sullivan, Dorothy Lamour, Eddie Bracken, Gil Lamb (c). Bracken and companions crash land in the Pacific. Islanders treat him as a god

See Here, Private Hargrove (MGM) d.Wesley Ruggles: Donna Reed, Robert Walker. Walker's bashful charm works well in warm treatment of Marion Hargrove's memoirs of army camp life

The Youngest Profession (MGM) d.Edward Buzzell: Virginia Weidler, Marta Linden, Edward Arnold. Lana Turner, William Powell, Greer Garson, Robert Taylor guest in vehicle for autograph-hunting Weidler

Miracle of Morgan's Creek (Paramount) d.Preston Sturges: Porter Hall, Betty Hutton, Eddie Bracken. Betty's fling at an all-night party results in a surprise package nine months later

Johnny Doesn't Live Here Any More (Mon) d.Joe May: William Terry, Simone Simon. Whimsical comedy romance about wartime housing shortage. Robert Mitchum has small part

Lost in a Harem (MGM) d.Charles Reisner: Lou Costello, Bud Abbott. Sets and costumes from *Kismet* and an appearance by Jimmy Dorsey bolster sagging A & C desert farce

See My Lawyer (Universal) d.Edward F Cline: Chic Johnson, Ole Olsen. O & J are nightclub performers trying to get out of a contract. Universal quickly took the hint and let them go

The Town Went Wild (PRC) d.Ralph Murphy: Freddie Bartholomew, Ruth Lee, Edward Everett Horton. A muddle over birth certificates and a small-town feud turn Freddie's fianceé into his sister

Hi Good Lookin' (Universal) d.Edward Lilley: Eddie Quillan, Betty Kean, Milburn Stone. Lively comedy with Harriet Hilliard as a singer from the Mid-West making it in Hollywood as a radio vocalist

The Dough Girls (Warner) d.James Kern: Eve Arden, Jane Wyman, Alexis Smith, Ann Sheridan. Overcrowded Washington hotel and a bevy of man-hungry women in screen version of Broadway hit

Hail the Conquering Hero (Paramount) d.Preston Sturges: Eddie Bracken, Ella Raines. Wickedly satirical Sturges tour de force with army reject Bracken mistaken for war hero by his home town

It Happened Tomorrow (UA) d.René Clair: Linda Darnell, Dick Powell. Disappointing comedy-fantasy in which reporter Dick Powell stumbles on the ability to predict the future

San Diego, I Love You (Universal) d.Reginald LeBorg: Buster Keaton, Jon Hall, Louise Allbritton. Small bottom-of-the-bill classic full of Allbritton's warm skills and a moment of magic from Buster Keaton

WESTERNS

Renegades of the Rio Grande (Universal) d.Howard Bretherton: Rod Cameron (l), Fuzzy Knight. Cameron poses as bank robber to round up bunch of thieves who have murdered his brother

The Cowboy and the Senorita (Republic) d.Joseph Kane: Roy Rogers, Mary Lee, Guinn 'Big Boy' Williams. Senorita of the title was Dale Evans appearing in the first of 20 successive Rogers films

The Singing Sheriff (Universal) d.Leslie Goodwins: Andrew Tombes, Bob Crosby, Fuzzy Knight. Comedy Western with Broadway star Crosby strapping on the holster to deal with Joe Sawyer's gang

Oklahoma Raiders (Universal) d.Lewis Collins: Jennifer Holt, Dennis Moore. Holt, sister of cowboy star Tim, is the masked vigilante El Vengador in Tex Ritter's last for Universal

Zorro's Black Whip (Republic) d.Spencer Bennet: George J Lewis, Linda Stirling. Stirling assumes her brother's role of masked avenger the Black Whip, in pacy 12-part serial

Cowboy Canteen (Columbia) d.Lew Landers: Guinn 'Big Boy' Williams, Vera Vague, Jane Frazee. Series Western version of *Hollywood Canteen*, notable for rare film appearance of country singer Roy Acuff

ROMANCE

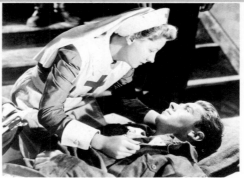

The White Cliffs of Dover (MGM) d.Clarence Brown: Irene Dunne, Peter Lawford. American Dunne loses husband in First War, son in Second in Miniver-type fantasy of England

Since You Went Away (Selznick) d.John Cromwell: Jennifer Jones, Claudette Colbert, Shirley Temple. No-holds-barred tearjerker with Claudette steering her family through heartaches of World War II

In Our Time (Warner) d.Vincent Sherman: Ida Lupino, Paul Henreid. Insipid romance set in pre-war Poland with nobleman Henreid marrying English tourist Lupino. Principally a plug for the Poles

Marriage is a Private Affair (MGM) d.Robert Z Leonard: Lana Turner, John Hodiak. Studio gloss can't save hasty wartime marriage tale with Lana giving glowering Hodiak the runaround

Blonde Fever (MGM) d.Richard Whorf: Marshall Thompson, Gloria Grahame. Gloria provides stately widow Mary Astor with competition of a more sultry kind over charms of boring Philip Dorn

The Hour Before Dawn (Paramount) d.Frank Tuttle: Franchot Tone, Veronica Lake. A mixture of melodrama and romance as Tone marries then murders Nazi spy Lake. Implausible

Mr Skeffington (Warner) d.Vincent Sherman: Claude Rains, Bette Davis. Society flirt Davis discovers meaning of marriage after she has lost her looks and Rains has lost his sight

Jane Eyre (Fox) d.Robert Stevenson: Joan Fontaine, Orson Welles, John Abbott. Welles is a darkly romantic Rochester bestriding studio-bound Yorkshire moors in adaptation of Bronte novel

A Song to Remember (Columbia) d.Charles Vidor: Paul Muni, Cornel Wilde. Superior schlock casting Wilde as a muscular Chopin, but Merle Oberon as Georges Sand is as wooden as his piano

MUSICALS

Lake Placid Serenade (Republic) d.Steve Sekely: Stephanie Bachelor, Vera Hruba Ralston, Ruth Terry. Vera's glinting blades propel her towards the arms of husky Robert Livingston. Roy Rogers guests

Pin-Up Girl (Fox) d.H Bruce Humberstone: Betty Grable, Joe E Brown. Secretary Grable pretends to be a Broadway star to be near sailor John Harvey. Naturally she is asked to perform

Follow the Boys (Universal) d.Edward Sutherland: George Raft, Vera Zorina. Raft's roving eye – he's married to Zorina – is slender pretext for a star-studded tribute to Hollywood Victory Committee Shows

Cover Girl (Columbia) d.Charles Vidor: Gene Kelly, Rita Hayworth, Phil Silvers. Key film in Kelly's career marks his transition from hoofer to dancer and gives pointers to triumphs to come in *On The Town* (1949)

Shine on Harvest Moon (Warner) d.David Butler: Ann Sheridan, Dennis Morgan. Backstage story of vaudeville girl Sheridan and composer Morgan. Opening number in Technicolor, rest of film b/w

Hey Rookie (Columbia) d.Charles Barton: Ann Miller. Drafted producer Larry Parks puts on a show for the boys in the camp. Stanley Donen choreographed lively programmer

Show Business (RKO) d.Edwin L Marin: George Murphy, Constance Moore, Eddie Cantor, Joan Davis. Rags-to-riches tale carries Cantor from Bowery to Ziegfeld in celebration of his 35 years in the business

Going My Way (Paramount) d.Leo McCarey: Barry Fitzgerald, Bing Crosby. Multiple-award-winning story of Crosby's Father Chuck O'Malley winning over Fitzgerald's prickly Father Fitzgibbon

Four Jills in a Jeep (Fox) d.William Seiter: Carole Landis. Based on a USO Camp Tour of England and North Africa made by Landis (who married on tour and in film), Kay Francis, Martha Raye, Mitzi Mayfair

Can't Help Singing (Universal) d.Frank Ryan: Deanna Durbin. Deanna wows them all out West in lavish Technicolor outing with score by Jerome Kern, E Y Harburg and Robert Paige as romantic interest

Casanova in Burlesque (Republic) d.Leslie Goodwins: Joe E Brown, June Havoc. Brown is unlikely college professor, Havoc burlesque queen with Shakespearian ambitions. Anticipates *Kiss Me Kate* (1953)

Here Comes the Waves (Paramount) d.Mark Sandrich: Bing Crosby. Singing star Bing joins the navy hoping for combat but finds himself in charge of benefit shows presented by the Waves

Sensations of 1945 (UA) d.Andrew L Stone: Dennis O'Keefe, C Aubrey Smith, Eleanor Powell. Slaphappy screenplay lands publicity-conscious Powell in a succession of daffy promotion stunts

Hollywood Canteen (Warner) d.Delmer Daves: Jack Carson, Jane Wyman, John Garfield, Bette Davis. Soldiers Robert Hutton, Dane Clark spend two unforgettable nights with the studio's stars

Greenwich Village (Fox) d.Walter Lang: Carmen Miranda, William Bendix. 1920s-set extravaganza found Miranda top-billed for the first time with support from aspiring composer Don Ameche and Vivian Blaine

Meet the People (MGM) d.Charles Reisner: Bert Lahr, Dick Powell, Lucille Ball. Broadway big shot Powell takes job in a shipyard to 'meet the people' and propel sacked singer Ball back to stardom

Step Lively (RKO) d.Tim Whelan: Gloria de Haven, Frank Sinatra. Frank is the singing playwright whose show is facing a cash flow crisis in remake of Marx Brothers' *Room Service* (1938)

Chip off the Old Block (Universal) d.Charles Lamont: Donald O'Connor, Ann Blyth. O'Connor is naval school cadet whose romance with daughter of musical comedy star (Blyth) takes him into showbiz

Pardon My Rhythm (Universal) d.Felix Feist: Patric Knowles, Gloria Jean. Gloria's romance with drummer Mel Torme runs into trouble with the arrival of pretty Marjorie Warren

Music for Millions (MGM) d.Henry Koster: June Allyson, Margaret O'Brien. Pregnant cellist Allyson agonizes over absent serviceman husband. More fun is Jimmy Durante singing 'Umbriago'

Moonlight and Cactus (Universal) d.Edward F. Cline: Shemp Howard, Tom Kennedy, Patty Andrews. Rancher Tom Seidel returns from the war to find all his cowhands replaced by women

Two Girls and a Sailor (MGM) d.Richard Thorpe: Van Johnson, Gloria de Haven, June Allyson. Gloria and June both fall for bashful millionaire Van, who secretly finances a servicemen's canteen

And the Angels Sing (Paramount) d.George Marshall: Fred MacMurray, Betty Hutton, Dorothy Lamour. Betty and Dorothy form half of the singing Angel Sisters fleeced by bandleader MacMurray

Sing a Jingle (Universal) d.Edward Lilley: Allan Jones, June Vincent, Gus Schilling. Famous tenor Jones goes to work in a defence plant. Vincent is the romantic foil

Bathing Beauty (MGM) d.George Sidney: Red Skelton, William Goodwin, Esther Williams. Worth it just for the climactic water ballet featuring a superbly kitschy interpretation of 'Blue Danube Waltz'

Bowery to Broadway (Universal) d.Charles Lamont: George Dolenz, Susanna Foster, Turhan Bey. Beer garden owners Donald Cook, Jack Oakie joins forces to become the toast of Broadway

Meet Me in St Louis (MGM) d.Vincente Minnelli: Margaret O'Brien, Judy Garland. Tender turn-of-the-century family saga retains all its beguiling charm. Judy sings 'The Trolley Song'

She's a Sweetheart (Columbia) d.Del Lord: Jimmy Lloyd, Larry Parks, Jane Frazee. Jane Darwell turns her boarding house into canteen for servicemen with short-time passes in brisk programmer

Belle of the Yukon (RKO) d.William Seiter: Randolph Scott, Florence Bates, Gypsy Rose Lee. Gypsy Rose is the queen of the notorious dance hall haunted by Scott. Dinah Shore sings 'Sleigh Ride in July'

Irish Eyes are Smiling (Fox) d.Gregory Ratoff: June Haver, Dick Haymes. Haver is Mary 'Irish' O'Brien in fictitious biopic of real-life composer Ernest Ball (Haymes) who co-wrote title song

Knickerbocker Holiday (UA) d.Harry Joe Brown: Constance Dowling, Charles Coburn. Anti-fascist message of Kurt Weill-Maxwell Anderson original whittled down in tale of 17th-century New York

Lady in the Dark (Paramount) d.Mitchell Leisen: Mischa Auer, Phyllis Brooks, Ginger Rogers. Ginger in Gertrude Lawrence Broadway role as lady recounting her fantasies to shrink Barry Sullivan

Lady Let's Dance (Mon) d.Frank Woodruff: Belita. Megabudget time on poverty row in an attempt to showcase poor-man's Sonja Henie. Features no less than five production numbers

Tonight and Every Night (Columbia) d.Victor Saville: Lee Bowman, Rita Hayworth, Janet Blair. Set in London's famous Windmill Theatre and featuring Marc Platt dancing a Hitler speech

Song of the Open Road (UA) d.S Sylvan Simon: W C Fields, Jill Browning. Introducing Jane Powell as a child star running away to a youth hostel. One of Fields' final appearances. Cute, ain't he?

Carolina Blues (Columbia) d.Leigh Jason: Ann Miller, Kay Kyser. Kay sets out to raise money for a warship through a series of war bond rallies. Sammy Cahn, Jule Styne do their best with the score

Louisiana Hayride (Columbia) d.Charles Barton: Judy Canova. Movie-mad hick Canova outsmarts a couple of con-men and makes it in the picture business. Songs include 'Rainbow Road'

Swing in the Saddle (Columbia) d.Lew Landers: Jane Frazee, Mary Treen. Actress Jane is mistaken for kitchen help in breezy parade of country and western radio favourites

Something for the Boys (Fox) d.Lewis Seiler: Vivian Blaine. Snappy 'putting on a show' Carmen Miranda vehicle which introduced laid-back Perry Como to cinema audiences

AMERICANA

HORROR

Wilson (Fox) d.Henry King: Alexander Knox. Ambitious biopic traces Woodrow Wilson's progress from Presidency of Princeton to that of the United States. From common room to White House

Buffalo Bill (Fox) d.William Wellman: Joel McCrea, Linda Darnell. Colourful biopic of William Cody (McCrea) promoted to fame by wily press agent Ned Buntline (Thomas Mitchell)

Andy Hardy's Blonde Trouble (MGM) d.George B Seitz: Lynn and Lee Wilde, Mickey Rooney. Ebullient Rooney sets off for college where he finds himself unable to resist the female attractions

An American Romance (MGM) d.King Vidor: Ann Richards, Brian Donlevy, John Qualen. Donlevy excellent as the immigrant who becomes a tycoon, capturing vigour of Dos Passos' original

The Lodger (Fox) d.John Brahm: Laird Cregar. Brahm creates fog-shrouded London, Cregar is riveting as 'Jack the Ripper'. Sadly he died the same year

The Uninvited (UA) d.Lewis Allen: Donald Crisp, Gail Russell. Russell haunted by dead mother in classic ghost story, long on atmosphere and suggestion, set in haunted house on the Cornish cliffs

Curse of the Cat People (RKO) d.Robert Wise: Kent Smith, Jane Randolph, Eve March, Elizabeth Russell, Julia Dean. Haunting meditation on the strange poetry of childhood recalls *Turn of the Screw*

The Lady and the Monster (Republic) d.George Sherman: Erich von Stroheim, Richard Arlen, Vera Hruba Ralston. First screen version of Curt Siodmak's novel *Donovan's Brain*

Weird Woman (Universal) d.Reginald LeBorg: Lon Chaney, Jr, Anne Gwynne. 'Inner Sanctum' mystery with Gwynne the target of witch Evelyn Ankers. Remade in 1962 as *Burn, Witch, Burn*

Cry of the Werewolf (Columbia) d.Henry Levin: Stephen Crane, Osa Massen, Barton MacLane. Nina Foch is Celeste La Tour, Queen of the Trioga gypsies, inheriting crown and wolf curse from her mother

Captive Wild Woman (Universal)
d.Edward Dmytryk: John Carradine,
Acquanetta. Crazy Carradine turns ape into
Acquanetta (or vice versa). Much stock footage
from Clyde Beatty's *The Big Cage* (1933)

Return of the Ape Man (Mon) d.Phil
Rosen: Bela Lugosi, George Zucco. Scientist
Bela revives frozen prehistoric man, inserts
John Carradine's brain and turns him into
George Zucco – all too confusing

Dead Man's Eyes (Universal) d.Reginald
LeBorg: Acquanetta, Edward Fielding, Lon
Chaney, Jr. 'Inner Sanctum' mystery.
Chaney tries to restore sight with tissue
from the eyes of another man

The Mummy's Ghost (Universal)
d.Reginald LeBorg: Lon Chaney, Jr. 3000-
year-old Princess Ananka is reincarnated in
small American town only to find swampy
resting place with Chaney's Kharis

Jungle Captive (Universal) d.Donald
Young: Vicky Lane. Dotty Otto Kruger has a
stab at reviving the corpse of an ape
woman with predictably distressing results.
Rondo Hatton also features

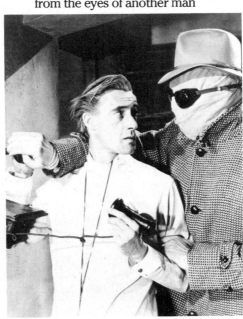

The Man in Half Moon Street
(Paramount) d.Ralph Murphy: Nils Asther,
Reinhold Schunzel. Asther preserves his
youth with gland transplants. Remade as
The Man Who Could Cheat Death (1959)

The Invisible Man's Revenge (Universal)
d.Ford Beebe: John Carradine, Jon Hall.
Embittered Hall does the disappearing trick
with designs on Evelyn Ankers and her
parents' property

Bluebeard (PRC) d.Edgar Ulmer: John
Carradine. Expressionist B masterpiece
with Carradine as the haunted strangler
terrorizing Paris. A triumph of imagination
over budget

B MOVIES

The Unwritten Code (Columbia)
d.Herman Rotsten: Roland Varno, Ann
Savage, Tom Neal. Far-fetched tale of Nazi
Varno posing as Englishman until exposed
by Army sergeant Neal

The Racket Man (Columbia) d.D Ross
Lederman: Tom Neal, Jeanne Bates, Hugh
Beaumont. Neal is a mobster reformed by
the Army and sent back to break up black
market ring

My Buddy (Republic) d.Steve Sekely: Don
Barry (l). Flashback tale of World War I
hero Barry drifting into unemployment and
then gangsterism. Straight lift from *The
Roaring Twenties* (1939)

Strange Affair (Columbia) d.Alfred E
Green: Frank Jenks, Evelyn Keyes, Allyn
Joslyn. Jaunty thriller with amateur
detective Joslyn investigating the murder of
a refugee and uncovering a nest of spies

Two-Man Submarine (Columbia) d.Lew
Landers: Tom Neal, Ann Savage. Scientist
Savage parachutes into Pacific Isle to help
penicillin research workers (!) closely
followed by the Japanese

U-Boat Prisoner (Columbia) d.Lew
Landers: John Abbott, Arno Frey, Eric Rolf,
John Wengrof. Bruce Bennett poses as a
spy the better to wreak havoc inside Nazi
submarine

Action in Arabia (RKO) d.Leonide Moguy:
George Sanders, Virginia Bruce. Newsman
Sanders stumbles on Nazi plot to get the
Arab tribes to rise en masse against British
and French

There's Something About a Soldier
(Columbia) d.Alfred E Green: Bruce
Bennett (l), Tom Neal (r). Usual training
camp drama with Evelyn Keyes filling the
love interest spot

Bermuda Mystery (Fox) d.Benjamin
Stoloff: Ann Rutherford, Preston Foster. Ann
Rutherford's uncle finds smoking can
damage your health – permanently. Foster
investigates poisoned cigarette murder

The Missing Juror (Columbia) d.Budd
Boetticher: Janis Carter, George Macready.
Embittered ex-con Macready sets out to
murder his way through the jury which
wrongly convicted him of murder

Youth on Trial (Columbia) d.Budd
Boetticher: Eric Sinclair, Cora Sue Collins.
The adolescent daughter of a juvenile court
judge falls in with a well-bred hoodlum who
robs and kills his own father

The Falcon in Hollywood (RKO)
d.Gordon Douglas: Rita Corday, Tom
Conway, Veda Ann Borg. Tongue-in-cheek
film-capital murder mystery. Borg is a
talkative taxi driver

The Whistler (Columbia) d.William Castle:
Byron Foulger, Richard Dix. Depressed Dix
hires a man to kill him, changes his mind,
but can't contact his executioner. J Carrol
Naish is the scrupulous assassin

The Mark of the Whistler (Columbia)
d.William Castle: Paul Guilfoyle, Richard
Dix. A drifter discovers a dormant bank
account with a name similar to his own,
impersonates party to obtain the money

Shadows in the Night (Columbia)
d.Eugene Forde: Nina Foch, Warner Baxter.
The 'Crime Doctor' discovers that Foch's
brother-in-law is trying to drive her mad
with his fiendish hypnotic gas

The Pearl of Death (Universal) d.Roy
William Neill: Basil Rathbone, Nigel Bruce.
Evelyn Ankers steals the fabulous Borgia
pearl and hides it in one of six busts of
Napoleon

**Sherlock Holmes and the Spider
Woman** (Universal) d.Roy William Neill:
Basil Rathbone, Gale Sondergaard.
Rathbone dons a variety of disguises to
smash exotic Sondergaard's crime ring

The Scarlet Claw (Universal) d.Roy
William Neill: Nigel Bruce, Basil Rathbone,
Arthur Hohl. A killer stalks the fog-
shrouded Canadian countryside in eerie
luminous clothing. Ingenious screenplay

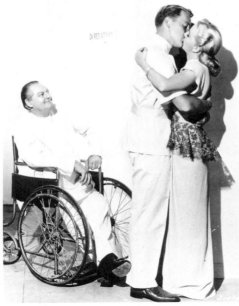

Between Two Women (MGM) d.Willis
Goldbeck: Lionel Barrymore, Van Johnson,
Marilyn Maxwell. Johnson cures Gloria de
Haven's hang-ups over eating, romances
Maxwell in 14th entry in medical saga

One Mysterious Night (Columbia) d.Budd
Boetticher: Janis Carter, Chester Morris.
Boston Blackie is called in by the cops to
help them recover the stolen Blue Star of
the Nile diamond

Maisie Goes to Reno (MGM) d.Harry Beaumont: Ann Sothern. Go-getter Sothern plays a date in Reno, sorts out Ava Gardner's marital and financial problems and still has time to sing 'Panhandle Pete'

Tahiti Nights (Columbia) d.Will Jason: Mary Treen, Jinx Falkenburg. Mild South Seas comedy with band leader South Seas prince romancing the lovely Falkenburg. Comedy from the Four Vagabonds

Block Busters (Mon) d.Wallace Fox: Leo Gorcey, Gabriel Dell, Huntz Hall. The East Side Kids discover to their amazement that a recently arrived French boy is a whizz at baseball

The Ghost that Walks Alone (Columbia) d.Lew Landers: Matt Willis, Arthur Space, Arthur Lake, Frank Sully. Honeymooning Lake stumbles across a murder, giving usual impersonation of amiable nitwit

Beautiful but Broke (Columbia) d.Charles Barton: Judy Clark, Joan Davis, Jane Frazee, Byron Foulger. An all-girl orchestra's adventures include seeking overnight shelter in a hut on an army firing range

Hot Rhythm (Mon) d.William Beaudine: Harry Langdon, Donna Drake (c), Irene Ryan (r). Drake and Robert Lowery are the romantic interest in a gentle spoof on radio stations and jingle writers

Dancing in Manhattan (Columbia) d.Henry Levin: William Wright, Ann Savage, Fred Brady, Jeff Donnell. A garbage man accidentally discovers a large sum of money meant for some blackmailers

Jam Session (Columbia) d.Charles Barton: Charlie Barnett and his orchestra. Zippy Ann Miller vehicle crammed with swing music including Duke Ellington Orchestra playing 'C-Jam Blues'

Slightly Terrific (Universal) d.Edward F Cline: Leon Errol (r). Ne'er do well Errol wants to encourage a group of young actors but causes havoc by impersonating his rich twin brother

Trocadero (Republic) d.William Nigh: Rosemary Lane, Johnny Downs. Lane inherits a nightclub and makes a success of it with a parade of swing bands. Cartoonist Dave Fleischer contributes some drawings

A Wave, a Wac and a Marine (Mon) d.Phil Karlson: Elyse Knox, Charles Marshall, Henry Youngman, Ann Gillis. A pair of understudies are mistakenly given Hollywood contracts

Meet Miss Bobby Socks (Columbia) d.Glenn Tryon: Lynn Merrick, Louise Erickson. Bob Crosby is cast as war veteran who finds fame as a Sinatra-style crooner in tedious quickie

Sweethearts of the USA (Mon) d.Lewis Collins: Parkyarkus, Una Merkel, Lillian Cornell. War worker Merkell knocks herself out and literally dreams up a cut-rate musical

Stars on Parade (Columbia) d.Lew Landers: Larry Parks, Lynn Merrick, Jeff Donnell. No stars at all really but Landers still delivers a pleasant little 'let's put on a show' musical

Swing out the Blues (Columbia) d.Malcolm St Clair: Joyce Compton, Bob Haymes, The Vagabonds. The Vagabonds have a hard time hanging on to meal-ticket Haymes after he marries

Kansas City Kitty (Columbia) d.Del Lord: Joan Davis. Song plugger Davis acquires a music publishing house only to be plunged precipitately into a plagiarism suit over song of title

Weekend Pass (Universal) d.Jean Yarbrough: Noah Beery, Jr, Martha O'Driscoll. Beery's plans for a restful weekend fly out of the window when he meets nightclub singer O'Driscoll

Take it Big (Paramount) d.Frank McDonald: Jack Haley (r). Haley inherits a ramshackle dude ranch, turns it into a hot night spot and accidentally wins a $15,000 rodeo prize

Seven Days Ashore (RKO) d.John H Auer: Gordon Oliver, Elaine Shepard. Playboy turned merchant seaman Oliver has only a week to sort out his complicated love life in Wally Brown-Alan Carney musical comedy

Youth Runs Wild (RKO) d.Mark Robson. Juvenile delinquency melodrama set in a typical defence plant town and starring Bonita Granville, Kent Smith and Lawrence Tierney

They Live in Fear (Columbia) d.Josef Berne. Wartime melodrama in which a former member of the Hitler Youth struggles to readjust to life in an American high school. Otto Kruger plays the head

Destiny (Universal) d.Reginald LeBorg: Gloria Jean, Alan Curtis. Embittered fugitive Curtis redeemed by blind girl Jean in programmer rescued from discarded episode of *Flesh and Fantasy* (1943)

Three Men in White (MGM) d.Willis Goldbeck: Lionel Barrymore, Alma Kruger, Keye Luke. Van Johnson and Luke are the interns vying for post of Dr Gillespie's assistant. Ava Gardner also turns up

When Strangers Marry (Mon) d.William Castle: Robert Mitchum, Kim Hunter, Neil Hamilton. Newly wed Hunter finds husband Dean Jagger is a stranger and possible murderer. One of the best Bs ever made

My Pal Wolf (RKO) d.Alfred Werker: Sharyn Moffet, Grey Shadow. Lonely little rich girl takes in stray Alsatian which has wandered off from nearby Army Dog Training Camp. Sickly sweet conclusion

BRITISH & FOREIGN

Henry V (Two Cities) d.Laurence Olivier: Laurence Olivier. Imaginative blend of stylised design and dramatic location shooting owing much to the epic tradition of Eisenstein.

The Way Ahead (Two Cities) d.Carol Reed: Leslie Dwyer, Jimmy Hanley, Raymond Huntley, James Donald, John Laurie. Army equivalent of *In Which We Serve* with recruits progressing from training to battle

Waterloo Road (Gainsborough) d.Sidney Gilliat: Stewart Granger, John Mills. Private John Mills goes AWOL to check up on wife Joy Shelton's affair with petty crook Granger. Early exercise in social realism

Tawny Pipit (Two Cities) d.Bernard Miles: Lucie Mannheim, Bernard Miles (c). Preservation of rare migrant birds' nest becomes national obsession, disrupts army manouevres, in hymn to 'Englishness'

Two Thousand Women (Gainsborough) d.Frank Launder: Renée Houston, Phyllis Calvert, Flora Robson (r). The women in an internment camp in France help some downed RAF airmen to escape

A Canterbury Tale (Archers) d.Michael Powell: John Sweet, Sheila Sim, Dennis Price, Eric Portman. Magistrate Portman's mystical infatuation with his native Kent leads to odd goings-on in sleepy village

Western Approaches (Crown Film Unit) d.Pat Jackson. Brilliant documentary reconstruction of duel between convoy straggler and U-boat in Atlantic. Colour photography by Jack Cardiff

Hotel Reserve (RKO) d.Lance Comfort: James Mason, Lucie Mannheim. Intricately plotted cloak-and-dagger thriller set in a pre-war hotel in the Riviera. Starts well but quickly falls away

The Yellow Canary (RKO) d.Herbert Wilcox: Richard Greene, Anna Neagle. Neagle makes no secret of her pro-Nazi views but in reality she is a British secret agent infiltrating spy ring

English Without Tears (Two Cities) d.Harold French: Penelope Ward, Lilli Palmer, Michael Wilding, Claude Dauphin. Society lady's daughter falls in love with the butler, who is now an officer and a gentleman

Dear Octopus (Gainsborough) d.Harold French: Roland Culver, Michael Wilding, Margaret Lockwood. Screen version of Dodie Smith's family romance. Celia Johnson excellent as long-lost daughter

This Happy Breed (GFD) d.David Lean: Stanley Holloway, Robert Newton. Noel Coward's tribute to the 'ordinary people' of Britain as personified by the Gibbons family of 17 Sycamore Road, Clapham

Love Story (Gainsborough) d.Leslie Arliss: Margaret Lockwood, Stewart Granger. Escapist tosh centring on romance between pilot losing his sight and concert pianist dying of incurable disease

Halfway House (Ealing) d.Basil Dearden: Mervyn Johns, Glynis Johns. Lumbering exercise in allegory adapted by T E B Clarke from *The Peaceful Inn* by Denis Ogden

Madonna of the Seven Moons (Gainsborough) d.Arthur Crabtree: Stewart Granger, Peter Glenville. Splendid melodrama in which schizophrenic Phyllis Calvert is banker's wife/cut-throat's moll

Bees in Paradise (Gainsborough) d.Val Guest: Arthur Askey, Ronald Shiner. A ferry pilot and his crew crash land on an island governed entirely by women. For Askey fans only

Fanny by Gaslight (Gainsborough) d.Anthony Asquith: Phyllis Calvert, Wilfrid Lawson, John Laurie. Victorian melodrama greatly enlivened by James Mason as snarling misogynistic aristocrat

They Came to a City (Ealing) d.Basil Dearden: Frances Rowe, Mabel Terry Lewis. Nine civilians are transported to a dream city and are presented with the choice of embracing or rejecting its values

Fiddlers Three (Ealing) d.Harry Watt: Frances Day, Sonnie Hale, Tommy Trinder. Broad comedy-musical in which Trinder and Hale take a trip back to Ancient Rome. Extensively reshot by Robert Hamer

Nora (Germany) d.Harald Braun. Fluent adaptation of 'The Doll's House' is saddled with Ibsen's alternative 'happy ending' in line with Nazi doctrine of sanctity of marriage

Champagne Charlie (Ealing) d.Alberto Cavalcanti: Jean Kent (lc), Tommy Trinder. Lovingly mounted comedy-drama set in the world of Victorian music hall. Trinder's best film

Grosse Freiheite No 7 (Germany) d.Helmut Kautner: Illse Werner, Hans Söhnker. Hans Albers vehicle is romance in baroque setting of a sailor who lands up in a nightclub

Junge Adler (Germany) d.Alfred Wiedenmann: Propaganda film centred around an aircraft factory features an appearance by a very young Hardy Kruger

1945

In Europe the war came to an end with VE Day on 8 May. In the Pacific theatre VJ arrived on 15 August. The struggle was over but war subjects still had an important place in the mainstream, as was demonstrated by John Ford's *They Were Expendable*, William Wellman's *GI Joe* and Lewis Milestone's *A Walk in the Sun*. Warner provided a corrective to mindless heroics with *Pride of the Marines*, in which John Garfield played a veteran coming to terms with blindness.

The movie of the year was Billy Wilder's *The Lost Weekend*, which won the Academy Award for Best Picture and a Best Actor Award for Ray Milland as the writer enslaved by booze. In the same film Frank Faylen gave one of the most telling cameos of the decade as a sadistic male nurse in a psychiatric ward. James Dunn won the Best Supporting Actor Award for his performance in *A Tree Grows in Brooklyn*.

Joan Crawford had left MGM in 1943. She had made no film for almost two years (save for a brief appearance in *Hollywood Canteen*) but came back with a bang in *Mildred Pierce* – playing a mother for the first time and also playing on her seemingly limitless capacity for suffering. It was a signal triumph, winning her the Best Actress Oscar and setting her on course for a string of roles in which she played driven business women hovering on the edge of middle age. The New York Critics chose Ingrid Bergman as the year's Best Actress for her performance in *Spellbound*. Bette Davis completed a triptych of resourceful leading ladies with a riveting performance in *The Corn is Green*, adapted from the play by Emlyn Williams. Anne Revere picked up the Academy's Best Actress Award for *National Velvet*.

The film musical was at its peak, but MGM's brilliant producer Arthur Freed overreached himself when he tried to push the genre's boundaries back even further in the ambitious fantasy *Yolanda and the Thief*. The film was a box-office failure, but it pointed the way to the more adventurous MGM musicals of the late 1940s and early 1950s.

New entries in the Top Ten were Van Johnson, child star Margaret O'Brien and singing cowpoke Roy Rogers, who was now firmly established as 'King of the Cowboys'. New faces included action hero Rory Calhoun, and Hurd Hatfield, who was cast in the title role in *The Picture of Dorian Gray*. Another newcomer, Lawrence Tierney, starred in *Dillinger*, Monogram's effort to revive the gangster cycle which had been dormant since the beginning of the decade. The posters for MGM's *Adventure* proclaimed 'Gable's Back, And Garson's Got Him!' but the King's return after war service was a limp affair. Some of the old magic seemed to have flaked away. Laird Cregar died after a drastic diet before surgery fatally weakened his heart.

In Britain the film industry entered the postwar period in a spirit of great optimism. Annual cinema admissions crept up towards 1600 million. Olivier's *Henry V* had scored an immense prestige success in the United States and films like producer Sydney Box's *The Seventh Veil* were also making inroads into the American market. The most powerful figure in the industry, J Arthur Rank, was determined to build a film empire on traditional Hollywood lines and take on the Americans in their own territory. But a more reliable pointer to the future of British films in the 1940s was the modest, parochial, highly efficient output of Ealing Studios. In 1945 they released the classic portmanteau collection of tales of the supernatural, *Dead of Night*, and the period melodrama *Pink String and Sealing Wax*. The latter starred Googie Withers, whose powerful screen presence was often too big for the narrow confines of British cinema.

ACTION

Objective Burma (Warner) d.Raoul Walsh: Roderic Red Wing, James Brown. The film, notorious in Britain, in which Errol Flynn appeared to overrun Burma singlehanded. Superb photography by James Wong Howe

A Walk in the Sun (Fox) d.Lewis Milestone: Lloyd Bridges, Dana Andrews. The war in microcosm. A platoon of infantrymen are ordered to capture an isolated farmhouse. Rhythmically scripted

G I Joe (UA) d. William Wellman: Robert Mitchum. Gritty, unheroic hymn of praise for the ordinary infantryman. Based on the writings of war correspondent Ernie Pyle played by Burgess Meredith

Counter Attack (Columbia) d.Zoltan Korda: Paul Muni, Marguerite Chapman, Roman Bohnen. No-better-than-average drama of partisans operating behind German lines sabotaging vital installations

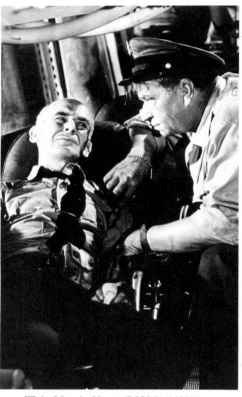

This Man's Navy (MGM) d.William Wellman: James Gleason, Wallace Beery. Usual rehash of all the Beery formulae, this time casting Tom Drake as the old battler's surrogate son

They Were Expendable (MGM) d.John Ford: James Pennick, John Wayne, Robert Montgomery, Ward Bond. Measured account of the role played by torpedo boats during withdrawal from the Philippines

God is My Co-Pilot (Warner) d.Robert Florey: Alan Hale, Dennis Morgan. Religious sentiment drenches story of Army reject who becomes hero with the 'Flying Tigers'. Based on Colonel Robert Lee Scott's book

Back to Bataan (Republic) d.Edward Dmytryk: John Wayne. Big John teaches the Filipino natives – among them Anthony Quinn – how to fight the Japanese guerrilla style

Pride of the Marines (Warner) d.Delmer Daves: John Garfield, Eleanor Parker. Antidote to gung-ho action heroics as blinded serviceman Garfield faces new battle adjusting to civilian life

Blood on the Sun (UA) d.Frank Lloyd: Rhys Williams, Sylvia Sidney, James Cagney. Pacy thriller with newsman Cagney stumbling over Japanese plans for conquest in pre-war Tokyo

Salty O'Rourke (Paramount) d.Raoul Walsh: Alan Ladd, Gail Russell, Bruce Cabot. Crisply told gangster melodrama with a racetrack background. Ladd is the luckless gambler in trouble with the mob

Paris Underground (UA) d.Gregory Ratoff: Gracie Fields, Constance Bennett. One of cinema's odder pairings has Fields and Bennett continuing the Resistance work in Nazi POW camp

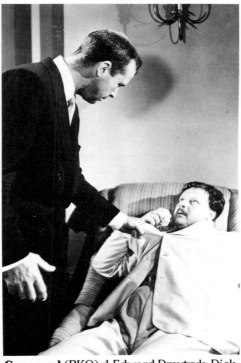

Cornered (RKO) d.Edward Dmytryk: Dick Powell, Walter Slezak. Powell in fine vengeful form as airman hunting the collaborators who murdered his French wife

The House on 92nd Street (Fox) d.Henry Hathaway: Lloyd Nolan. Signe Hasso leads spy ring attempting to snatch atomic secrets in quasi-realistic reconstruction of FBI counter-espionage activities

Captain Eddie (Fox) d.Lloyd Bacon: Fred MacMurray. Floating in a life raft awaiting rescue, World War I fighter ace Rickenbacker (MacMurray) reminisces about his career

Dangerous Partners (MGM) d.Edward L Cahn: Edmund Gwenn, James Craig, Signe Hasso. Serviceable programmer in which Craig and Hasso play a couple of shady characters who break up Gwenn's spy ring

Confidential Agent (Warner) d.Herman Shumlin: Lauren Bacall, Arthur Gould-Porter, Charles Boyer. Disappointing Greene adaptation finds Spanish loyalist Boyer tangling with fascist heavies in England

ADVENTURE

Men of the Deep (Columbia) d.Del Lord: Victor McLaglen, Veda Ann Borg. McLaglen and Chester Morris walk their way through routine comedy drama of deep sea diving experts who join up

Captain Kidd (UA) d.Rowland V Lee: Charles Laughton, Randolph Scott. Laughton hams and blusters away engagingly but cannot disguise the skimpy nature of this would-be swashbuckler

A Thousand and One Nights (Columbia) d.Alfred E Green: Adele Jergens, Cornel Wilde, Evelyn Keyes. Colourful production values boost Arabian Nights hokum. Rex Ingram repeats famous genie role

Tarzan and the Amazons (RKO) d.Kurt Neumann: Johnny Weissmuller, Johnny Sheffield, Brenda Joyce. Tarzan protects a tribe of warrior women from archaeologists overcome by lust for gold

Sudan (Universal) d.John Rawlins: Jon Hall, Andy Devine, Maria Montez. Maria is Ancient Egyptian queen snatched by slave traders. George Zucco plays unctuously scheming chamberlain

National Velvet (MGM) d.Clarence Brown: Elizabeth Taylor, Micky Rooney. Spunky kids train horse to win legendary Grand National steeplechase. Followed by feeble sequel *International Velvet* in 1978

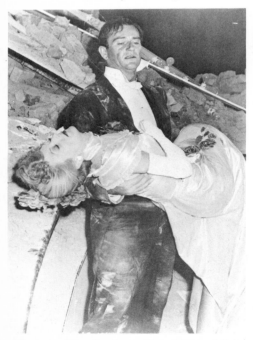

Song of the Sarong (Universal) d.Harold Young: George Dolenz, Nancy Kelly. William Gargan explores a remote island in search of fabulous pearls. Weird mixture of adventure, comedy and musical

Flame of the Barbary Coast (Republic) d.Joseph Kane: John Wayne, Ann Dvorak. Wayne vies with Joseph Schildkraut for hand of saloon singer Dvorak while San Francisco earthquake waits in the wings

The Great John L (UA) d.Frank Tuttle: Wallace Ford, Linda Darnell, Greg McClure, George Matthews. Deftly told tale of the rise and fall of boxing champion John L Sullivan with McClure in title role

Son of Lassie (MGM) d.S Sylvan Simon: Peter Lawford. The noble canine puts in a woof or two for the war effort in capable sequel to *Lassie Come Home* (1943) with espionage background

MELODRAMA

And Then There Were None (Fox) d.René Clair: June Duprez. Briskly orchestrated adaptation of Agatha Christie mystery with guests on a lonely island going down like ninepins. Some neat visual touches

Scarlet Street (Universal) d.Fritz Lang: Edward G Robinson, Joan Bennett. Scheming Bennett and Dan Duryea draw Robinson into world of crime and deception. Remake of Renoir's *La Chienne* (1931)

Conflict (Warner) d.Curtis Bernhardt: Alexis Smith, Humphrey Bogart. Wife-murderer Bogart is trapped in web woven by jovial psychiatrist Sydney Greenstreet. Stylish but rather empty exercise

Fallen Angel (Fox) d.Otto Preminger: Anne Revere, Alice Faye, Dana Andrews. Cynical press agent Andrews marries Faye for money and is then suspected of the murder of his mistress Linda Darnell

Johnny Angel (RKO) d.Edwin L Marin: Claire Trevor, George Raft. Sea captain Raft hunts down the mutineers who killed his father and hijacked consignment of gold bullion. Suspenseful

Tomorrow is Forever (RKO) d.Irving Pichel: Orson Welles, Claudette Colbert. Orson is reported missing in WWI but returns with new face to find wife Colbert remarried to George Brent

Escape in the Desert (Warner) d.Edward A Blatt: Philip Dorn, Hans Schumm, Jean Sullivan. Remake of *Petrified Forest* (1936) updated to accommodate Nazis on the run from a desert prison camp

The Suspect (Universal) d.Robert Siodmak: Ella Raines, Charles Laughton. Unhappy Laughton murders his ghastly wife, marries charming Raines. Then blackmailer Henry Daniell turns up

The Lost Weekend (Paramount) d.Billy Wilder: Ray Milland. Milland brilliant as the writer too dreamily trapped in the romance of booze to make the 'happy ending' convincing

Hangover Square (Fox) d. John Brahm: Laird Cregar, Glenn Langan, Linda Darnell. Full-blooded Gothic adaptation of Patrick Hamilton novel with Cregar as unhinged composer. Fine score by Bernard Herrmann

Bewitched (MGM) d. Arch Oboler: Edmund Gwenn, Phyllis Thaxter. Intriguing tale of murdering schizophrenic Thaxter anticipates *Lizzie* (1957) *The Three Faces of Eve* (1957)

Love Letters (Paramount) d. William Dieterle: Jennifer Jones, Joseph Cotten, Cecil Kellaway. Victor Young's haunting title song is best thing in tearjerker of amnesiac Jones cured by Cotten's devotion

The Brighton Strangler (RKO) d. Max Nosseck: June Duprez, John Loder. Loder is actor driven mad by air raid injury who starts to live out murderous stage role. Hints at *A Double Life* (1948)

The Southerner (UA) d. Jean Renoir: Zachary Scott, J Carrol Naish. Renoir brings gentle poetry to drama of sharecroppers struggling for survival, but the underlying feel is curiously phoney

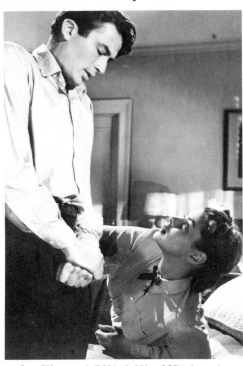

Spellbound (UA) d. Alfred Hitchcock: Gregory Peck, Ingrid Bergman. Psychiatrist Bergman delves deep into Peck's subconcious, revealing Salvador Dali-designed dream sequences

Our Vines Have Tender Grapes (MGM) d. Roy Rowland: Margaret O'Brien, Jackie 'Butch' Jenkins, Edward G Robinson, Agnes Moorehead. Syrupy account of American-Norwegian life in Wisconsin

Hotel Berlin (Warner) d. Peter Godfrey: Faye Emerson, Kurt Kreuger. Vicki Baum story set during the fall of the Third Reich. Peter Lorre riveting as disillusioned academic

Danger Signal (Warner) d. Robert Florey: Zachary Scott, Faye Emerson. Indecisive Zachary wobbles hopelessly between fiancée Faye Emerson and younger, wealthier sister Mona Freeman

The Strange Affair of Uncle Harry (Universal) d.Robert Siodmak: Samuel Hinds, George Sanders, Ella Raines. Sanders abandons his cad persona to play meek man fatally bullied by his sisters

Mildred Pierce (Warner) d.Michael Curtiz: Zachary Scott, Joan Crawford. Joan's portrayal of the ferociously driven over-achieving Mildred is paradigm of her own unhappy life. It won her an Oscar

The Corn is Green (Warner) d.Irving Rapper: John Dall, Bette Davis. Suitably padded up Davis steps into Ethel Barrymore role of selfless schoolmistress coaching Welsh miner Dall for university

A Tree Grows in Brooklyn (Fox) d.Elia Kazan: Peggy Ann Garner, Dorothy McGuire, Ted Donaldson. Richly detailed picture of a family struggling to make ends meet. Joan Blondell as Aunt Cissie

Weekend at the Waldorf (MGM) d.Robert Z Leonard. Leon Ames, Moroni Olsen, Ginger Rogers, Irving Bacon. Polished remake of 1932 hit *Grand Hotel* with Rogers and Walter Pidgeon stealing the honours

COMEDY

Christmas in Connecticut (Warner) d.Peter Godfrey: Barbara Stanwyck, Dennis Morgan. Stanwyck's career as cookery writer is threatened when boss orders her to entertain war hero

A Medal for Benny (Paramount) d.Irving Pichel: J Carrol Naish, Frank McHugh, Arturo de Cordova, Dorothy Lamour. Pointed comedy of town hypocritically honouring one of its war dead

Murder, He Says (Paramount) d.George Marshall: Jean Heather, Fred MacMurray, Helen Walker. Zany comedy in which insurance man MacMurray encounters a family of homicidal hayseeds

Junior Miss (Fox) d.George Seaton: Peggy Ann Garner. Garner is ebullient match-making teenager meddling in her family's affairs in lively adaptation of Broadway hit

Don Juan Quilligan (Fox) d.Frank Tuttle: Joan Blondell, William Bendix, Phil Silvers. Oafish Hudson Bay barge captain Bendix devises novel way of escaping a charge of bigamy

Over 21 (Columbia) d.Charles Vidor: Irene Dunne, Alexander Knox, Charles Coburn. Middle-aged Knox struggles through World War II officer training with help of wife Dunne, in adaptation of Ruth Gordon play

Practically Yours (Paramount) d.Mitchell Leisen: Fred MacMurray, Gil Lamb, Claudette Colbert. Pilot MacMurray is reported missing in action, but his last message causes complications

Kiss and Tell (Columbia) d.Richard Wallace: Katherine Alexander, Walter Abel, Shirley Temple, Jerome Courtland. The feud between two families forces a secret marriage and myriad muddles

Love, Honour and Goodbye (Republic) d.Albert Rogell: Nils Asther, Edward Ashley, Virginia Bruce. A husband tries to wreck wife's career by secretly backing dud play in which she is to star

A Royal Scandal (Fox) d.Ernst Lubitsch, Otto Preminger: Tallulah Bankhead, William Eythe. Amorous Tallulah cast as Catherine the Great pampering young protegé Eythe. Finished by Preminger

Colonel Effingham's Raid (Fox) d.Irving Pichel: Charles Coburn. Military diehard Coburn fights to save a town's historical landmark with good support from Joan Bennett, Allyn Joslyn, Donald Meek

Hold that Blonde (Paramount) d.George Marshall: Veronica Lake, Eddie Bracken. Kleptomaniac Bracken joins forces with beautiful crook Lake in breezy comedy outing

She Wouldn't Say Yes (Columbia) d.Alexander Hall: Rosalind Russell, Adele Jergens. Psychiatrist Russell steers well clear of marriage until she meets famous cartoonist Lee Bowman

The Bullfighters (Fox) d.Malcolm St Clair: Oliver Hardy, Stan Laurel. Looking sadly old, L & H thrash around in Mexico in search of a lady criminal. A long, long way from their best

Abbott and Costello in Hollywood (MGM) d.S Sylvan Simon. Strain on A & C's basically limited repertoire beginning to show as they crash Tinsel Town in guise of barber and porter

The Sailor Takes a Wife (MGM) d.Richard Whorf: June Allyson, Hume Cronyn, Robert Walker, Reginald Owen, Audrey Totter. Pleasant domestic comedy occasionally succumbs to the cutes

Road to Utopia (Paramount) d.Hal Walker: Bob Hope, Dorothy Lamour, Bing Crosby, Robert Barrat, Nestor Paiva. Bob and Bing in the Klondike, Dorothy sings, Robert Benchley provides commentary

Here Comes the Co-Eds (Universal) d.Jean Yarbrough: Lou Costello, Martha O'Driscoll, Bud Abbott, Peggy Ryan. A & C are caretakers rescuing a school from bankruptcy

The Naughty Nineties (Universal) d.Jean Yarbrough: Rita Johnson, Alan Curtis, Frank Bailey, Lou Costello, Bud Abbott, Henry Travers. The usual complications follow A & C on to a Mississippi river boat cruise

Out of This World (Paramount) d.Hal Walker: Cass Daley, Veronica Lake, Eddie Bracken, Diana Lynn. Bracken is crooning telegram boy hitching an eventful ride with Diana Lynn's all-girl orchestra

Roughly Speaking (Warner) d.Michael Curtiz: Rosalind Russell, Jack Carson. Breezy account of the life of the eccentric pioneer feminist Louise Randall Pierson and her large family

Pardon My Past (Columbia) d.Leslie Fenton: Marguerite Chapman, Fred MacMurray. Hapless MacMurray incurs the debts and enemies of famous playboy lookalike

Pillow to Post (Warner) d.Vincent Sherman: William Prince, Ida Lupino. Circumstances force salesperson Ida Lupino to acquire a temporary husband in ill-advised excursion by Sherman into farce

What Next, Corporal Hargrove? (MGM): d.Richard Thorpe: Robert Walker, Jean Porter. Episodic sequel to *See Here Private Hargrove* (1944) with Walker in France accompanied by buddy Keenan Wynn

The Horn Blows at Midnight (Warner) d.Raoul Walsh: Jack Benny, Alexis Smith, Guy Kibbee. Trumpeter Benny falls asleep and dreams he is an angel in almost unrelievedly unfunny comedy

It's in the Bag (UA) d.Richard Wallace: Fred Allen, William Bendix. Flea-circus promoter Allen pursues inheritance in plot similar to Mel Brooks' *The Twelve Chairs* (1970)

That's the Spirit (Universal) d.Charles Lamont: June Vincent, Jack Oakie. Long-dead hoofer Oakie returns to Earth to help daughter Peggy Ryan in fantasy musical comedy

She Went to the Races (MGM) d.Willis Goldbeck: Charles Halton, Ava Gardner, James Craig, Frances Gifford. A team of scientists attempt to devise a foolproof betting system

Lady on a Train (Universal) d.Charles David: Edward Everett Horton, Deanna Durbin. Mystery writer David Bruce helps murder witness Deanna to track down a killer in entertaining comedy-thriller

Guest Wife (UA) d.Sam Wood: Don Ameche, Claudette Colbert. Marital mix-ups with Claudette posing as Ameche's wife to confusion of real hubby Dick Foran

Man Alive (RKO) d.Ray Enright: Pat O'Brien, Ellen Drew, Minna Gombell. Magician Adolphe Menjou urges jealous husband O'Brien to masquerade as a ghost and haunt wife Drew

I'll Tell the World (Universal) d.Leslie Goodwins: Lee Tracy (c), June Preisser, Raymond Walburn (centre back row). Fast-talking Tracy puts a radio station on the map with a lonely hearts programme

SNAFU (Columbia) d.Jack Moss: Robert Benchley, Conrad Janis, Vera Vague. A young demobilised soldier returns from the war to find family treating him as if he was still a young boy

WESTERNS

Saratoga Trunk (Warner) d.Sam Wood: Gary Cooper, Ingrid Bergman. Overlong melodrama with fortune-hunting Bergman wavering between railroad entrepreneur John Warburton and Cooper

The Bells of Rosarita (Republic) d.Frank McDonald: George 'Gabby' Hayes (r). Gimmick western in which Roy Rogers summons up a small army of sagebrush stars to dish the heavies

San Fernando Valley (Republic) d.John English: Dale Evans, Roy Rogers. Roy receives his first screen kiss, albeit a chaste one from Jean Porter in a rather odd dream sequence

Dakota (Republic) d.Joseph Kane: Mike Mazurki, John Wayne, Vera Hruba Ralston, Grant Withers. Wayne and Ralston are the young couple who get mixed up in plans to buy land along a proposed railroad route

The Cisco Kid Returns (Mon) d.John P McCarthy: Martin Garralaga, Cecilia Callejo, Duncan Renaldo. First of three Renaldo Cisco movies after Cesar Romero left the series to join the Navy. Routine stuff

Return of the Durango Kid (Columbia) d.Derwin Abrahams: John Calvert (2nd l), Jean Stevens. The Durango Kid (Charles Starrett) clears his dead father's name and saves a stagecoach line

Frontier Gal (Universal) d.Charles Lamont: Yvonne De Carlo, Rod Cameron. De Carlo and Cameron are feuding lovers in broad comedy Western modelled on *Destry Rides Again* (1939)

Along Came Jones (International) d.Stuart Heisler: Gary Cooper, William Demarest, Loretta Young. Comedy western in which Cooper guys his screen image as tenderfoot mistaken for killer Dan Duryea

Lawless Empire (Columbia) d.Vernon Keays: Charles Starrett (l). The Durango Kid rescues some homesteaders from landgrabbers led by a doctor and saloon keeper

ROMANCE

The Bells of St Mary's (Paramount) d. Leo McCarey: Ingrid Bergman, Bing Crosby. Sequel to *Going My Way* (1944), in which Bing tells Ingrid, 'If you're ever in trouble, dial O for O'Malley'

The Enchanted Cottage (RKO) d. John Cromwell: Robert Young, Dorothy McGuire. Unashamedly sentimental account of disfigured, Young and Plain Jane McGuire finding that love overcomes all

A Bell for Adano (Fox) d. Henry King: Fortunio Bonanova, John Hodiak, Gene Tierney. Hodiak is American officer administering small Italian town, falling for Tierney, retrieving bell taken by Germans

Under the Clock (MGM) d. Vincente Minnelli: Robert Walker, Judy Garland. Dewy love story with New York girl Garland meeting and marrying soldier Walker on his 48-hour leave

The Affairs of Susan (Paramount) d. William Seiter: Joan Fontaine, Vera Marshe, Dennis O'Keefe. Romantic comedy in which O'Keefe is just one of four men in Fontaine's crowded life

Adventure (MGM) d. Victor Fleming: Greer Garson, Joan Blondell, Clark Gable. Gable's first for three years focuses on misfiring marriage between hardbitten merchant seaman and librarian Garson

Without Love (MGM) d. Harold S Bucquet: Spencer Tracy, Katharine Hepburn. Misogynist inventor Tracy marries man-wary widow Hepburn in sparkling, generally underrated comedy

A Letter for Evie (MGM) d. Jules Dassin: John Carroll, Marsha Hunt. Marsha's wimpish pen pal Hume Cronyn sends her a photograph of he-man Carroll. Remake of 1922 silent hit *Don't Write Letters*

Valley of Decision (MGM) d. Tay Garnett: Greer Garson, Marsha Hunt, Marshall Thompson. Romantic drama with steel industry background. Servant girl Greer marries mill-owner's son Gregory Peck

Her Highness and the Bellboy (MGM) d. Richard Thorpe: Hedy Lamarr, Robert Walker. Absolute turkey in which hotel employee Walker imagines visiting princess Lamarr is in love with him

Those Endearing Young Charms (RKO)
d. Lewis Allen: Robert Young, Ann Harding,
Laraine Day, Bill Williams. Philandering
Young is laid low by sweetly innocent Day.
Harding is worldly wise mother

This Love of Ours (Universal) d. William
Dieterle: Merle Oberon, Charles Korvin, Sue
England. England imagines her mother to
be dead. But she's alive, she's Oberon and
she's trying to patch it up with Korvin

I'll Be Seeing You (UA) d. William
Dieterle: Joseph Cotten, Walter Baldwin,
Ginger Rogers. Shell-shocked soldier
Cotten falls in love with reformatory
parolee Rogers. Tender and affecting

MUSICALS

Duffy's Tavern (Paramount) d. Hal Walker:
Sonny Tufts, Paulette Goddard. Ed Gardner,
Victor Moore come to the rescue of a
recording studio in contrived parade of the
studio's contract stars

Masquerade in Mexico (Paramount)
d. Mitchell Leisen: Dorothy Lamour.
Nightclub singer Lamour finds herself
mixed up in a jewel robbery in Mexico City.
Remake of *Midnight* (1939)

Rhapsody in Blue (Warner) d. Irving
Rapper: Joan Leslie. Music speaks louder
than words in lavish but largely fictitious
biopic of George Gershwin (Robert Alda).
Oscar Levant has the best lines

The Dolly Sisters (Fox) d. Irving
Cummings: Betty Grable, John Payne, June
Haver. Gaudy, vulgar account of two
Hungarian sisters rocketing to fame at
Oscar Hammerstein's Musical Hall

Patrick the Great (Universal) d. Frank
Ryan: Peggy Ryan, Donald O'Connor.
O'Connor and father Donald Cook fall out
over the same part in a Broadway show.
Wisecracking support from Eve Arden

On Stage Everybody (Universal) d. Jean
Yarbrough: Jack Oakie, Peggy Ryan. Slender
plot has diehard vaudevillian Oakie coming
to terms with radio, which he professes
to despise

Billy Rose's Diamond Horseshoe (Fox) d. George Seaton: Betty Grable. Betty is the shopgirl with the 'mink coat complex', Dick Haymes a medic with greasepaint in his veins, in tribute to showman Rose

Wonder Man (RKO) d. H Bruce Humberstone: Danny Kaye. Danny in dual role as brothers, the serious one taking the place of his devil-may-care singing sibling when the latter is killed by mobsters

Sunbonnet Sue (Mon) d. Ralph Murphy: Alan Mowbray, Gale Storm, Minna Gombell. Turn-of-the-century Bowery provides background to pleasant effort from poverty row

Thrill of a Romance (MGM) d. Richard Thorpe: Esther Williams, Van Johnson. War hero Johnson chases newly wed Williams in between trips to the swimming pool in Sierra Nevada-set entertainment

George White's Scandals of 1945 (RKO) d. Felix Feist: Joan Davis, Gene Krupa, Jack Haley. Paper-thin 'putting on a show' musical's high spot is Ethel Smith's organ rendition of the Gershwin's 'Liza'

State Fair (Fox) d. Walter Lang: Percy Kilbride, Charles Winninger, Fay Bainter. Jeanne Crain repeats 1933 Janet Gaynor role in gentle bucolic romance with Dana Andrews. Remade in 1962

The Stork Club (Paramount) d. Hal Walker: Betty Hutton. Hat-check girl Betty saves a millionaire's life, but his gratitude leads to complications with returning serviceman boyfriend Don Defore

Yolanda and the Thief (MGM) d. Vincente Minnelli: Fred Astaire, Lucille Bremer. Remarkable, stylized blend of song, dance and colour with con-man Astaire falling for gullible young heiress Bremer

The Three Caballeros (RKO) d. Norman Ferguson: Aurora Miranda, Donald Duck. Dazzlingly inventive animation achievement with Donald opening up a series of birthday presents

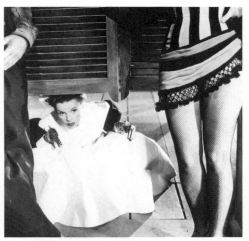

The Harvey Girls (MGM) d. George Sidney: Judy Garland. Judy is enchanting as straitlaced waitress in the Wild West, singing 'On the Atchison, Topeka and the Sante Fe'

Hit the Hay (Columbia) d.Del Lord: Fortunio Bonanova, Judy Canova. Ross Hunter grooms hayseed Canova for career in opera. Only trouble is she can't act (so what's new?)

Anchors Aweigh (MGM) d.George Sidney: Gene Kelly, Frank Sinatra. Ultra-energetic archetypal Kelly movie, with Gene and Frank trying to help Kathryn Grayson to stardom

Bring On the Girls (Paramount) d.Sidney Lanfield: Sonny Tufts, Veronica Lake, Eddie Bracken. Millionaire Sonny hopes to escape gold diggers by joining the Navy. Cigarette girl Lake stays on his trail

It's a Pleasure (RKO) d.William Seiter: Sonja Henie. Sonja swoops around the rink and romances hockey star Michael O'Shea in bland skating mini-spectacular. Best kept on ice

Eadie Was a Lady (Columbia) d.Arthur Dreifuss: William Wright, Ann Miller. Miller is straitlaced college girl by day, queen of burlesque by night, in entertaining programmer

Eve Knew her Apples (Columbia) d.Will Jason: Ann Miller. Runaway radio singer Miller is mistaken for a murderess by newspaper man William Wright. Ann sings but, alas, does not dance

That Night With You (Universal) d.William Seiter: Susanna Foster, David Bruce, Franchot Tone, Louise Allbritton. Soprano Foster tries to convince producer Tone that she's his daughter

Nob Hill (Fox) d.Henry Hathaway: Vivian Blaine, George Raft. Patchwork of old Fox musical hits, notably *Hello, Frisco, Hello* (1943), set on San Francisco's Barbary Coast

Incendiary Blonde (Paramount) d.George Marshall: Betty Hutton. Betty tears hell for leather into biopic of Texas Guinan, the lady whose favourite phrase was 'Hello Suckers'

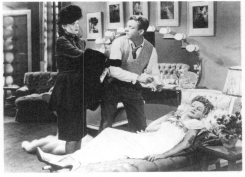

Earl Carroll Vanities (Republic) d.Joseph Santley: Stephanie Bachelor, Dennis O'Keefe, Constance Moore. Ruritanian princess Moore visits New York and gets caught up in a Broadway extravaganza

HORROR

The Picture of Dorian Gray (MGM)
d. Albert Lewin: Hurd Hatfield. Hatfield is
the ageless one, contemplating his
depraved portrait, George Sanders the
ironic heavy, in stylish Wilde adaptation

Pillow of Death (Universal) d. Wallace
Fox: Brenda Joyce, Lon Chaney, Jr.
Schizophrenic Chaney goes on a murder
rampage but all is revealed in spooky,
psychic climax

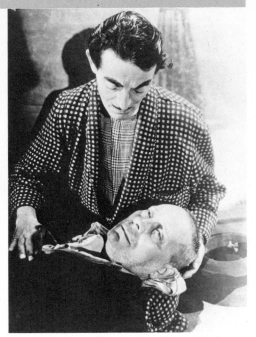

The Great Flamarion (Republic)
d. Anthony Mann: Lester Allen, Erich von
Stroheim. Von Stroheim is the circus
sharpshooter driven to murder by vixenish
flirt Mary Beth Hughes

The Unseen (Paramount) d. Lewis Allen:
Herbert Marshall, Gail Russell. Dismal
sequel to *The Uninvited* (1944) finds Gail
Russell once again on the receiving end of
ghostly attention. Feeble ending

Isle of the Dead (RKO) d. Mark Robson:
Boris Karloff, Katherine Emery. Plague and
vampires stalk a Greek island. Karloff
mesmeric as general succumbing to
superstition

The Body Snatcher (RKO) d. Robert Wise:
Boris Karloff, Bela Lugosi, Henry Daniell.
Atmospheric variation on the Burke and
Hare theme with Daniell outstanding as
tormented man of science

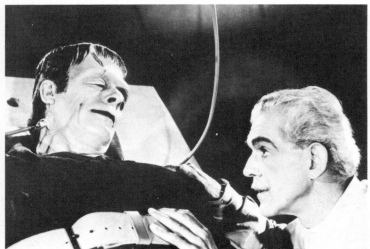

House of Frankenstein (Universal) d. Erle
C Kenton: Glenn Strange, Boris Karloff. Mad
doctor Karloff goes monster collecting,
befriends Count Dracula, Frankenstein
Monster and the Wolf Man

The Vampire's Ghost (Republic) d. Lesley
Selander: John Abbott (1). Abbott puts his
sinister charm to good use as the vampiric
leader of West Africa's underworld sucking
blood since the days of Good Queen Bess

The Frozen Ghost (Universal) d.Harold Young: Evelyn Ankers, Lon Chaney, Jr, Elena Verdugo. Chaney is a hypnotist whose strange powers result in the death of a member of his audience

A Game of Death (RKO) d.Robert Wise: Gene Stutenroth, Audrey Long, Edgar Barrier, Russell Wade. Remake of *The Most Dangerous Game* (1932) with Barrier as hunter who prefers human game

House of Dracula (Universal) d.Erle C Kenton: Onslow Stevens, Lon Chaney, Jr. Concerned scientist Stevens cures the Wolf Man, eliminates Dracula, but draws a fatal blank on Frankenstein's Monster

B MOVIES

China's Little Devils (Mon) d.Monta Bell: 'Duckie' Louie. The story of a Chinese boy, orphaned and adopted by some Flying Tigers, who organizes mission children into a guerrilla unit to harass the Japanese

First Yank into Tokyo (RKO) d.Gordon Douglas: Barbara Hale, Tom Neal. Neal undergoes plastic surgery for mission to rescue imprisoned American scientist. First topical reference to A-bomb

Betrayal from the East (RKO) d.William Berke: Philip Ahn, Lee Tracy, Abner Biberman. Likeable rogue Tracy is double agent playing along with Japanese attempts to seize Panama Canal defence plans

Shady Lady (Universal) d.George Waggner: Robert Paige, Ginny Simms. State Attorney Paige falls in love with the niece of a notorious card sharp, tangles with a night-club racketeer

Grissly's Millions (Republic) d.John English: Virginia Grey, Paul Kelly. Grey inherits a fortune but finds herself at the mercy of a pack of fortune hunters and accused of a brace of murders

Allotment Wives (Mon) d.William Nigh: Kay Francis, Bernard Nedell, Gertrude Michael. Kay is lured into crooked scheme in which loose women wed soldiers to get their federal paychecks

Dillinger (Mon) d.Max Nosseck: Anne Jeffreys, Lawrence Tierney. Hard-hitting gangster melo padded out with generous chunks of action footage from Fritz Lang's *You Only Live Once* (1937)

My Name is Julia Ross (Columbia) d.Joseph H Lewis: George Macready, Nina Foch. Unsuspecting Foch is pawn in plot to cover up the murder of psychopath Macready's wife. Small masterpiece

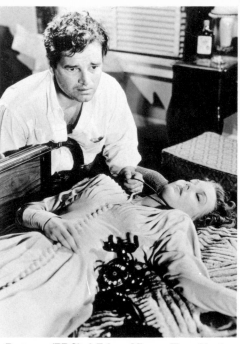

Detour (PRC) d.Edgar Ulmer: Tom Neal, Ann Savage. Intriguingly incoherent film noir with bleak dénounment and cult reputation. One of the best films to come out of poverty row

The Hidden Eye (MGM) d.Richard Whorf: Edward Arnold, William Phillips, Frances Rafferty, Paul Langton, 'Friday'. Arnold reprises the blind detective role he first played in *Eyes in the Night* (1942)

Strange Illusion (PRC) d.Edgar Ulmer: James Lydon. Ingenious psychological melodrama in which a dream leads Lydon into solving the riddle of his father's death

Divorce (Mon) d.William Nigh: Helen Mack, Kay Francis, Bruce Cabot. Old flame Kay vamps unsettled war hero away from his wife, but not for long, in sentimental programmer

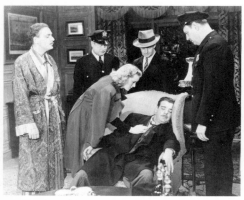

Strange Confession (Universal) d.John Hoffman: Brenda Joyce, Lon Chaney, Jr. Chaney is a chemist who decides to murder his drug-peddling boss. Weak entry in 'Inner Sanctum' series

Why Girls Leave Home (Mon) d.William Berke: Constance Worth, Pamela Blake. Dastardly goings on at the infamous Kitten club lead to the death of a hostess. Lola Lane a convincing heavy

Two O'Clock Courage (RKO) d.Anthony Mann: Jack Norton, Tom Conway, Ann Rutherford. Amnesia victim Conway is fingered on murder rap in remake of *Two in the Dark* (1936)

Sing Your Way Home (RKO) d.Anthony Mann: Jack Haley, Anne Jeffreys, Marcy McGuire, Glenn Vernon. Haley is in charge of a group of American teenagers trapped in Europe by the war

Radio Stars on Parade (RKO) d.Leslie Goodwins: Tony Romano, Frances Langford. Songs include 'I Couldn't Sleep a Wink Last Night'. Unlikely after sitting through this leaden programmer

Bedside Manner (UA) d.Andrew L Stone: John Carroll, Ruth Hussey. Romantic comedy with doctor Hussey tending crashed pilot Carroll, who feigns madness to keep her around

Swing Out Sister (Universal) d.Edward Lilley: Jacqueline de Wit, Frances Raeburn. Raeburn spends her time warbling in a nightclub when she should be pursuing her operatic studies

Easy to Look At (Universal) d.Ford Beebe: J Edward Bromberg, Dick French, Gloria Jean. Gloria Jean plays a singing fashion designer who comes to New York only to be accused of plagiarism

Swingin' on a Rainbow (Republic) d.William Beaudine: Harry Langdon, Jane Frazee. Composer Frazee enters a radio song competition, wins first prize and lyricist Brad Taylor. Langdon's last film

Blonde from Brooklyn (Columbia) d.Del Lord: Mary Treen, Lynn Merrick. Merrick breaks into radio under the assumed name of Susanna Belwithers, finds it's also name of missing heiress

Ten Cents a Dance (Columbia) d.Will Jason: Joan Woodbury, Robert Scott, Jimmy Lloyd, Jane Frazee. Pleasant little second feature has nothing to do with the 1931 film directed by Lionel Barrymore

Delightfully Dangerous (UA) d.Arthur Lubin: Jane Powell. Little Miss Fixit Powell sets about boosting sister Constance Moore's showbiz career and marrying her off to Ralph Bellamy

Twice Blessed (MGM) d.Harry Beaumont: Preston Foster, Lynn and Lee Wilde. Identical twins switch their identities in a bid to reunite estranged parents Foster and Gail Patrick

A Guy, a Girl and a Pal (Columbia)
d.Budd Boetticher: Ted Donaldson, Lynn
Merrick, Ross Hunter. Hunter and Merrick
pretend to be man and wife to secure
Merrick a train seat

Hitchhike to Happiness (Republic)
d.Joseph Santley: Willy Trenk, Brad Taylor,
Dale Evans. Irritating Hungarian producer
Trenk is conned into believing waiter Al
Pearce has penned masterpiece

Her Lucky Night (Universal) d.Edward
Lilley: The Andrews Sisters, Martha
O'Driscoll. O'Driscoll takes a fortune teller
at her word and devises loopy scheme to
snare the man of her dreams

Mama Loves Papa (RKO) d.Frank Strayer:
Leon Errol, Elisabeth Risdon. Errol is the
dithering clerk whose job as playground
commissioner lands him in a sea of
troubles. Remake of 1933 Paramount film

Getting Gertie's Garter (UA) d.Allan
Dwan: Sheila Ryan, Jerome Cowan. Strained
comedy of marital mix-ups is a variant of
the ancient plot used in *Up in Mabel's
Room* (1926)

She Gets Her Man (Universal) d.Erle C
Kenton: Leon Errol, Joan Davis. Joan mugs
happily through role of special investigator
extraordinaire solving murder mystery in
this bouncy comedy

What a Blonde (RKO) d.Leslie Goodwins:
Chef Milani, Leon Errol, Richard Lane,
Dorothy Vaughn. Topical comedy in which
Errol is the lingerie millionaire who finds an
amusing way out of the gas rationing crisis

Steppin' in Society (Republic)
d.Alexander Esway: Edward Everett Horton,
Frank Jenks (r). A judge is accidentally
stranded at an inn with some crooks, who
take him to be a master racketeer

Brewster's Millions (UA) d.Allan Dwan:
June Havoc, Mischa Auer, Dennis O'Keefe.
Monty Brewster inherits 8 million dollars
from eccentric uncle on condition he
spends a million in two months

The Power of the Whistler (Columbia) d. Lew Landers: Richard Dix (c). Dix is a homicidal maniac who escapes from an asylum, bent on murdering the judge who committed him

The Red Dragon (Mon) d. Phil Rosen: Benson Fong, Sidney Toler, Fortunio Bonanova. Charlie Chan arrives in Mexico City to investigate attempted theft of atomic device. Several murders ensue

Pursuit to Algiers (Universal) d. Roy William Neill: Nigel Bruce, Basil Rathbone. Holmes foils assassins' plans to kill heir to a Far Eastern throne on board a transatlantic ocean liner

Voice of the Whistler (Columbia) d. William Castle: Richard Dix, Rhys Williams, Lynn Merrick. Dix outlines the perfect murder to his wife's former fiancée, who decides to test it out

Boston Blackie Booked on Suspicion (Columbia) d. Arthur Dreifuss: Chester Morris, Lynn Merrick, Steve Cochran. Blackie poses as an auctioneer, accidentally sells bogus first edition

The House of Fear (Universal) d. Roy William Neill: Nigel Bruce, Basil Rathbone. Scottish-set mystery with Holmes unmasking the murderer at work among 'The Good Comrades'

The Woman in Green (Universal) d. Roy William Neill: Tom Bryson, Basil Rathbone, Nigel Bruce. Could the sinister Professor Moriarty (Henry Daniell) be the evil genius behind 'The Finger Murders'?

Crime Doctor's Courage (Columbia) d. George Sherman: Hillary Brooke, Warner Baxter. Dr Robert Ordway stumbles across the inevitable skullduggery, this time among California's swimming-pool set

Boston Blackie's Rendezvous (Columbia) d. Arthur Dreifuss: Chester Morris. Blackie has to deal with an escaped homicidal maniac (Steve Cochran) holding Nina Foch hostage

Up Goes Maisie (MGM) d. Harry Beaumont: Ann Sothern, Lewis Howard (r). Maisie dons horn-rims, gets a job as helicopter inventor George Murphy's secretary, and saves him from ruin

Life with Blondie (Columbia) d.Abby
Berlin: Marjorie Kent, Penny Singleton,
Bobby Larson, Larry Sims. The Bumsteads'
dog Daisy hits the headlines as 'Pin-up Dog
of the Navy'

Leave it to Blondie (Columbia) d.Abby
Berlin: Penny Singleton, Mary Newton.
Daisy the Dog gets most of the laughs in
this below-par entry in the interminable
Bumstead saga

The Purple Monster Strikes (Republic)
d.Spencer Bennet, Fred C Brannon: Roy
Barcroft, Linda Stirling, Mary Moore.
Barcroft arrives as the advance guard of a
Martian invasion in engagingly dotty serial

Secret Agent X-9 (Universal) d.Ray
Taylor, Lewis Collins: Keye Luke, Lloyd
Bridges. Can Bridges prevent the beautiful
Japanese master spy Nabura from stealing
synthetic fuel formula? Gripping serial

BRITISH & FOREIGN

Great Expectations (Cineguild) d.David
Lean: John Mills, Martita Hunt, Valerie
Hobson. Fluent, magisterially organized
Dickens adaptation. One of the best British
films of the decade

The Wicked Lady (Gainsborough)
d.Leslie Arliss: Margaret Lockwood, James
Mason. Beauty with cruelty as the vixenish
Lockwood becomes highwayperson in fine
example of 'Gainsborough Gothic'

A Place of One's Own (Gainsborough)
d.Bernard Knowles: James Mason, Margaret
Lockwood, Barbara Mullen. Haunting ghost
story adapted from an Osbert Sitwell novel.
Beautiful sets by Rex Whistler

Caesar and Cleopatra (Pascal) d.Gabriel
Pascal: Claude Rains, Vivien Leigh. No-
expenses-spared epic version of Shaw
founders under weight of its own
production values

Latin Quarter (British National) d.Vernon
Sewell: Derrick de Marney, Joan Seton,
Frederick Valk. A medium is used to expose
a murder in melodrama set among artists
in 19th-century Paris

Pink String and Sealing Wax (Ealing)
d.Robert Hamer: Garry Marsh, Googie
Withers. Googie in viperish form, poisoning
her drunken husband, then pinning the
blame on an infatuated admirer

Dead of Night (Ealing) d.Alberto
Cavalcanti: Michael Redgrave. Redgrave is
the ventriloquist possessed by his dummy
in the most famous segment of this
collection of supernatural tales

They Were Sisters (Gainsborough)
d.Arthur Crabtree: James Mason, Phyllis
Calvert, Dulcie Gray. Mason is the domestic
tyrant driving Gray to suicide, Calvert the
sister who exposes him

The Seventh Veil (Ortus) d.Compton
Bennett: Ann Todd, James Mason. Mason is
concert pianist Todd's sardonic, brooding
guardian in quintessentially British
psychological melodrama

Brief Encounter (Cineguild) d.David Lean:
Joyce Carey, Stanley Holloway, Celia
Johnson. A piece of grit in the eye leads to
Johnson's doomed romance with Trevor
Howard. From play by Noel Coward

The Agitator (British National) d.John
Harlow: Mary Morris, Moore Marriott, John
Laurie. An embittered young mechanic
(William Hartnell) is left a factory and the
responsibility mellows him

The Way to the Stars (Two Cities)
d.Anthony Asquith: Michael Redgrave, Basil
Radford, David Tomlinson. Understated
drama of American and British airmen and
their relationships with local people

Johnny Frenchman (Ealing) d.Charles
Frend: Alfie Bass, Francoise Rosay. The
strains of war unite the people of a Cornish
fishing village with their age-old enemies
across the Channel in Brittany

I Live in Grosvenor Square (ABPC)
d.Herbert Wilcox: Dean Jagger, Nancy
Price, Robert Morley. Anna Neagle is the
Duke's daughter pursued by American
Jagger and a British officer (Rex Harrison)

I Know Where I'm Going (Archers) d.Michael Powell: John Laurie, Roger Livesey, Wendy Hiller. Hiller falls under the spell of Celtic twilight, helps Laird Livesey lay an ancient family curse

Painted Boats (Ealing) d.Charles Crichton: Bill Blewitt, May Hallatt. Characteristic Ealing clash between old ways and new in semi-documentary tale of river life. Photographed by Douglas Slocombe

Blithe Spirit (Two Cities) d.David Lean: Kay Hammond, Rex Harrison, Constance Cummings. Harrison is the novelist plagued by two ghostly wives, Margaret Rutherford the eccentric medium Madame Arcati

I Didn't Do It (Columbia) d.Marcel Varnel: Marjorie Brown, George Formby. Gormless variety artist Formby gets caught up in a murder mystery. Lashings of slapstick and ukelele-bashing

The Rake's Progress (Independent) d.Sidney Gilliat: Lilli Palmer, Rex Harrison. Harrison is the modern-day ne'er do well who finally finds an outlet for his destructive talents in the war

Les Enfants du Paradis (France) d.Marcel Carné: Pierre Brasseur, Arletty, Jean-Louis Barrault. Sprawling, picaresque masterpiece set in the interlocking worlds of theatre and crime in 1830s Paris

Rome, Open City (Italy) d.Roberto Rossellini: Anna Magnani. Semi-documentary film, shot in very trying conditions at the end of the war, gave immense impetus to Italian neo-realism

Marie Louise (Switzerland) d.Leopold Lindtberg. A young French refugee is reluctant to return to her home from the comfort of Switzerland. Academy Original Screenplay Award 1945

Die Letzte Chance (Switzerland) d.Leopold Lindtberg: John Hoy. Three escaped airmen conduct a column of refugees from northern Italy to the safety of Switzerland

1946

The year saw cinema audiences at their peak. Every week 90 million Americans went to the movies. In Britain the figure was 30 million, and in France eight million. Paramount's profits leapt to $39 million and both Fox and Warner's balance sheets were in the black to the tune of $22 million. It was also a good year for Columbia. *The Jolson Story*, starring Larry Parks in the title role, was a huge hit, as was *Gilda*, the quintessential showcase for Rita Hayworth at the height of her beauty.

Postwar readjustment movies featured in all the studios' programmes. Head and shoulders above the rest was William Wyler's *The Best Years of Our Lives*, a Samuel Goldwyn production, which was chosen as the year's Best Picture. It also gained William Wyler the Best Director Award, the cinematography award for Gregg Toland and an Oscar for screenwriter Robert Sherwood. Fredric March scooped the Best Actor Award, and the Best Supporting Actor Oscar went to the armless veteran Harold Russell, whose only film this was. Olivia de Havilland won the Best Actress Award for her performance in *To Each His Own*, a well-turned weepie directed by Mitchell Leisen. Anne Baxter was voted Best Supporting Actress for her portrayal of the alcoholic whom Tyrone Power romances on the rebound from Gene Tierney in *The Razor's Edge*.

Among the year's outstanding films were Clarence Brown's exquisitely photographed *The Yearling*; *Blue Skies*, which reunited Crosby and Astaire for the first time since *Holiday Inn*; Howard Hawks' *The Big Sleep*, with Humphrey Bogart as Raymond Chandler's Philip Marlowe; and Hitchcock's *Notorious*, which contains the justly famous crane shot which begins at the top of a sweeping staircase and then swoops down to the floor below, where a party is in progress, finally to focus in close-up on a key clutched in Ingrid Bergman's hand.

Bergman broke into the 1946 Top Ten, joining Bing Crosby, Van Johnson, Gary Cooper, Bob Hope, Humphrey Bogart, Greer Garson, Margaret O'Brien, Betty Grable and Roy Rogers. Burt Lancaster made a sensational debut in Robert Siodmak's *The Killers* and other newcomers included John Lund, Kirk Douglas, Richard Basehart, Raymond Burr and Martha Hyer. By contrast William Boyd was coming up to his twelfth year on the Bar 20 Ranch as Hopalong Cassidy.

The year saw the death of one of the legendary cowboy stars, poker-faced William S Hart. Death also took Florence Turner, the original 'Vitagraph Girl', and George Arliss, the veteran British thespian who had been a top box-office draw in the early 1930s. Displaying his customarily immaculate sense of timing, W C Fields died on Christmas Day. He had always professed to loathe the Yuletide season.

In Britain cinema admissions reached an all-time high of 1635 million, a remarkable figure considering that 230 of the 5000 cinemas were still closed by bomb damage. J Arthur Rank initiated an ambitious programme of expansion. However, *London Town*, his attempt to make a lavish Hollywood-style musical, was an unmitigated disaster. Gainsborough continued to pump out costume melodramas, scoring a big hit with *The Magic Bow*, in which Stewart Granger gave an athletic impersonation of the violin virtuoso Paganini. Sidney Gilliat's *Green for Danger* was a charming pastiche of the detective thriller. Ealing's *The Captive Heart*, directed by Basil Dearden, was a well-organized war film set in a prisoner of war camp in Germany. It was not a great popular success – the public was now more interested in escapism and costume melodrama. Nevertheless, it established many of the themes, and the clichés, which were to run through the cycle of war films which dominated British cinema in the following decade. It also provided Jack Warner with his first role at Ealing Studios.

ACTION

Dead Reckoning (Columbia) d. John Cromwell: Lizabeth Scott, Humphrey Bogart. Scott is the lethal dame Bogart has to reckon with as he tries to solve murder of World War II comrade. Geronimo

The Chase (UA) d. Arthur Ripley: Robert Cummings, Michele Morgan. Weird Cuban-set thriller buckles under the weight of its own pretensions. Peter Lorre provides engagingly creepy touches

The Lady in the Lake (MGM) d. Robert Montgomery: Robert Montgomery, Audrey Totter. Unique Chandler adaptation told in first person. As Marlowe, Montgomery is seen only in occasional mirror

The Big Sleep (Warner) d. Howard Hawks: Humphrey Bogart. Complex Chandler plot defeated screenwriters Faulkner, Brackett, Furthman, but the principals ensured a triumph of style over content

The Killers (Universal) d. Robert Siodmak: Burt Lancaster, Albert Dekker. Intricate, explosive crime melodrama developed from a Hemingway sketch. In his debut Lancaster strikes sparks off Ava Gardner

The Blue Dahlia (Paramount) d. George Marshall: Alan Ladd, William Bendix. Chandler-scripted drama with war veteran Ladd returning to find wife first unfaithful and then dead

Cloak and Dagger (Warner) d. Fritz Lang: Gary Cooper. Nuclear scientist Cooper parachutes into Germany to extricate Italian atomic expert kidnapped by Nazis. Much mangled by studio

ADVENTURE

Night in Paradise (Universal) d. Arthur Lubin: Merle Oberon, Turhan Bey. Fairytale set in hokum Ancient Greece. Bey plays Aesop of fable fame, Oberon the beautiful princess he weaves a tale around

Bandit of Sherwood Forest (Columbia) d. George Sherman: Cornel Wilde. Colourful but decidedly cut-rate actioner with Wilde cast as the son of Robin Hood taking charge of Dad's Merry Men

Thieves' Holiday (UA) d. Douglas Sirk: George Sanders, Carole Landis. Sanders purveying villainy at its silkiest as master thief working his way into the position of prefect of police

The Spanish Main (RKO) d.Frank Borzage: Paul Henreid, Maureen O'Hara. Cast against type as an athletic swashbuckler, Henreid enjoys himself foiling Spanish grandee Walter Slezak

Magnificent Doll (Universal) d.Frank Borzage: David Niven, Burgess Meredith, Ginger Rogers. Ginger all at sea as Dolly Madison. Meredith, Niven give valiant support as President Madison and Aaron Burr

The Macomber Affair (UA) d.Zoltan Korda: Gregory Peck, Joan Bennett. Thoughtful adaptation of Hemingway story of strife-torn safari expedition, given added weight by principals' strong performances

Tarzan and the Leopard Woman (RKO) d.Kurt Neumann: Acquanetta, Johnny Weissmuller. Sultry Acquanetta is the high priestess of a leopard cult terrorizing law-abiding citizens of the jungle

Kitty (Paramount) d.Mitchell Leisen: Paulette Goddard. Penniless artist Ray Milland helps transform guttersnipe Goddard into the toast of 18th-century English society

Two years Before the Mast (Paramount) d.John Farrow: Barry Fitzgerald, Alan Ladd. Limping account of crusade by Richard Henry Dana (Brian Donlevy) to improve conditions at sea

Gallant Journey (Columbia) d.William Wellman: Glenn Ford, Janet Blair. Glenn Ford as the 19th-century inventor who pioneered the glider 'plane. Like his models, film drifts with the wind

Smoky (Fox) d.Louis King: Anne Baxter, Fred MacMurray. Cowboy MacMurray searches Utah for his beautiful black stallion stolen in a cattle raid. Adapted from Will James' classic story

Courage of Lassie (MGM) d.Fred Wilcox: Elizabeth Taylor. Lassie's wartime service as killer dog is all too much for the noble canine, who is straightened out by devoted Taylor

Gallant Bess (MGM) d.Andrew Marton: Alan Curtis, Marshall Thompson. A lonely Texan soldier adopts a wounded horse on a Pacific island, in confusingly scripted equine tear-jerker

Black Beauty (Fox) d.Max Nosseck: J M Kerrigan, Mona Freeman. No more than routine version of Anna Sewell's 19th-century girl and horse tale. Filmed in b/w

The Yearling (MGM) d.Clarence Brown: Claude Jarman, Jr, Gregory Peck, Henry Travers. Exquisitely photographed account of the love of a young boy (Jarman) for a deer. Peck, Jane Wyman his parents

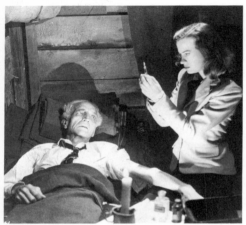

Strange Journey (Fox) d.James Tinling: Fritz Leiber, Osa Massen. Reformed gangster Paul Kelly crash lands on a Caribbean Island, discovers the survivors of a shipwreck and a uranium deposit

Boys' Ranch (MGM) d.Roy Rowland: Skippy Homeier. Son of *Boys Town* in a western setting. Homeier demonstrates that elimination of all subtlety is no pre-requisite in juvenile roles

Tangier (Universal) d.George Waggner: Robert Paige, Maria Montez, Preston Foster. Dancer Montez is on the trail of Nazi war criminals, journalist Paige is looking for diamonds, police chief Foster looking bored

MELODRAMA

The Spiral Staircase (RKO) d.Robert Siodmak: Ethel Barrymore, Dorothy McGuire. Tension mounts to breaking point as deaf-mute McGuire is singled out by homicidal maniac George Brent

Dragonwyck (Fox) d.Joseph L Mankiewicz: Gene Tierney, Vincent Price. Price starts over the top and keeps on going as tyrannical landlord marrying beautiful Tierney in 19th-century drama

Diary of a Chambermaid (UA) d.Jean Renoir: Francis Lederer, Paulette Goddard. One of Goddard's best performances as the pert servant driving all the local menfolk wild with desire

The Verdict (Warner) d.Don Siegel: Sydney Greenstreet, Peter Lorre. In Siegel's directing debut Greenstreet plays disgraced policeman planning 'perfect murder', Lorre his artist friend

The Strange Woman (UA) d.Edgar Ulmer: June Storey, Louis Hayward, Hedy Lamarr. George Sanders wildly miscast as a lumberjack tangling with man-eating New England femme fatale Lamarr

Till the End of Time (RKO) d.Edward Dmytryk: Guy Madison, Robert Mitchum, Bill Williams. Postwar readjustment saga features famous bar-room brawl between the three veterans and Klan-like thugs

The Best Years of Our Lives (RKO) d.William Wyler: Michael Hall, Teresa Wright, Myrna Loy, Fredric March. March is senior of three returning veterans in most successful postwar readjustment movie

The Stranger (RKO) d.Orson Welles: Orson Welles, Loretta Young. Escaped Nazi war criminal Welles settles into a small town, but is smoked out by war crimes investigator Edward G Robinson

To Each His Own (Paramount) d.Mitchell Leisen: Olivia de Havilland, John Lund. De Havilland won Best Actress Oscar as unwed mother who must remain 'aunt' to her son. Lund played both father and son

From This Day Forward (RKO) d.John Berry: Joan Fontaine, Mark Stevens. Returned war hero Stevens and young wife Fontaine struggle to make ends meet. Adapted from *All Brides are Beautiful*

Somewhere in the Night (Fox) d.Joseph L Mankiewicz: Fritz Kortner, John Hodiak, Margo Wood. Amnesiac combat casualty Hodiak pieces together clues about his past which suggest he is a murderer

Sentimental Journey (Fox) d.Walter Lang: Maureen O'Hara, William Bendix, John Payne, Connie Marshall (r). Actress O'Hara dies shortly after she and producer husband Payne adopt a winsome orphan

The Secret Heart (MGM) d.Robert Z Leonard: June Allyson, Walter Pidgeon, Claudette Colbert. Allyson steals film as the daughter who makes a hero out of her dead wastrel father

Deception (Warner) d.Irving Rapper: Bette Davis, Claude Rains. Rains is the composer who blows his top when he finds that Bette has a yen for handsome rival Paul Henreid

Notorious (RKO) d.Alfred Hitchcock: Ingrid Bergman, Cary Grant. Bergman is ruthlessly manipulated by Grant to trap spy Claude Rains in tense World War II espionage thriller

Undercurrent (MGM) d.Vincente Minnelli: Robert Taylor, Katharine Hepburn. Taylor is moody big-business man with much charm but dangerous undercurrents, most of them swirling towards wife Hepburn

The Searching Wind (Paramount) d.William Dieterle: Robert Young, Sylvia Sidney. Flashback tale, from Lillian Hellman play, in which diplomat Young agonizes over failure to stand up to fascism

The Razor's Edge (Fox) d.Edmund Goulding: Anne Baxter, Herbert Marshall, John Payne, Gene Tierney, Clifton Webb. Tyrone Power's comeback vehicle after war was tortuous Somerset Maugham drama

My Reputation (Warner) d.Curtis Bernhardt: Barbara Stanwyck, George Brent. Smart society widow Stanwyck falls for womanizing bachelor Brent to the general scandal of her circle

A Stolen Life (Warner) d.Curtis Bernhardt: Glenn Ford, Bette Davis. Bette is unprincipled lady who assumes her dead twin sister's identity to win Glenn Ford. Originally filmed by Paramount in 1929

Wake Up and Dream (Fox) d.Lloyd Bacon: June Haver, Connie Marshall, John Payne, Oliver Blake. Odd little fantasy, tinged with humour, about child's quest to find brother missing in World War II

Spectre of the Rose (Republic) d.Ben Hecht: Judith Anderson, Michael Chekhov, Viola Essen. Weird, wordy drama of schizophrenic ballet dancer Ivan Kirov leaping crazily to his doom

Leave Her to Heaven (Fox) d.John M Stahl: Cornel Wilde, Gene Tierney. Deeply disturbed Tierney will stop at nothing to keep Wilde, including allowing his crippled brother to drown

Humoresque (Warner) d.Jean Negulesco: John Garfield, Joan Crawford. Rich bitch Crawford falls for violinist Garfield, utters immortal line 'Bad manners, the infallible sign of genius!' Walks into sea at end

The Dark Mirror (Universal) d.Robert Siodmak: Lew Ayres, Olivia de Havilland. Psychiatrist Ayres tries to discover which one of identical twins – one nice, one nasty – has committed a murder

The Strange Love of Martha Ivers (Paramount) d.Lewis Milestone: Van Heflin, Barbara Stanwyck, Kirk Douglas. A crime committed in the past comes back to haunt driven Stanwyck. High-octane melodrama

The Postman Always Rings Twice (MGM) d.Tay Garnett: John Garfield, Hume Cronyn, Lana Turner. The lipstick rolls across the floor and dooms drifter Garfield into murdering Lana's elderly husband

The Locket (RKO) d.John Brahm: Robert Mitchum, Laraine Day. John Brahm's compelling flashback extravaganza in which kleptomaniac Day's problems are rooted in childhood trauma

Shock (Fox) d.Alfred Werker: Vincent Price, Lynn Bari. Price murders his wife then joins forces with poisonous Bari to bump off the eye witness (Annabel Shaw). But her husband is a cop

Deadline at Dawn (RKO) d.Harold Clurman: Susan Hayward, Bill Williams. Feisty singer Hayward is drawn into fight to clear Bill Williams of suspected murder, in taut Clifford Odets-scripted drama

Whistle Stop (UA) d.Leonide Moguy: Jimmy Conlin, George Raft, Ava Gardner. Ava is torn between sleazy but rich nightclub owner Tom Conway and lazy but nice (?) boyfriend George Raft

Salome, Where She Danced (Universal) d.Charles Lamont: Yvonne De Carlo. Exotic dancer De Carlo progresses from the Franco-Prussian War to fame and fortune in the American West. Rod Cameron co-stars

Gilda (Columbia) d.Charles Vidor: Rita Hayworth. Hayworth was never more provocative than in this love triangle with George Macready, Glenn Ford. But the only thing that really happens is Rita

Nobody Lives Forever (Warner) d.Jean Negulesco: John Garfield, Geraldine Fitzgerald, Walter Brennan. Swindler Garfield fleeces rich widow Fitzgerald, then falls in love with her and redeems himself

Miss Susie Slagle's (Paramount) d.John Berry: Lillian Gish, Veronica Lake. Drama revolving around a boarding house for medical students. Gish dominates proceedings with quiet authority

Three Strangers (Warner) d.Jean Negulesco: Sydney Greenstreet, Geraldine Fitzgerald, Peter Lorre. Three desperate characters hold winning sweepstake tickets in weird circumstances. It all ends in tears

Angel on My Shoulder (UA) d.Archie Mayo: Paul Muni. Rather odd fantasy in which murdered convict Muni gets a reprieve from Hell and returns to Earth in the guise of a judge

Crack-Up (RKO) d.Irving Reis: Pat O'Brien. Cracking little thriller in which amnesiac O'Brien tumbles headlong into an art-forgery racket. Good support from Herbert Marshall, Claire Trevor

Hoodlum Saint (MGM) d.Norman Taurog: Esther Williams, William Powell. Powell encourages some crooks to start a charity in the name of St Dismas, patron saint of hoodlums. More dismal than Dismas

Swell Guy (Universal) d.Frank Tuttle: Ruth Warrick, Sonny Tufts. Unscrupulous waster Tufts trades on his reputation as war correspondent to the despair of his family. Finally, he redeems himself

The Dark Corner (Fox) d.Henry Hathaway: Lucille Ball, Mark Stevens, Kurt Kreuger. Outstanding *film noir* with tough private eye Stevens framed for murder. They just can't make 'em like this any more

Child of Divorce (RKO) d.Richard
Fleischer: Sharyn Moffett, Regis Toomey.
Super-sensitive little Sharyn can't reconcile
herself to the divorce of parents Toomey
and Madge Meredith. No happy ending

The Unfaithful (Warner) d.Vincent
Sherman: Zachary Scott, Eve Arden. A
reworking of *The Letter* (1940) with a
strong central performance from Ann
Sheridan in the Bette Davis role

Little Mister Jim (MGM) d.Fred
Zinnemann: James Craig, Jackie 'Butch'
Jenkins, Frances Gifford. Sickly sweet tale
of father and son coping after mother dies
in childbirth. Cynics, you have been warned

Sister Kenny (RKO) d.Dudley Nichols:
Rosalind Russell, Alexander Knox.
Reverential biopic of Australian nurse who
achieved fame with her treatment of
infantile paralysis

Of Human Bondage (Warner) d.Edmund
Goulding: Paul Henreid, Eleanor Parker,
Patric Knowles. Second film version of
Somerset Maugham novel flounders in
morass of miscasting

COMEDY

So Goes My Love (Universal) d.Frank
Ryan: Myrna Loy, Bobby Driscoll, Don
Ameche. Sentimental period romantic
comedy based on the life of inventor Hiram
Stephen Maxim

The Cockeyed Miracle (MGM) d.S Sylvan
Simon: Richard Quine, Keenan Wynn,
Audrey Totter, Frank Morgan. Recently
deceased Morgan and his rakish
father (Wynn) return from the dead

Because of Him (Universal) d.Richard
Wallace: Charles Laughton, Deanna Durbin,
Franchot Tone. Stagestruck Deanna sings
'Danny Boy' to Laughton and becomes his
leading lady in Tone's new play

Monsieur Beaucaire (Paramount)
d.George Marshall: Bob Hope. Spoof of 1924
Valentino hit seems somewhat laboured
now. Joseph Schildkraut provides some
excellent villainy

The Bride Wore Boots (Paramount)
d.Irving Pichel: Patric Knowles, Barbara
Stanwyck, Robert Cummings. Quarrelling
Cummings and Stanwyck are reunited by a
racehorse. Makes a change from children

The Perfect Marriage (Paramount)
d.Lewis Allen: David Niven, Loretta Young.
Pacy domestic comedy with Niven and
Young as thoroughly modern couple
bickering and then making up

The Well-Groomed Bride (Paramount)
d.Sidney Lanfield: Ray Milland, Olivia de
Havilland. The US Navy need a magnum of
champagne to christen a new aircraft
carrier but Olivia has the only one in town

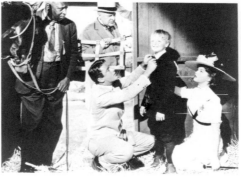

My Brother Talks to Horses (MGM)
d.Fred Zinnemann: Peter Lawford, Jackie
'Butch' Jenkins, Beverly Tyler. Gimmick
comedy which starts in spritely fashion but
quickly falls away

Three Wise Fools (MGM) d.Edward
Buzzell: Margaret O'Brien, Edward Arnold,
Lionel Barrymore, Lewis Stone. Romantic
comedy in which three crusty bachelors try
to sell Irish orphan O'Brien's inheritance

Bachelor Girls (UA) d.Andrew Stone:
Claire Trevor, Adolphe Menjou, Ann
Dvorak. Four shopgirls and a floorwalker go
social climbing on Long Island, posing as a
wealthy family

Little Giant (Universal) d.William Seiter:
Bud Abbott, Jacqueline de Wit, Pierre
Watkin. Unusual A & C effort in that this
time they play two separate characters who
meet in the course of the film

White Tie and Tails (Universal) d.Charles
Barton: Ella Raines, Dan Duryea. While the
family's away butler Duryea masquerades
as a gentleman and gets mixed up
with the Mob

The Time of Their Lives (Universal)
d.Charles Barton: Lou Costello, Marjorie
Reynolds, Bud Abbott, John Shelton, Lynne
Baggett, Binnie Barnes. Costello and
Reynolds are ghosts, Abbott a psychiatrist (!)

Two Guys from Milwaukee (Warner) d.
David Butler: Rosemary De Camp, Patti
Brady, Jack Carson, Joan Leslie, Janis Paige.
Cab driver Carson meets dream girl Lauren
Bacall, only to be upstaged by Bogart

She Wrote the Book (Universal)
d.Charles Lamont: Joan Davis, Jack Oakie,
Kirby Grant. Plain Jane teacher Davis gets a
knock on the head, wakes up believing
she's a famous writer with torrid sex life

The Show-Off (MGM) d. Harry Beaumont: Marilyn Maxwell, Red Skelton. Fourth time around for tale of backslapping braggart who succeeds in creating chaos all around him

Two Smart People (MGM) d. Jules Dassin: John Hodiak, Lloyd Nolan, Lucille Ball. Romance flourishes between Ball and con-man Hodiak under the watchful eye of the latter's accommodating police escort

Her Adventurous Night (Universal) d. John Rawlins: Dennis O'Keefe, Helen Walker, Scotty Beckett. Beckett's stories land his parents and teacher in jail but he makes amends by solving murder mystery

No Leave, No Love (MGM) d. Charles Martin: Marie Wilson, Van Johnson, Pat Kirkwood, Keenan Wynn. Thudding failure which torpedoed studio's attempts to launch British star Kirkwood in Hollywood

It Shouldn't Happen to a Dog (Fox) d. Herbert I Leeds: Carole Landis. Crime mystery cum comedy in which Carole plays a detective trailing a mobster with the help of her Doberman and Allyn Joslyn

The Kid from Brooklyn (RKO) d. Norman Z McLeod: Danny Kaye. Mild-mannered milkman Kaye becomes boxing champ in lavish remake of Harold Lloyd's *The Milky Way* (1936)

Cinderella Jones (Warner) d. Busby Berkeley: Joan Leslie, Roberta Alda. Leslie will inherit a million if she can marry a man of unusual intelligence by a certain date

Cluny Brown (Fox) d. Ernst Lubitsch: Charles Boyer, Reginald Gardiner, Jennifer Jones. Unconventional maid Jones and equally unconventional Czech writer Boyer conduct scandalous romance

WESTERNS

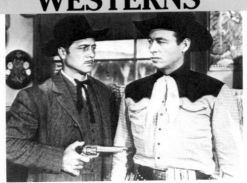

San Antonio (Warner) d. David Butler: Alexis Smith, Errol Flynn. Flynn is the rustler tangling with crooked saloon bar owner Victor Francen over singer Smith. Final shoot-out in the Alamo

Wild West (PRC) d. Robert Tansey: Terry Front, Eddie Dean. Dean, Lash La Rue (the poor man's Bogart) and Roscoe Ates are battling Texas Rangers. Reissued in 1948 in b/w as *Prairie Outlaw*

My Pal Trigger (Republic) d. Frank McDonald: Roy Rogers, Dale Evans. Watch this film, allegedly Roy's favourite, and discover just where the faithful Trigger came from

My Darling Clementine (Fox) d.John Ford: Henry Fonda, Victor Mature, Linda Darnell: 'I knew Wyatt Earp ... and he told me about the fight at the OK Corral. So we did it . . . the way it had been.' John Ford

The Sea of Grass (MGM) d.Elia Kazan: Katharine Hepburn, Spencer Tracy. Mainly studio-shot epic features Tracy as rugged rancher and Hepburn as his equally tough wife, Robert Walker their wayward son

The Man from Rainbow Valley (Republic) d.Robert Springsteen: Adrian Booth, Monte Hale, Jo Ann Marlowe. Hale tracks down a rodeo horse stolen from a strip cartoonist's ranch

Duel in the Sun (Selznick) d.King Vidor: Gregory Peck, Jennifer Jones. Peck and Joseph Cotten are Cain and Abel brothers fighting over Jones in overblown dynastic Western dubbed 'Lust in the Dust'

The Virginian (Paramount) d.Stuart Gilmore: Barbara Britton, Joel McCrea. McCrea is excellent as stoic hero but this is no more than a routine remake of Victor Fleming's 1929 hit with Gary Cooper

Badman's Territory (RKO) d.Tim Whelan: Lawrence Tierney, Morgan Conway. Randolph Scott rides against a small army of outlaws to bring Oklahoma Territory into the Union

Bad Bascomb (MGM) d.S Sylvan Simon: Wallace Beery, Margaret O'Brien. Bank robber Beery hides out in a Mormon wagon train. O'Brien helps fight off Indian attack with a pea shooter

Canyon Passage (Universal) d.Jacques Tourneur: Brian Donlevy, Susan Hayward, Dana Andrews. Donlevy and Andrews are friendly rivals for Hayward's affections in slow-paced almost dreamlike Western

Abilene Town (UA) d.Edwin L Marin: Ann Dvorak. Randolph Scott cleans up the rip-roaring town at the end of the Chisolm Trail. Delicious sozzled cameo from Edgar Buchanan

The Devil's Playground (UA) d. George Archainbaud: Rand Brooks, William Boyd, Andy Clyde. Brisk oater relaunched Hopalong Cassidy in a series of twelve made by Boyd's own production company

Drifting Along (Mon) d. Derwin Abrahams: Lynn Carver, Douglas Fowley, Johnny Mack Brown. Tough guy Mack Brown indulges in some painful range warbling at the start of this amiable actioner

Gunning for Vengeance (Columbia) d. Ray Nazarro: Smiley Burnette. Charles Starrett in his familiar role of The Durango Kid pins on a Marshal's star and cleans up a lawless town

ROMANCE

Devotion (Warner) d. Curtis Bernhardt: Paul Henreid, Olivia de Havilland, Arthur Kennedy, Ida Lupino, Nancy Coleman. Absurdly romanticized biography of the Bronte sisters, held up for three years

Without Reservations (RKO) d. Mervyn Le Roy: John Wayne, Claudette Colbert. Best-selling writer Colbert falls for hunky Marine flier Wayne, even though he thinks her books are a lot of rubbish

Love Laughs at Andy Hardy (MGM) d. Willis Goldbeck: Lina Romay, Mickey Rooney, Lewis Stone, Fay Holden. GI Andy returns from the war to Wainwright College and to a misfiring romance

It's a Wonderful Life (RKO) d. Frank Capra: James Stewart, Donna Reed. Angel Henry Travers shows would-be suicide Stewart what the world would have been like if he hadn't been born

Breakfast in Hollywood (UA) d. Harold Schuster: Tom Breneman, Bonita Granville, Eddie Ryan. Madcap romance against background of zany radio programme hosted by Breneman

Temptation (Universal) d. Irving Pichel: Charles Korvin, Merle Oberon. Creaking romantic melodrama in which Oberon throws over archaeologist husband George Brent for sleek roué Korvin

Claudia and David (Fox) d.Walter Lang: Dorothy McGuire, Robert Young. Slick, sentimental sequel to *Claudia* (1943) with good support from John Sutton and Mary Astor

Anna and the King of Siam (Fox) d.John Cromwell: Irene Dunne, Rex Harrison. Dunne at her most intelligently charming as secretary-tutor-confidante to Harrison's potentate. Harrison's Hollywood debut

Heartbeat (RKO) d.Sam Wood: Basil Rathbone, Ginger Rogers. Ginger is a French pickpocket, coached by Rathbone, who falls for one of her victims. Remake of *Battement de Coeur* (1939)

Faithful in My Fashion (MGM) d.Sidney Salkow: Donna Reed, Tom Drake. Reed has kept up a pretence of loving Drake during the war so that he would not be heartbroken on active service

Her Kind of Man (Warner) d.Frederick de Cordova: Zachary Scott, Janis Paige. Paige is wooed by big-time gambler Scott and newspaperman Dane Clark in throwback to the studio's 1930s crime melos

Lady Luck (RKO) d.Edwin L Marin: Barbara Hale, Robert Young. Confirmed gambler Young promises his bride Hale that he is a reformed character, but within an hour he's at it again. Lively comedy

Lover Come Back (Universal) d.William Seiter: Lucille Ball, George Brent. War correspondent Brent returns home with a roving eye, which sends Ball off to Las Vegas with divorce in mind

Margie (Fox) d.Henry King: Glenn Langan, Lynn Bari, Jeanne Crain. Charming evocation of life in an Ohio high school in the late 1920s with Crain romancing handsome French teacher Langan

Janie Gets Married (Warner) d.Vincent Sherman: Joan Leslie, Margaret Hamilton. Mild comedy chronicling the various upsets and domestic crises which befall a pair of young marrieds

One More Tomorrow (Warner) d.Peter Godfrey: Ann Sheridan, Dennis Morgan, Jane Wyman, Danny Jackson. Story of a wealthy playboy who marries a left-wing photographer and then buys her magazine

MUSICALS

Ziegfeld Follies (MGM) d.Vincente Minnelli: Fred Astaire, Gene Kelly. Lavish revue dreamed up in heaven by Flo Ziegfeld (William Powell). Astaire and Kelly's only screen appearance together

Night and Day (Warner) d.Michael Curtiz: Estelle Sloan. Utterly fictitious biopic of Cole Porter with Cary Grant as composer. Porter's reaction. 'It must be good, none of it's true.'

The Time, the Place and the Girl (Warner) d.David Butler: Jack Carson, Janis Paige, Martha Vickers, Dennis Morgan. Well-worn 'putting on a show' formula is well served by LeRoy Prinz choreography

Two Sisters from Boston (MGM) d.Henry Koster: Jimmy Durante, Kathryn Grayson. Grayson and June Allyson are two sisters in New York with Grayson singing in Durante's bar, yearning for the Met

Doll Face (Fox) d.Lewis Seiler: Perry Como, Vivian Blaine. Stripper Blaine takes a snappy route to the legitimate theatre in standard backstage musical. Como sings 'Dig You Later'

Till the Clouds Roll By (MGM) d.Richard Whorf: Van Heflin, Robert Walker. Star-studded tribute to Jerome Kern features nearly two dozen classics and climaxes with Sinatra singing 'Ol' Man River'

Blue Skies (Paramount) d.Stuart Heisler: Bing Crosby, Fred Astaire. Bing and Fred reunited for the first time since *Holiday Inn* with score by Irving Berlin. Astaire gives magical version of 'Puttin' On the Ritz'.

Three Little Girls in Blue (Fox) d.H Bruce Humberstone: Vivian Blaine, June Haver, Vera-Ellen. Reworking of *Moon over Miami* (1941) with lively trio off to Atlantic City in search of wealthy husbands

Song of the South (RKO) d.Wilfred Jackson: Glenn Leedy, James Baskett, Bobby Driscoll. Baskett is Uncle Remus in syrupy Disney confection, salvaged by some delightful cartoon sequences.

Earl Carroll Sketchbook (Republic) d.Albert Rogell: Constance Moore. Romantic misunderstandings between singing star Moore and composer boyfriend William Marshall

Holiday in Mexico (MGM) d. George Sidney: Walter Pidgeon, Roddy McDowall, Jane Powell. Powell's first for MGM finds her keeping house for widowed diplomat father Pidgeon, mooning over Jose Iturbi

Easy to Wed (MGM) d. Edward Buzzell: Esther Williams, Van Johnson. Williams and Johnson fill the roles originally played by Loy and Powell in glossy Technicolor remake of *Libeled Lady* (1936)

The Jolson Story (Columbia) d. Alfred E Green: Larry Parks. Artful collection of every showbiz cliché in the book proved the studio's biggest moneyspinner up to the time. Jolson dubbed the songs

If I'm Lucky (Fox) d. Lewis Seiler: Vivian Blaine, Harry James, Phil Silvers, Carmen Miranda. Crooner Perry Como goes into politics in mediocre musical remake of the studio's *Thanks a Million* (1937)

Make Mine Music (RKO) d. (among others) Robert Cormack, Jack Kinney. Disney does for popular music what *Fantasia* did for the classics, includes music from Benny Goodman, Nelson Eddy

The Thrill of Brazil (Columbia) d. S Sylvan Simon: Ann Miller. Hyperactive show revolves around producer Keenan Wynn's efforts to stop ex-wife Evelyn Keyes marrying Allyn Joslyn

Swing Parade of 1946 (Mon) d. Phil Karlson: Gale Storm. Gale's desperate to become a nightclub singer but all kinds of legal complications get in the way. Also featured are the Three Stooges

Centennial Summer (Fox) d. Otto Preminger: Walter Brennan, Cornel Wilde. Attempt to copy success of *Meet Me in St Louis* (1944) with musical set during Philadelphia Exposition of 1876

Do You Love Me? (Fox) d. Gregory Ratoff: Dick Haymes, Maureen O'Hara, Harry James. O'Hara looks stunning in Technicolor as the music student who gets involved with Haymes and James

The Bamboo Blonde (RKO) d. Anthony Mann: Frances Langford, Russell Wade. Nightclub singer Langford finds her face adorning the fuselage of Wade's B-29 bomber in diverting musical romance

HORROR

The Catman of Paris (Republic) d.Lesley Selander: Lenore Aubert, Robert Wilkes. Wilkes pastes on a fetching pair of whiskers but fails signally to raise a frisson of terror in below-par horror outing

The Brute Man (Mon) d.Jean Yarbrough: Rondo Hatton. Tasteless exercise casts hideously disfigured Hatton as the homicidal backbreaking 'Creeper' rampaging over jungle-clad island

The Flying Serpent (PRC) d.Sam Newfield: Ralph Lewis, Hope Kramer. Crazed archaeologist George Zucco protects Montezuma's treasure with a prehistoric bird trained to kill

Bedlam (RKO) d.Mark Robson: Boris Karloff. Atmospheric chiller set in 18th-century insane asylum and inspired by eighth painting in Hogarth's series The Rake's Progress

The Beast with Five Fingers (Warner) d.Robert Florey: Peter Lorre, Robert Alda, Andrea King. Marvellous exercise in hysteria by Lorre as he is pursued by the severed hand of his dead master

B MOVIES

The Mighty McGurk (MGM) d.John Waters: Wallace Beery, Dean Stockwell. The turn of the century Bowery provides a background to collection of Beery clichés, mostly taken from *The Champ*

Partners in Time (RKO) d.William Nigh: Chester Lauck, Norris Goff (both centre), John James, Teala Loring. Small-town comedy based on the Jot 'Em Down store made famous by radio series

It's Great to be Young (Columbia) d.Del Lord: Jimmy Lloyd, Robert Stanton, Leslie Brooks. Some demobilized soldiers take jobs as entertainers-cum-dishwashers at a hotel in a summer mountain resort

Meet Me on Broadway (Columbia) d.Leigh Jason: Marjorie Reynolds, Allen Jenkins. Arrogant director Fred Brady is reduced to putting on a show with amateurs. Jinx Falkenburg provides the glamour

Sioux City Sue (Republic) d.Frank McDonald: Stirling Holloway, Lynne Roberts, Richard Lane. Comedy in which Gene Autry is tricked into playing the voice of a singing cartoon donkey

Riverboat Rhythm (RKO) d.Leslie Goodwins: Harry Harvey, Marc Kramer, Leon Errol, Jonathan Hale. A showboat runs aground opposite a smart hotel, pitching its owner into a complicated family feud

The Great Morgan (MGM) d.Nat Perrin:
Ben Blue. Frank Morgan is allowed to make
a film, but in the cutting room it is mixed up
with a number of shorts and extracts from
other movies

People Are Funny (Paramount) d.Sam
White: Jack Haley, Helen Walker. Agreeable
little radio spin-off casts Haley as a
small-town announcer with big-time
ambitions. Frances Langford guests

High School Hero (Mon) d.Arthur
Dreifuss: Freddie Stewart, Isabelita, Bobby
Stone, Noel Neill, Frankie Darro, Jackie
Moran. A bunch of lively teenagers restore
the fortunes of their high school

One Way to Love (Columbia) d.Ray
Enright: Willard Parker, Chester Morris,
Janis Carter, Marguerite Chapman.
Chapman tries to break up the Parker-
Morris radio-writing team

Susie Steps Out (UA) d.Reginald LeBorg:
David Bruce, Nita Hunter. Complications
follow Hunter when she gets a job singing
in a nightclub by pretending to be older
than she is

Girl on the Spot (Universal) d.William
Beaudine: George Dolenz, Ludwig Stossel,
Lois Collier. Comedy-thriller cum musical
with an enterprising newsman trapping a
music-loving mobster

Dangerous Millions (Fox) d.James
Tinling: Kent Taylor. Idiotic China-set
melodrama in which a magnate summons
eight relatives to his mountain-top home,
the better for them to fight over his fortune

Smooth as Silk (Universal) d.Charles
Barton: Kent Taylor (l), Virginia Grey.
Criminal lawyer Taylor murders ambitious
actress Grey after she throws him over for a
big-time producer. Will he get away with it?

The Mask of Dijon (PRC) d.Lew Landers:
Erich von Stroheim, Edward Van Sloan.
Macabre thriller in which illusionist von
Stroheim goes on a murder rampage before
literally losing his head

Shadow of a Woman (Warner) d.Joseph
Santley: Andrea King, Helmut Dantine.
Innocent Andrea marries Dantine little
knowing that he is a psychopath planning
to murder her

The Man who Dared (Columbia) d.John Sturges: Leslie Brooks, George Macready. Reporter Macready allows himself to be convicted of murder when innocent to confound legal system

Strange Triangle (Fox) d.Ray McCarey: Annabel Shaw, John Shepperd, Preston Foster, Signe Hasso. Seductive Signe Hasso drives husband Shepperd to gambling and bank supervisor Foster to embezzlement

Queen of Burlesque (PRC) d.Sam Newfield: Craig Reynolds, Carleton Young, Evelyn Ankers. (r) Hardboiled reporter Young wisecracks his way to solving murder mystery in a burlesque show

Rendezvous 24 (Fox) d.James Tinling: Pat O'Moore, William Gargan. An American and a British agent smash a secret atom lab in the Hartz Mountains established by a band of diehard Nazis

Johnny Comes Flying Home (Fox) d.Benjamin Stoloff: Richard Crane, Charles Russell, Martha Stewart, Henry Morgan. Three pilots return from the war and pool their money to start an air freight line

Behind Green Lights (Fox) d.Otto Brower: William Gargan, John Ireland, Carole Landis. Private eye's body is found outside police station. Lieutenant falls in love with chief suspect

Black Angel (Universal) d.Roy William Neill: Dan Duryea, June Vincent, Peter Lorre. A beautiful blackmailer is found murdered. Lorre is seductively slimy and Duryea plays a drunk

The Runaround (Universal) d.Charles Lamont: Rod Cameron, Broderick Crawford, Ella Raines. Private eyes Cameron and Crawford try to prevent a millionaire's daughter from eloping

Danger Woman (Universal) d.Lewis Collins: Brenda Joyce, Milburn Stone, Patricia Morison. Atom scientist Don Porter's estranged wife (Morison) turns up with some crooks to steal his secret formula

Mysterious Intruder (Columbia) d.William Castle: Nina Vale, Richard Dix. Briskly handled entry in the 'Whistler' series, this time involving a hunt for a missing heiress

Shadow of Blackmail (Mon) d.Phil Karlson: Kay Francis. Francis ironically cast as a fading film star foolishly investing her savings in a phoney marriage bureau. Sad low-budget outing

The Truth about Murder (RKO) d.Lew Landers: Bonita Granville, Morgan Conway. Lie detectors play a big part in lawyer Granville's attempts to clear a man on trial for murder

Crime Doctor's Manhunt (Columbia) d.William Castle: Warner Baxter. Ellen Drew is the psychopath who assumes the physical appearance of her dead sister in order to kill. She nearly gets Baxter, too

Step by Step (RKO) d.Phil Rosen: Lawrence Tierney, George Cleveland, Anne Jeffreys. Demobilized Marine Tierney meets a mystery girl on the beach and stumbles into a complicated spy plot

Dark Alibi (Mon) d.Phil Karlson: Sidney Toler. The inscrutable one is on the trail of a criminal who has a plant which can 'forge' fingerprints and thus frame innocent people

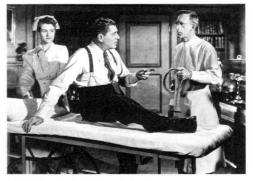

Just Before Dawn (Columbia) d.William Castle: Warner Baxter, Charles Lane. This Crime Doctor tale has the lot – kidnapping, murder, a girl locked in a mortuary, and a stomach pump for the Doctor

Blonde Alibi (Universal) d.d.Will Jason: Tom Neal, Donald MacBride. Cop Donald MacBride brings his usual touch of comedy to the third degree routines in competent murder mystery

Criminal Court (RKO) d.Robert Wise: Tom Conway, Pat Gleason. Attorney Conway's girlfriend is arrested for murder. Only he knows the real answer – and nobody will believe him

A Close Call for Boston Blackie (Columbia) d.Lew Landers: Erik Rolf, Richard Lane, Lynn Merrick, Chester Morris. Boston Blackie slips into disguise to clear himself of a murder charge

Boston Blackie and the Law (Columbia)
d.D. Ross Lederman: George E Stone,
Chester Morris. A female convict escapes
from the pen and murders her former
partner in a magic act

Deadline for Murder (Fox) d.James
Tinling: Kent Taylor, Sheila Ryan, Paul
Kelly. Gambler Taylor and detective Kelly
combine to solve series of murders with
espionage background

Terror by Night (Universal) d.Roy William
Neill: Basil Rathbone, Nigel Bruce. Holmes
and Watson are aboard the London-
Edinburgh express guarding the priceless
Star of Rhodesia diamond

Notorious Lone Wolf (Columbia) d.D
Ross Lederman: Eric Blore, Gerald Mohr.
Michael Lanyard and his butler
impersonate a pair of Eastern princes in
their bid to recover the Shalimar sapphire

Hop Harrigan (Columbia) d.Derwin
Abrahams: Jennifer Holt, William Bakewell,
Sumner Getchell. Airman Harrigan defends
a revolutionary new power unit from the
evil 'Chief Pilot' in snappy serial

Blondie's Lucky Day (Columbia) d.Abby
Berlin: Arthur Lake, Angelyn Orr. Dagwood
is left in charge of the Dithers Construction
Co and hires an ex WAC architect with the
usual complicated results

Dick Tracy (RKO) d.William Berke: Mike
Mazurki, Anne Jeffreys, Morgan Conway.
Conway takes over the role of Chester
Gould's comic strip hero originally made
famous by Ralph Byrd

Daughter of Don Q (Republic) d.Spencer
Bennet, Fred C Brannon: Roy Barcroft, Kirk
Alyn, Adrian Booth. 12-part serial in which
Booth plays the descendant of a Spanish
grandee fighting to save her inheritance

BRITISH & FOREIGN

The Captive Heart (Ealing) d.Basil
Dearden: Michael Redgrave. Thoughtful
POW camp drama in which the stories of
the inmates are interwoven with the lives of
their families back at home

Cage aux Rossignols (France) d.Jean
Dréville: Noel Noel. A young writer brings a
touch of humanity to the harsh regime of a
reform school and wins the respect and
affection of the boys

Piccadilly Incident (ABPC) d.Herbert
Wilcox: Michael Wilding, Anna Neagle.
Wilding marries Neagle, loses her at sea,
remarries, has child. Neagle returns from
the dead and is bumped off in air raid

School for Secrets (Two Cities) d.Peter
Ustinov: Raymond Huntley, Ralph
Richardson. Optimistic, uncritical view of
wartime research into radar. Certain to
outrage feminists

The Years Between (Box) d.Compton
Bennett: Michael Redgrave, Valerie Hobson.
Redgrave returns from a top-secret
wartime mission (in which he is presumed
dead) to find his wife Hobson an MP

I See a Dark Stranger (Individual)
d.Frank Launder: Trevor Howard, Deborah
Kerr. Utterly delightful chase thriller with
Kerr as Anglophobe Irish girl and Howard
as young British officer who falls for her

Green for Danger (Individual) d.Sidney
Gilliat: Alastair Sim, Trevor Howard.
Charming pastiche of the detective thriller
with whimsical detective Sim solving a
hospital murder in V-bomb blitz

Wanted for Murder (Fox) d.Lawrence
Huntington: Dulcie Gray, Eric Portman.
Mother's boy Portman is driven out of his
mind by his father's gruesome reputation
as the public hangman

Bedelia (Gainsborough) d.Lance Comfort:
Barry K Barnes, Margaret Lockwood.
Lockwood is murderess in well-mannered
British cross between *Double Indemnity*
and *Laura* by way of *The Wicked Lady*

Night Boat to Dublin (ABPC) d.Lawrence
Huntington: Robert Newton, Herbert Lom.
Crisp wartime melodrama in which
German agents kidnap a vital Swedish atom
scientist

Carnival (Two Cities) d.Stanley Haynes:
Sally Gray. Patchy adaptation of
Compton Mackenzie novel, with Gray
as ballerina contracting a
disastrous marriage

Caravan (Gainsborough) d.Arthur Crabtree: Jean Kent. Enjoyably ludicrous 19th-century melodrama, much of it set in Spain. Dennis Price enjoys himself hugely as a drawling, aristocratic villain

Gaiety George (Warner) d.George King: Richard Greene, Ann Todd. Greene stars in a meticulous but rather dull biopic of the musical comedy producer George Edwardes

George in Civvy Street (Columbia) d.Marcel Varnel: George Formby. Demobbed George inherits a run-down pub and a bucketful of trouble. Formby's last film

Beware of Pity (Two Cities) d.Maurice Elvey: Albert Lieven, Lilli Palmer. Palmer is the young Austrian cripple who imagines that Lieven's attentions are motivated by love rather than pity

The Green Years (MGM) d.Victor Saville: Dean Stockwell, Charles Coburn. Irish orphan Dean is raised by dour Scottish relations, grows up to be Tom Drake. Just about every cliché in the book

Quiet Weekend (ABPC) d.Harold French: Derek Farr, Barbara White. Mild domestic comedy set in a holiday cottage in the country. One nice sequence when the local squire is lured into some salmon poaching

The Magic Bow (Gainsborough) d.Bernard Knowles: Jean Kent, Stewart Granger, Cecil Parker. Granger looks suitably romantic as dashing violin virtuoso Paganini, dubbed by Menuhin

The Curse of the Wraydons (Ambassador) d.Victor M Gover: Tod Slaughter (c). Slaughter, the last of the great hams, in one of his famous stage roles, master spy Philip Wraydon

London Town (Eagle Lion) d.Wesley Ruggles: Kay Kendall, Sid Field. Completely disastrous attempt by J Arthur Rank to mount a lavish musical to rival those of MGM and Fox. Cast sink without trace

La Foire aux Chimères (France) d.Pierre Chenal: Madeleine Sologne. Overwrought melodrama in which blind circus girl marries hideously disfigured Erich von Stroheim, who is sadly wasted

La Danse de la Mort (France-Italy) d.Marcel Cravenne: Erich von Stroheim, Denise Varnac. Disappointing Strindberg adaptation. Von Stroheim wrote, then junked the script. An intriguing might-have-been

Martin Roumagnac (France) d.Georges Lacombe: Marlene Dietrich, Jean Gabin. Small-town contractor Gabin becomes fatally infatuated with slinky adventuress Dietrich. Complicated flashback structure

Vivere in Pace (Italy) d.Luigi Zampa. A comedy involving two escaped American soldiers in a mountain village which is occupied by only one German soldier

La Belle et la Bête (France) d.Jean Cocteau: Jean Marais, Josette Day. Masterly fantasy whose dreamlike atmosphere is underpinned throughout by a haunting score from Georges Auric

Les Portes de la Nuit (France) d.Marcel Carné: Yves Montand. Drama of the reunion of a group of Resistance fighters after the liberation of Paris and their revenge on a collaborator

Shoeshine (Italy) d.Vittorio de Sica: Rinaldo Smordoni, Franco Interlinghi. Two urchins set out to buy a horse but a brush with the black market leads to prison and heart-rending tragedy

Paisa (Italy) d.Roberto Rossellini: Maria Michi, Gar Moore. Bitter, episodic account of the end of the war in Italy concentrates on the misery and isolation of both soldiers and civilians. One sequence by Fellini

A Matter of Life and Death (Archers) d.Michael Powell: David Niven, Marius Goring. Remarkable fantasy – filled with dazzling effects – built around a young airman's miraculous escape from death

1947

Slowly but surely, seismic shifts were taking place beneath Hollywood's topography. Although MGM remained a byword for glamour, its profits were lagging behind those of Paramount, Warner and Fox. Top-heavy with expensive talent, the mighty studio was in danger of becoming becalmed.

The motion picture industry was on the point of entering a prolonged period of crisis. The wartime boom, when almost anything on celluloid was guaranteed an uncritical audience, was now at an end. Spiralling production costs were compounded by the British government's imposition of a 75 per cent *ad valorem* customs duty on all imported films. Foreign revenue dipped by 30 per cent, while at the same time box-office income in America declined by 20 per cent. Hovering on the horizon was the growing power of television.

The shadow of McCarthyism also fell over Hollywood. J Parnell Thomas' House Un-American Activities Committee began its investigation into alleged Communist infiltration into the film industry, rapidly sowing the seeds of fear, paranoia and betrayal. Eight writers, a producer and a director – who became known as 'The Hollywood Ten' – declined to testify before the Committee and were cited for contempt of Congress. The witch hunt spread deeper and wider, and many writers, directors and actors were blacklisted for supposed Communist sympathies. Notable casualties of McCarthyism included actors Larry Parks, Marsha Hunt and Gale Sondergaard, and director Abraham Polonsky. The blacklist also played a baleful part in hastening John Garfield's death, from a heart attack, in 1952. Charles Chaplin's political views also attracted controversy, and the year saw his first commercial failure with *Monsieur Verdoux*, an intriguing black comedy several years ahead of its time which clearly influenced Robert Hamer's 1949 Ealing classic *Kind Hearts and Coronets*.

The director and producer among the 'Hollywood Ten' were Edward Dmytryk and Adrian Scott, two of RKO's top talents who, ironically, were responsible for *Crossfire*, the studio's biggest financial and critical success of the year. *Crossfire* was a hard-hitting indictment of anti-Semitism, as was Elia Kazan's *Gentleman's Agreement*. The Academy voted the latter the year's Best Film and Kazan the Best Director. The film also gained Celeste Holm the Best Supporting Actress Award for her performance as the chic but lonely fashion editor. The Best Actress Award took everyone by surprise, but was deservedly won by Loretta Young for *The Farmer's Daughter*. Ronald Colman was voted Best Actor for his performance in *A Double Life*, while Edmund Gwenn carried off the Best Supporting Actor Award as 'Kris Kringle' in *Miracle on 34th Street*. Flop of the year was RKO's ambitious screen version of Eugene O'Neill's *Mourning Becomes Electra*, which racked up a record-breaking loss of $2,310,000. More successful for the studio were the frothy *Bachelor and the Bobby Soxer* and *Out of the Past*, the definitive *film noir* which has fixed Robert Michum's laconic, heavy-lidded screen persona for several generations of filmgoers.

Filmed books were all the rage, among them *Forever Amber*, *The Secret Life of Walter Mitty*, *Nightmare Alley*, *The Egg and I*, *The Late George Apley* and *The Paradine Case*. Plays successfully adapted for the screen included *Life with Father*, *Voice of the Turtle* and *Dear Ruth*.

The year saw the death of director Ernst Lubitsch, opera singer Grace Moore, cowboy star Harry Carey – who had become one of Hollywood's best-loved character actors – and J Warren Kerrigan, matinée idol of the silent screen. Barbara Bel Geddes made her screen debut alongside Henry Fonda in *The Long Night*. Another newcomer was stern-faced Jeff Chandler in *Johnny O'Clock*. Richard Widmark's film career got off to a flying start with his performance as the thin-lipped giggling killer Tommy Udo in *Kiss of Death*.

The British mogul J Arthur Rank was one of the prime movers in telescoping Universal, International and United World Pictures into Universal-International Productions. The British film industry was still on the crest of a wave, scoring critical and commercial successes with Michael Powell's *Black Narcissus*, Carol Reed's *Odd Man Out* and the Boultings' *Brighton Rock*. Gainsborough's *Holiday Camp* and Ealing's *It Always Rains on Sunday* provided evocative pictures of life in Britain towards the end of the decade. As an antidote to postwar austerity Herbert Wilcox produced the immensely successful *The Courtneys of Curzon Street*, a whimsical fantasy of upper-class life starring Michael Wilding and Anna Neagle.

ACTION

Dark Passage (Warner) d.Delmer Daves: Lauren Bacall, Humphrey Bogart. Escaped convict Bogart undergoes plastic surgery before tracking down his wife's killer. Brilliant opening 40 minutes

Crossfire (RKO) d.Edward Dmytryk: Robert Ryan, Robert Young. Taut *film noir* with a message, as homicidal anti-Semite Ryan is exposed by fellow GI Robert Mitchum and detective Robert Young

Intrigue (UA) d.Edwin L Marin: George Raft. Court-martialled airman Raft is reduced to flying black market food into postwar Shanghai. Reporter Helena Carter is on hand to straighten him out

Brute Force (Universal) d.Jules Dassin: Howard Duff, Burt Lancaster. Explosive prison-break drama with Hume Cronyn in sadistic form as psychopathic Wagner-loving prison captain

Kiss of Death (Fox) d.Henry Hathaway: Richard Widmark, Victor Mature. Small-time crook Mature is forced to turn informer. Stunning debut by Widmark as the insanely giggling killer Tommy Udo

Nocturne (RKO) d.Edwin L Marin: Walter Sande, Myrna Dell, George Raft. Impassive detective Raft investigates the suspicious death of a lady-killing composer. The ten suspects are all beautiful women

The Brasher Doubloon (Fox) d.John Brahm: Nancy Guild, George Montgomery. Efficient, underrated version of Raymond Chandler's *The High Window* with Montgomery cast as Philip Marlowe

Johnny O'Clock (Columbia) d.Robert Rossen: Dick Powell. Tight-lipped thriller in which gambling-den owner Powell is involved in more ways than one with the death of a bent cop and his moll

T-Men (Eagle Lion) d.Anthony Mann: Wallace Ford, Jack Overman, Alfred Ryder, Dennis O'Keefe. Two Treasury agents pose as wanted men to infiltrate Detroit's Vantucci gang. Pacy thriller

13 Rue Madeleine (Fox) d.Henry Hathaway: James Cagney. Cagney leads a group of Allied agents searching behind German lines for a secret rocket site. Documentary feel

The Web (Universal) d.Michael Gordon: Edmond O'Brien, Ella Raines. Incisive thriller finds attorney O'Brien hired as crooked Vincent Price's bodyguard, walking into murder frame-up

Christmas Eve (UA) d.Edwin L Marin: George Raft. Fugitive Raft, playboy George Brent and rodeo rider Randolph Scott answer a call for help from their eccentric 'Aunt Matilda' in snappy comedy-thriller

Song of the Thin Man (MGM) d.Edward Buzzell: Myrna Loy, Asta, William Powell. Sadly, the Martinis had to stop and this was the last in the series. Nick investigates slaying on a gambling ship

Riff-Raff (RKO) d.Ted Tetzlaff: Percy Kilbride, Anne Jeffreys, Pat O'Brien. Panama-based adventurer O'Brien races Walter Slezak for valuable oil concessions. Superbly orchestrated opening 10 minutes

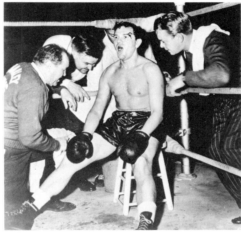

Body and Soul (MGM) d.Robert Rossen: John Garfield. A boxing champion who has been corrupted by success regains his self-respect. Garfield plays the fighter with a fierce, dumb eloquence

Wild Harvest (Paramount) d.Tay Garnett: Alan Ladd, Robert Preston, Dorothy Lamour. Turbulent saga of contract harvesting folk set among the boundless acres of the Midwest

Mr District Attorney (Columbia) d.Robert Sinclair: Michael O'Shea, Dennis O'Keefe, Adolphe Menjou, Marguerite Chapman. Hard-boiled but attractive murderess (Chapman) falls for DA O'Keefe, gets her comeuppance

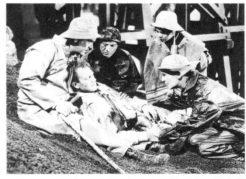

Tycoon (RKO) d.Richard Wallace: John Wayne (c). Arrogant, hard-driving engineer Wayne battles to build a railroad through the Andes for magnate Cedric Hardwicke. Laraine Day the love interest

Golden Earrings (Paramount) d.Mitchell Leisen: Ray Milland, Marlene Dietrich. Dusky gypsy Marlene helps secret agent Milland filch Nazi poison gas formula in utterly preposterous espionage melodrama

The Perils of Pauline (Paramount) d.George Marshall: Betty Hutton. Spirited action-comedy traces the career of Pearl White, queen of the early movie serials. Hutton in energetic form

The Corpse Came C.O.D. (Columbia) d.Henry Levin: Joan Blondell, George Brent. Enterprising reporters Blondell and Brent solve a bizarre murder mystery with Hollywood background

ADVENTURE

Forever Amber (Fox) d.Otto Preminger: Cornel Wilde, Richard Greene, Linda Darnell. Gaudy, dull version of block-busting novel. Sole delight is George Sanders' sardonic Charles II

Captain from Castile (Fox) d.Henry King: Tyrone Power, Cesar Romero (c). Dispossessed Spanish nobleman Power joins bold Cortez (Romero) in colourful expedition to Mexico

The Exile (Universal) d.Max Ophuls: Robert Coote, Douglas Fairbanks, Jr, Paule Croset (later Paula Corday). Fairbanks is appropriately debonair as Charles II planning his return to England

Green Dolphin Street (MGM) d.Victor Saville: Linda Christian, Van Heflin, Lana Turner. Tidal waves, family conflicts, triangle romances, Maori uprisings in tale of pioneering days of New Zealand

Last of the Red Men (Columbia) d.George Sherman: Jon Hall. Chaotic adaptation of Fenimore Cooper's *Last of the Mohicans*. Dreadful colour process only adds to the ordeal

Unconquered (Paramount) d.Cecil B DeMille: Paulette Goddard, Cecil Kellaway, Gary Cooper. Sprawling epic set in 18th-century Virginia with Cooper taking on vil-lainous Howard da Silva and his redskins

Pirates of Monterey (Universal) d.Alfred Werker: Maria Montez, Rod Cameron. Gun-running soldier of fortune Cameron takes time off to dally with the ripe Montez in old Monterey

Wife of Monte Cristo (PRC) d.Edgar Ulmer: Lenore Aubert, John Loder. Playful, cut-rate outing in which Aubert takes the place of her imprisoned husband, the masked 'Avenger'

Slave Girl (Universal) d.Charles Lamont: Yvonne De Carlo, George Brent. Misfiring send-up of adventure films set on North African coast. Most animated performance comes from a talking camel

Sinbad the Sailor (RKO) d.Richard
Wallace: Douglas Fairbanks, Jr, Anthony
Quinn, Maureen O'Hara. Wordy, torpid
Arabian Nights adventure with Fairbanks
after treasure of Alexander the Great

Tarzan and the Huntress (RKO) d.Kurt
Neumann: Johnny Sheffield, Johnny
Weissmuller. Pioneer ecologist Tarzan
thwarts a dastardly plot to trap wild life
wholesale for the world's zoos

MELODRAMA

Desire Me (MGM) d.George Cukor: Greer
Garson, Richard Hart. Missing-believed-
dead soldier Robert Mitchum comes home
to find wife Garson in arms of former
comrade Hart

The Guilt of Janet Ames (Columbia)
d.Henry Levin: Rosalind Russell, Melvyn
Douglas. Two elegant farceurs tackle soggy
psychological drama of war widow and guilt-
racked former officer

Out of the Past (RKO) d.Jacques
Tourneur: Jane Greer, Robert Mitchum.
Richly textured, definitive *film noir* gave
Mitchum his first starring role supported by
femme fatale Greer

Possessed (Warner) d.Curtis Bernhardt:
Joan Crawford, Van Heflin. Ultra-neurotic
Joan is driven crazy by unrequited love for
Van Heflin. Way over the top study of
schizophrenia

Daisy Kenyon (Fox) d.Otto Preminger:
Dana Andrews, Joan Crawford, Henry
Fonda. Another chance for Joan to suffer in
mink as old flame Andrews tries to prise
her away from husband Fonda

Smash-Up – The Story of a Woman
(Universal) d.Stuart Heisler: Lee Bowman,
Susan Hayward, Marsha Hunt. Torch singer
Hayward gives up husband Bowman for the
booze in female rerun of *Lost Weekend*

The Paradine Case (Vanguard) d.Alfred
Hitchcock: Gregory Peck, Ann Todd.
Barrister Peck falls under the spell of his
beautiful client (Valli), a woman accused of
murder. Opulent but very static

The Woman on the Beach (RKO) d.Jean Renoir: Joan Bennett, Robert Ryan. Supercharged triangle between bored bitch Bennett, her blind husband Charles Bickford and tortured coastguard Ryan

A Woman's Vengeance (Universal) d.Zoltan Korda: Charles Boyer, Ann Blyth. The vengeance is wrought by jealous Jessica Tandy, who murders Boyer's wife (Rachel Kempson). Script by Aldous Huxley

Dishonored Lady (UA) d.Robert Stevenson: Dennis O'Keefe, Hedy Lamarr. Lamarr is the lady with a past, saved by psychiatry from the charge of murdering one of her admirers

Nightmare Alley (Fox) d.Edmund Goulding: Tyrone Power, Joan Blondell, Colleen Gray. Determined effort by Power to shrug off romantic image as a swindling mentalist who winds up as a fairground geek

Cry Wolf (Warner) d.Peter Godfrey: Errol Flynn, John Ridgely, Barbara Stanwyck. Flynn sets out to disprove Stanwyck's claims to his late brother's estate, in Gothic cat-and-mouse drama

I Walk Alone (Paramount) d.Byron Haskin: Lizabeth Scott, Kirk Douglas, Burt Lancaster. Racketeer Douglas finds his past catching up with him when former boot-legging partner Lancaster turns up

Gentleman's Agreement (Fox) d.Elia Kazan: Gregory Peck, Dorothy McGuire, John Garfield. Writer Peck poses as a Jew to discover the extent of anti-Semitism. Considered hard-hitting in its day

The Two Mrs Carrolls (Warner) d.Peter Godfrey: Barbara Stanwyck, Ann Carter, Humphrey Bogart. Bogie is the unhinged artist who paints his wives then disposes of them with a glass of poisoned milk

The Arnelo Affair (MGM) d.Arch Oboler: John Hodiak, Frances Gifford. A neglected wife is caught up in a murder web woven by ruthless Hodiak. *Brief Encounter* with bullets

Boomerang (Fox) d.Elia Kazan: Lee J Cobb, Karl Malden, Dana Andrews. Andrews is the lawyer defending a vagrant (Arthur Kennedy) accused of murder. Location-shot and based on a true story

The Unsuspected (Warner) d.Michael Curtiz: Joan Caulfield, Claude Rains. Radio presenter Rains lives out one of his own murder stories. Stylish example of 40s Hollywood plush

Framed (Columbia) d.Richard Wallace: Janis Carter, Glenn Ford. Alluring but ruthless Carter entices out-of-work engineer Ford into a complicated plot to pull bank heist

Desert Fury (Paramount) d.Lewis Allen: Lizabeth Scott, Mary Astor. Cop Burt Lancaster and slimy hoodlum John Hodiak both lust after casino owner Astor's daughter Scott. Guess who gets her

Kiss the Blood off My Hands (Universal) d.Norman Foster: Joan Fontaine, Burt Lancaster. Brooding Burt, on the run after accidental killing, falls into the clutches of blackmailing Robert Newton

If Winter Comes (MGM) d.Victor Saville: Dame May Whitty, Ian Wolfe, Walter Pidgeon, Janet Leigh. Pidgeon is torn between wife Angela Lansbury and true love Deborah Kerr

Tenth Avenue Angel (MGM) d.Roy Rowland: George Murphy, Margaret O'Brien, Angela Lansbury. Seventy-four minutes of tearjerking moppetry with winsome little O'Brien

The Hucksters (MGM) d.Jack Conway: Clark Gable, Sydney Greenstreet. Lively exposé of Madison Avenue with Greenstreet in fine form as the egomaniacal king of the Beautie Soap empire

High Wall (MGM) d.Curtis Bernhardt: Robert Taylor, Audrey Totter. Doctor Totter proves a dab hand with the truth serum while clearing war veteran Taylor of the murder of his wife

The Red House (UA) d.Delmer Daves: Judith Anderson, Edward G Robinson. Crippled farmer Robinson warns all and sundry not to go into spooky Ox Head Woods and kills them when they do

Ivy (Universal) d.Sam Wood: Joan Fontaine, Lillian Fontaine. Heartless Joan murders her husband and frames her lover to ensnare a millionaire but finally ends up at the bottom of an elevator shaft

The Private Affairs of Bel Ami (MGM) d.Albert Lewin: George Sanders, Marie Wilson, John Carradine. George Sanders is well cast as de Maupassant's cynical social-climbing careerist

Thunder in the Valley (Fox) d.Louis King: Peggy Ann Garner, Lon McCallister, Reginald Owen. Highland tale of sheepdogs and their owners based on novel *Bob, Son of Battle*. Edmund Gwenn an unlikely shepherd

Moss Rose (Fox) d.Gregory Ratoff: Victor Mature, Peggy Cummins. Edwardian murder mystery with a nice feel for period, though Mature is a little hard to swallow as a cultivated and wealthy young Englishman

Lured (UA) d.Douglas Sirk: Lucille Ball, George Sanders. Ball acts as a decoy to help Scotland Yard nail a killer who finds his victims in the Personal Columns of the newspapers

Night Song (RKO) d.John Cromwell: Merle Oberon, Ethel Barrymore, Hoagy Carmichael, Dana Andrews. Millionairess Oberon woos blind composer Andrews back to the piano

A Double Life (Universal) d.George Cukor: Edmond O'Brien, Signe Hasso, Ronald Colman. Colman won Oscar as actor who, taken over by the role of Othello, strangles sluttish Shelley Winters

The Fugitive (RKO) d.John Ford: Henry Fonda, J Carrol Naish. Graham Greene's *The Power and the Glory* loses out to Ford's bleary romanticism. Brilliant photography by Gabriel Figueroa

Singapore (Universal) d.John Brahm: Fred MacMurray, Ava Gardner, Maylia. Ex-sailor Fred returns to Singapore to find wife Ava, presumed dead in war, now amnesiac (probably caused by watching this film)

Unfinished Dance (MGM) d.Henry Koster: Margaret O'Brien, Cyd Charisse. The heartaches, triumphs and tears of a backstage musical transferred to a ballet school. Remake of *La Mort du Cygne* (1937)

Stallion Road (Warner) d.James Kern: Alexis Smith, Ronald Reagan. Veterinary surgeon Ronnie's devotion to duty nearly costs him the love of Smith, but he rallies to elbow aside 'other man' Zachary Scott

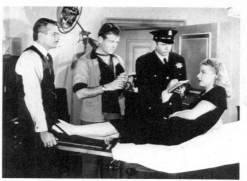

Nora Prentiss (Warner) d.Vincent Sherman: Kent Smith, Ann Sheridan. Happily married Dr Kent Smith is driven to his downfall by obsession with sleazy night-club singer Sheridan

They Won't Believe Me (RKO) d.Irving Pichel: Robert Young, Susan Hayward, Jane Greer. Flashback tale of sponging, murdering heel Young who gets his just desserts after his wife's suicide

The Long Night (RKO) d.Anatole Litvak: Henry Fonda, Barbara Bel Geddes. Faithful remake of *Le Jour se Lève* (1939) fails on every count, including the addition of a 'happy ending'

Ride the Pink Horse (Universal) d.Robert Montgomery: Robert Montgomery, Wanda Hendrix, Thomas Gomez. Blackmailer Montgomery tracks down a war-profiteer responsible for the death of a buddy

That's My Man (Republic) d.Frank Borzage: Don Ameche. Don's gambling wrecks his marriage and ruins him financially, but the noble equine Gallant Man saves the day in the race that matters

The Gangster (Allied Artists) d.Gordon Wiles: Joan Lorring, Barry Sullivan, John Ireland. The sands of time are running out for Sullivan, racketeer boss of Neptune Beach, in pacy shoot 'em up drama

The Man I Love (Warner) d.Raoul Walsh: Robert Alda, Ida Lupino. Lupino wasted in self-sacrificing role of singer who goes with nightclub owner Alda to save her brother and sister. Some good songs, though

The Beginning or the End (MGM) d.Norman Taurog: Robert Walker. Documentary-style outline of the scientific road that led to the bombing of Hiroshima and Nagasaki

COMEDY

Her Husband's Affairs (Columbia) d.S Sylvan Simon: Lucille Ball, Franchot Tone. Slick, improbable farce tangles advertising man Tone up with the schemes of a mad inventor

I'll Be Yours (Universal) d.William Seiter: Deanna Durbin, William Bendix. *The Good Fairy* (1935) revamped to provide Durbin with so-so musical comedy. Script by Preston Sturges

Mad Wednesday (RKO) d.Preston Sturges: Harold Lloyd, Jimmy Conlin. Sad attempt by Lloyd and the failing Sturges to revive the days of 'thrill comedy'. Originally titled *The Sin of Harold Diddlebock*

Monsieur Verdoux (UA) d.Charles Chaplin: Charles Chaplin, Martha Raye. Deeply misogynistic black comedy of a little wife murderer. Brassy Raye a delight as the 'wife' Chaplin just can't kill

The Farmer's Daughter (RKO) d.H C Potter: Charles Bickford, Loretta Young, Joseph Cotten. Loretta is the Swedish-American farm girl who wins politician Cotten's heart and a seat in Congress

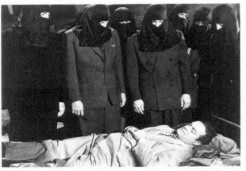

Where There's Life (Paramount) d.Sidney Lanfield: Bob Hope. New Yorker Bob finds that he is heir to the throne of Boravia. General Signe Hasso is determined to keep him off the throne

Dear Ruth (Paramount) d.William D Russell: Billy de Wolfe, Joan Caulfield, William Holden, Virginia Welles. Comedy of errors caused by Mona Freeman's pen-pal activities

Buck Privates Come Home (Universal) d.Charles Barton: Lou Costello, Bud Abbott. A & C get tangled up with the smuggling of a little French orphan into the USA. Formula stuff by now

The Bachelor and the Bobby Soxer (RKO) d.Irving Reis: Cary Grant, Shirley Temple, Rudy Vallee. Judge Myrna Loy sentences Cary to be adoring younger sister's constant escort. Cute

The Egg and I (Universal) d.Chester Erskine: Fred MacMurray, Claudette Colbert. Fred whisks sophisticated Claudette off to a life of chicken farming. Led to the 'Ma and Pa Kettle' series

Suddenly It's Spring (Paramount)
d.Mitchell Leisen: Macdonald Carey,
Paulette Goddard. Marriage guidance
expert Goddard finds her own marriage to
Fred MacMurray is on the rocks

Ladies' Man (Paramount) d.William D
Russell: Virginia Welles, Eddie Bracken,
Cass Daley. Country boob Bracken strikes it
rich and finds himself the first prize in a
New York radio show

Lost Honeymoon (Eagle Lion) d.Leigh
Jason: Ann Richards, Franchot Tone.
Amnesiac Tone has his memory jolted
when presented with the results of a
wartime marriage in England

Miracle on 34th Street (Fox) d.George
Seaton: Edmund Gwenn, Natalie Wood,
Maureen O'Hara. Charming comedy-fantasy
in which Macy's new Santa Claus, 'Kris
Kringle', just might be the real thing

The Trouble with Women (Paramount)
d.Sidney Lanfield: Brian Donlevy, Teresa
Wright. Reporter Wright sets her sights on
Professor Ray Milland whose masterwork is
a book entitled *The Subjugation of Women*

Fiesta (MGM) d.Richard Thorpe: Esther
Williams, Akim Tamiroff, Cyd Charisse.
Esther impersonates matador twin brother
Ricardo Montalban in the bull ring, and
looks just great in the outfit

Merton of the Movies (MGM) d.Robert
Alton: Virginia O'Brien, Red Skelton. Third
time around for the old George S Kaufman
play with Skelton as the sappy comic
making good in cinema's early days

Variety Girl (Paramount) d.George
Marshall: Billy de Wolfe, Olga San Juan.
Olga's quest for Hollywood stardom
provides Paramount with the excuse to
trundle out all their stars

The Secret Life of Walter Mitty (RKO)
d.Norman Z McLeod: Danny Kaye, Virginia
Mayo. Energetic performance by Kaye as
Thurber's wimpish daydreamer. He also
performs 'Anatole of Paris'

The Senator was Indiscreet (Universal)
d. George S Kaufman: William Powell, Peter
Lind Hayes. Powell superb as the
irredeemably fatuous politician whose
diaries cause a scandal

Road to Rio (Paramount) d. Norman Z
McLeod: Bob Hope, Dorothy Lamour, Bing
Crosby. After wrecking a carnival with their
high-wire bicycle act, Bob and Bing stow
away on a Rio-bound luxury liner

Something in the Wind (Universal)
d. Irving Pichel: Charles Winninger, Deanna
Durbin, Donald O'Connor. Musical comedy
of errors with Durbin mistaken for a
recently deceased tycoon's mistress

It Had to be You (Columbia) d. Rudolph
Maté: Ginger Rogers, Cornel Wilde.
Scatterbrained Rogers just can't nerve
herself for the wedding ceremony until the
appearance of literal 'dream lover' Wilde

The Wistful Widow of Wagon Gap
(Universal) d. Charles Barton: Bud Abbott,
Lou Costello, Marjorie Main. An old
Montana law is invoked to make A & C
responsible for battleaxe Main

Honeymoon (RKO) d. William Keighley:
Franchot Tone, Shirley Temple. Shirley
runs off to Mexico City to marry GI Guy
Madison but then gives harassed diplomat
Tone the runaround

WESTERNS

Cheyenne (Warner) d. Raoul Walsh:
Dennis Morgan. Morgan is the gambler
turned lawman who joins Bruce Bennett's
gang to stop him and then steals his wife
(Jane Wyman)

The Gunfighters (Columbia) d. George
Waggner: Randolph Scott, Steven Geray,
Charles Kemper. Scott is the grim-faced
hero who buckles on his holster just one
more time when he finds a friend murdered

The Fabulous Texan (Republic) d. Edward
Ludwig: John Carroll, Catherine McLeod.
Carroll and Wild Bill Elliott return from the
Civil War to find Texas turned into a police
state by the despotic Albert Dekker

King of the Bandits (Mon) d.Christy Cabanne: Gilbert Roland, Chris Pin Martin. The last of Roland's outings as the Cisco Kid, on the trail of an outlaw who's holding up stagecoaches in his name

Angel and the Badman (Republic) d.James Edward Grant: John Wayne, Gail Russell, Irene Rich. Leisurely tale of outlaw Wayne finding refuge with a Quaker family and falling for Russell

Pursued (Warner) d.Raoul Walsh: Robert Mitchum, Teresa Wright. Brooding psychological Western, full of landscapes of the mind brilliantly photographed by James Wong Howe

Bowery Buckaroos (Mon) d.William Beaudine: Jack Norman, Leo Gorcey, Gabriel Dell, Billy Benedict, Julie Gibson, Bobby Jordan, David Gorcey. Bowery Boys in search of gold. Only if you're desperate

Jessie James Rides Again (Republic) d.Thomas Carr, Fred C Brannon: Clayton Moore, Roy Barcroft. Pacy serial in which the famous outlaw (Moore) does his best to go straight

The Michigan Kid (Universal) d.Ray Taylor: Jon Hall, Stanley Andrews, Rita Johnson. Trouble looms for Hall when he foils an attempted stage robbery by outlaw Victor McLaglen

Robin Hood of Texas (Republic) d.Lesley Selander: Gene Autry, Lynne Roberts. Gene's last for Republic with the blame being pinned on him for a bank robbery. Between songs he finds the real culprits

The Last Round-Up (Columbia) d.John English: Gene Autry, Bobby Blake. Autry's first after leaving Republic finds him relocating an Indian tribe so that an aqueduct can be built on their barren land

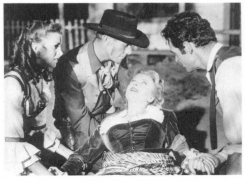

Trail Street (RKO) d.Ray Enright: Madge Meredith, Randolph Scott, Anne Jeffreys, Robert Ryan. Scott is lawman Bat Masterson, Ryan a proto-agribusinessman and Steve Brodie a would-be cattle baron

Heaven Only Knows (UA) d.Albert Rogell: Robert Cummings, Brian Donlevy. Fantasy Western in which the Archangel Michael (Cummings) is despatched to Earth to sort out Donlevy's destiny

Thunder Mountain (RKO) d.Lew Landers:
Jason Robards, Sr, Virginia Owen, Richard
Martin, Tim Holt. Tim Holt returns from
college and is plunged into an old family
feud stirred up by scheming villains

Northwest Outpost (Republic) d.Allan
Dwan: Peter Whitney, Ilona Massey, Nelson
Eddy. Nelson gallops to the rescue of a
Russian girl held captive in California, while
Dwan has some sly fun at his expense

ROMANCE

The Ghost and Mrs Muir (Fox) d.Joseph L
Mankiewicz: Gene Tierney, Rex Harrison.
Charming fantasy in which a young widow
is befriended by the ghost of a sea captain
who then falls in love with her

Cynthia (MGM) d.Robert Z Leonard:
Elizabeth Taylor, Mary Astor. Taylor
blossoms into a beautiful young teenager.
James Lydon was her first date. Since then
their careers have diverged

The Other Love (MGM) d.Andre de Toth:
Maria Palmer, David Niven. Maudlin story
of suave sanatorium doctor Niven marrying
dying concert pianist Barbara Stanwyck.
One of his many thankless roles

The Homestretch (Fox) d.H Bruce
Humberstone: Cornel Wilde, Helen Walker.
Racing almost comes between charming
gambler Wilde and his sheltered wife
Maureen O'Hara. Climax at Kentucky Derby

Time out of Mind (Universal) d.Robert
Siodmak: Phyllis Calvert, Robert Hutton.
Phyllis strives to help seafarer's son Hutton
realize his natural gifts as a pianist in soggy
romantic drama

Escape Me Never (Warner) d.Peter
Godfrey: Gig Young, Ida Lupino, Errol
Flynn. The mother of an illegitimate child
marries a composer whose heart belongs
to another

High Barbaree (MGM) d.Jack Conway:
Cameron Mitchell, Van Johnson. Downed
airman Johnson drifts across Pacific
wallowing in flashback romance with June
Allyson. Ending too preposterous for words

That Way with Women (Warner)
d.Frederick de Cordova: Barbara Brown,
Martha Vickers, Dane Clark, Sydney Greenstreet. Clark romances tycoon's daughter
Vickers. Remake of *The Millionaire* (1931)

Love and Learn (Warner) d.Frederick de Cordova: Janis Paige, Robert Hutton, Martha Vickers, Jack Carson. Two impoverished songwriters are snatched from the jaws of oblivion by an heiress

Welcome Stranger (Paramount) d.Elliott Nugent: Bing Crosby, Joan Caulfield, Barry Fitzgerald. Reprise of *Going My Way* with crotchety doctor Fitzgerald baulking at his new singing assistant Bing

Love from a Stranger (Eagle Lion) d.Richard Whorf: Sylvia Sidney, John Hodiak. Romance turns sour for sweepstake winner Sidney as suspicion grows that husband Hodiak is a killer

MUSICALS

This Time for Keeps (MGM) d.Richard Thorpe: Esther Williams, Jimmy Durante. On-off romance between aquaperson Williams and playboy Johnnie Johnston. Durante sings 'Inka Dinka Doo'

New Orleans (UA) d.Arthur Lubin: Billie Holiday, Louis Armstrong. Small army of immortal musicians wasted in trite tale of Dorothy Patrick dithering between the worlds of classical music and jazz

Copacabana (UA) d.Alfred E Green: Carmen Miranda, Groucho Marx. Groucho is an agent whose only artiste is Miranda – well, they were made for each other, weren't they

Hit Parade of 1947 (Republic) d.Frank McDonald: Constance Moore, Gil Lamb, Joan Edwards, Eddie Albert. The principals' nightclub act is signed up by a Hollywood producer but he only wants Miss Moore

It Happened in Brooklyn (MGM) d.Richard Thorpe: Frank Sinatra, Jimmy Durante. Frank falls for Kathryn Grayson but loses out to Peter Lawford after performing opera duet with her

The Fabulous Dorseys (UA) d.Alfred E Green: Tommy Dorsey, Janet Blair, Jimmy Dorsey. A family bereavement unites the bickering musical brothers in perfunctory biopic. The music speaks for itself

I Wonder Who's Kissing Her Now (Fox) d.Lloyd Bacon: June Haver, Mark Stevens. Very loose biopic of composer Joe Howard, set – as ever with Fox – in the Gay Nineties

Down to Earth (Columbia) d.Alexander Hall: Larry Parks, Rita Hayworth, Marc Platt. Clever reworking of *Here Comes Mr Jordan* with Roland Culver sending Rita back to Earth as musical comedy star

Good News (MGM) d.Charles Walters: June Allyson, Peter Lawford. Impressive directorial debut by Walters, breathing life into an old warhorse of a campus comedy. 'The Varsity Drag' illustrated here

Carnival in Costa Rica (Fox) d.Gregory Ratoff: J Carrol Naish, Cesar Romero, Vera-Ellen. Cesar is betrothed to Vera-Ellen but he really wants Celeste Holme. But she's mad about Dick Haymes

Mother Wore Tights (Fox) d.Walter Lang: Mike Dunn, Dan Dailey, Betty Grable. Dailey and Grable are a pair of vaudevillians whose lifestyle is resented by their finishing school-educated daughter Mona Freeman

Living in a Big Way (MGM) d.Gregory La Cava: Phyllis Thaxter, Gene Kelly, Marie MacDonald. Kelly returns from the war to find his overnight bride is a millionairess. Three numbers arranged by Stanley Donen

My Wild Irish Rose (Warner) d.David Butler: Dennis Morgan (r). Morgan essays the brogue to play composer Chauney Olcott ('When Irish Eyes Are Smiling'). Newcomer Arlene Dahl adds glamour

The Shocking Miss Pilgrim (Fox) d.George Seaton: Betty Grable, Dick Haymes. Typist Grable battles for women's suffrage in 1870s Boston. Not much chance to see those legs, but a big hit

Song of Scheherezade (Universal) d.Walter Reisch: Yvonne De Carlo, Jean-Pierre Aumont. Gloriously camp extravaganza with sultry dancer De Carlo inspiring Aumont's Rimsky-Korsakov

Song of Love (MGM) d.Clarence Brown: Katharine Hepburn, Robert Walker, Henry Daniell. Agreeably preposterous aberration in which Hepburn plays Clara Schumann, Walker is Brahms and Henry Daniell Liszt

Summer Holiday (MGM) d.Rouben Mamoulian: Mickey Rooney, Marilyn Maxwell. Rooney takes first, faltering steps into manhood in musical version of Eugene O'Neill's *Ah Wilderness*. Looks a treat

Carnegie Hall (UA) d.Edgar Ulmer: Jascha Heifetz, Marsha Hunt. Hunt's role as pushy custodian of Carnegie Hall is peg on which to hang some splendid performances by Heifetz, Rubinstein and Ezio Pinza

Calendar Girl (Republic) d.Allan Dwan: Irene Rich, Victor McLaglen, Jane Frazee. Former silent star Rich cast as a kindly landlady presiding over a motley collection of boarders

Beat the Band (RKO) d.John H Auer: Frances Langford, Phillip Terry. Country girl Langford comes to the city to take opera lessons but falls into the clutches of unscrupulous bandleader Terry

Fun and Fancy Free (RKO) d.William Morgan, Jack Kinney, Bill Roberts, Hamilton Luske. Two cartoon stories from Disney, the second featuring Mickey Mouse in a version of Jack and the Beanstalk

AMERICANA

The Romance of Rosy Ridge (MGM) d.Roy Rowland: Dean Stockwell, Selena Royle, Janet Leigh, Thomas Mitchell, Van Johnson. A Southern family struggles to get by in the days of Reconstruction

Cass Timberlane (MGM) d.George Sidney: Spencer Tracy, Lana Turner. Smooth adaptation of Sinclair Lewis novel with Tracy as wealthy judge and Turner the poor girl who marries him

Life with Father (Warner) d.Michael Curtiz: Irene Dunne, William Powell, Elizabeth Taylor (c). New York of the 1880s meticulously evoked in faithful screen version of Broadway hit

Deep Valley (Warner) d.Jean Negulesco: Dane Clark, Ida Lupino. Brutalized farm girl Lupino befriends escaped convict Clark in cross between *Tobacco Road* and *Cold Comfort Farm*

Mourning Becomes Electra (RKO) d.Dudley Nichols: Michael Redgrave, Rosalind Russell. Doomed attempt to film O'Neill's transposition of *Agamemnon* to a post-Civil War family

Magic Town (RKO) d.William Wellman: James Stewart, Jane Wyman. Stewart miscast as pollster who discovers a town which is perfect composite of the US. He should have been one of its citizens

The Foxes of Harrow (Fox) d.John M Stahl: Maureen O'Hara, Rex Harrison. Irish adventurer Harrison gambles his way into plantation society in ante-Bellum New Orleans. From a novel by Frank Yerby

The Late George Apley (Fox) d.Joseph L Mankiewicz: Ronald Colman, Vanessa Brown, Richard Ney. Colman in fine form as stuffed shirt Bostonian clinging to tradition but eventually having to compromise

B MOVIES

The Falcon's Adventure (RKO) d.William Berke: Madge Meredith, Tom Conway, Edward S Brophy. Svelte Conway rescues Brazilian Meredith from kidnappers and tumbles into diamond mystery

Dick Tracy's Dilemma (RKO) d.John Rawlins: Jack Lambert, Jason Robards, Sr. The original Dick Tracy, Ralph Byrd, resumes the title role, chasing fur thieves

Dick Tracy vs Cueball (RKO) d.Gordon Douglas: Morgan Conway, Esther Howard. Tongue-in-cheek thriller filled with exotic characters, including Vitamin Flintheart, Dripping Dagger and Jules Priceless

The Millerson Case (Columbia) d.George Archainbaud: Warner Baxter. The Crime Doctor arrives in the Blue Ridge Mountains on holiday only to find the locals going down like flies in a mysterious epidemic

The Chinese Ring (Mon) d.William Beaudine: Roland Winters, Victor Sen Yung, Mantan Moreland, Warren Douglas. First appearance by Winters in the role of the aphoristic Chinese detective

Undercover Maisie (MGM) d.Harry Beaumont: Barry Nelson, Ann Sothern, Mark Daniels. Sothern's hardboiled, heart-of-gold chorus girl bows out with a spell in the police force

Dark Delusion (MGM) d.Willis Goldbeck: James Craig, Lucille Bremer. Blair General Hospital closes its doors for the last time with Lionel Barrymore giving his 15th impersonation of Dr Gillespie

Philo Vance's Gamble (PRC) d.Basil Wrangell: Alan Curtis, Cliff Clark, James Burke. Tough guy Vance (Curtis) is involved with an underworld syndicate, stolen gems and a trio of homicides

The Thirteenth Hour (Columbia) d. William Clemens: Bernadene Hayes, Richard Dix, John Kellogg. Another instalment in the 'Whistler' series finds Dix framed on a hit and run murder

Second Chance (Fox) d. James Tinling: Kent Taylor, Louise Currie, Larry Blake, Frances Pierlot. Jewel thief Kent Taylor falls in love with insurance agent Currie imagining she is in the same line of business

Seven Keys to Baldpate (RKO) d. Lew Landers: Phillip Terry, Eduardo Ciannelli. Screen treatment No 5 with writer Terry's snowbound house the rendezvous of a murderous clutch of criminals

Desperate (RKO) d. Anthony Mann: Jason Robards, Sr, Steve Brodie. And well might trucker Brodie be as he flees with wife Audrey Long from the cops and a gang of vicious mobsters in taut little thriller

Born to Kill (RKO) d. Robert Wise: Isabel Jewell, Lawrence Tierney. Killer Tierney and grasping divorcee Claire Trevor make a splendidly unlovely couple in gripping melodrama

The Invisible Wall (Fox) d. Eugene Forde: Virginia Christine. Effective flashback tale of gambler (Don Castle) on the run from murder in Las Vegas, L.A., Denver and St Louis

The Devil Thumbs a Ride (RKO) d. Felix Feist: Lawrence Tierney, Nan Leslie. Tierney revels in the part of a psychopathic hoodlum leaving mayhem in his wake as he hitch hikes away from a hold-up

Whispering City (Quebec) d. Fedor Ozep: Paul Lukas. Amateurish effort, filmed in Canada, casts Lukas as a manipulative, murdering lawyer exposed by a young female reporter

So Dark the Night (Columbia) d. Joseph H Lewis: Steven Geray, Micheline Cheirel. Geray is vacationing Parisian detective who gradually realizes he's committed murders he's investigating

Killer McCoy (MGM) d. Roy Rowland: Sam Levene, Mickey Rooney, James Dunn. Remake of *The Crowd Roars* (1938) allows 25-year-old Rooney to act his age as feisty little boxer

Jewels of Brandenburg (Fox) d. Eugene Forde: Fernando Alvarado, Carol Thurston. American agent (Richard Travis) is sent to Europe to clear up theft of jewels by wartime spy (Leonard Strong)

Alias a Gentleman (MGM) d.Harry Beaumont: Tom Drake, Wallace Beery, Frank McGrath. Formula Beery vehicle about an ex-con trying to go straight almost writes and directs itself

Cigarette Girl (Columbia) d.Gunther Fritsch: Leslie Brooks (l). Flashback tale, told by Ludwig Donath, of a cigarette girl and the young man who believes she is a famous singer

Kilroy was Here (Mon) d.Phil Karlson: Pat Goldin, Jackie Cooper. Witless college comedy starring former child stars Cooper and Jackie Coogan which relies on the old 'Kilroy was Here' as its single gag

Roses are Red (Fox) d.James Tinling: Patricia Knight, Don Castle, Joseph Sawyer. Newly-elected DA Castle is kidnapped by a Mr Big who puts a lookalike in his place to run the City as he wants it

Sarge Goes to College (Mon) d.Will Jason: Joe Venuti (on guitar), Wingy Manone (on trumpet). Alan Hale, Jr, is the Sarge of the title, finding college ways a bit different from life at the camp

Linda Be Good (PRC) d.Frank McDonald: Elyse Knox, Marie Wilson. Author Knox joins burlesque show to find material and also finds her duties include entertaining 'tired' businessmen. This leads to trouble

A Likely Story (RKO) d.H C Potter: Lanny Rees, Barbara Hale, Bill Williams. Laboured comedy built around ex-GI Williams who thinks he has fatal disease. Williams and Hale became engaged during filming

Banjo (RKO) d.Richard Fleischer: Walter Reed, Jacqueline White. Faltering attempt to turn 10-year-old Sharyn Moffet into a Margaret O'Brien-style star in whimsical girl and dog tale

Black Gold (Allied Artists) d.Phil Karlson: Ducky Louie, Katherine DeMille, Anthony Quinn. Quinn's first starring role as Oklahoma Indian hoping to breed a racehorse that will win the Kentucky Derby

Son of Rusty (Columbia) d.Lew Landers: Stephen Dunne, Ted Donaldson, 'Flame'. Excellent small-town drama in which the humans and the dogs just about share the acting honours

BRITISH & FOREIGN

An Ideal Husband (London) d.Alexander Korda: Michael Wilding, Paulette Goddard. Colourful screen version of Wilde play. Vincent Korda's sets and Cecil Beaton's costumes rate higher than the acting

Hungry Hill (Two Cities) d.Brian Desmond Hurst: Dennis Price, Margaret Lockwood. Pallid interpretation of Daphne du Maurier's Victorian family saga with Lockwood trying hard to be Irish

Jassy (Gainsborough) d.Bernard Knowles: Margaret Lockwood. Gypsy girl Lockwood possesses second sight. However, this does not prevent her from being accused of poisoning her husband

Fame is the Spur (Two Cities) d.Roy Boulting: Hugh Burden, Michael Redgrave. Redgrave is the former fire-breathing Labour politician who sells out to the British establishment

Captain Boycott (Individual) d.Frank Launder: Stewart Granger. Cecil Parker is the Anglo-Irish rackrenter who gave his name to the language in well-handled historical drama

The Loves of Joanna Godden (Ealing) d.Charles Frend: Jean Kent, Googie Withers. Turn of the century sheepfarming drama. Tough Googie comes on like Stanwyck in *Cattle Queen of Montana*

A Man about the House (British Lion) d.Leslie Arliss: Kieron Moore, Dulcie Gray, Margaret Johnston. Two frumpish English spinsters inherit a beautiful Neapolitan villa and scheming major domo

Blanche Fury (Cineguild) d.Marc Allegret: Stewart Granger, Valerie Hobson. Exquisitely mounted melodrama with illegitimate Granger using Hobson to cheat and murder his way into a family fortune

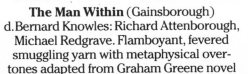

The Man Within (Gainsborough) d.Bernard Knowles: Richard Attenborough, Michael Redgrave. Flamboyant, fevered smuggling yarn with metaphysical overtones adapted from Graham Greene novel

The Master of Bankdam (Holbein) d.Walter Forde: Anne Crawford, Dennis Price. Turbulent three-generation story of mill-owning folk. Price is on the side of the angels, but gets crushed by a loom

The Courtneys of Curzon Street (British Lion) d.Herbert Wilcox: Michael Wilding, Gladys Young, Anna Neagle. Sentimental saga of a family founded by nobleman Wilding and Irish maid Neagle

Dear Murderer (Gainsborough) d.Arthur Crabtree: Dennis Price, Eric Portman. Well-mannered British *film noir* with Portman committing the 'perfect murder' on his wife's lover

They Made Me a Fugitive (Warner) d.Alberto Cavalcanti: Sally Gray, Trevor Howard. Howard is a down-on-his-luck former RAF pilot drawn into a gang of Soho racketeers. Griffith Jones is the slimy villain

The Brothers (Gainsborough) d.David Macdonald: Patricia Roc, Maxwell Reed. Pert city girl Roc arrives on a Hebridean island and sparks off a murderous blood feud in meaty adaptation of L A G Strong novel

Nicholas Nickleby (Ealing) d.Alberto Cavalcanti: Derek Bond (l). Attempt to film Dickens' huge novel collapses under the weight of characters and subplots. Stanley Holloway superb as Vincent Crummles

So Well Remembered (RKO) d.Edward Dmytryk: Martha Scott, Trevor Howard, John Mills. Martha Scott is the selfish woman at the centre of the James Hilton saga set in a northern mill town

Dual Alibi (British National) d.Alfred Travers: Herbert Lom. Two Loms for the price of one as he plays identical twins seeking the winning lottery ticket purloined from them by slippery Terence de Marney

The Upturned Glass (Box) d.Lawrence Huntington: Brefni O'Rourke, James Mason. Brain surgeon Mason murders the woman responsible for the death of a woman he loves in sub-Hitchcockian thriller

The Shop at Sly Corner (British Lion) d.George King: Muriel Pavlow, Derek Farr. A blackmailer threatens to expose affable antique dealer Oscar Homolka as a refugee from Devil's Island and a fence

Temptation Harbour (ABPC) d.Lance Comfort: William Hartnell, Robert Newton. Strong performance by Newton as the signalman who finds a suitcase full of money and decides not to turn it in

The White Unicorn (John Corfield) d.Bernard Knowles: Margaret Lockwood. Lockwood is the warden of a girl's reformatory. Her crisp hair-do and tailor-mades are sufficient to keep order

Daybreak (Triton) d. Compton Bennett: Ann Todd, Maxwell Reed. Hangdog melodrama in which bargee Eric Portman leads a secret life as the public hangman. Ann Todd is his wife

Black Narcissus (Independent) d. Michael Powell: Kathleen Byron, Deborah Kerr. A group of nuns move into an empty palace in the remote Himalayas. Erotic, pulsing with colour and with a remarkable score

It Always Rains on Sunday (Ealing) d. Robert Hamer: John McCallum, Patricia Plunkett, Googie Withers. Googie shelters old flame McCallum, who's on the run from prison

Frieda (Ealing) d. Basil Dearden: Mai Zetterling, David Farrar. Farrar's return home at war's end with a German wife unleashes a complex set of tensions within his family and in the town where they live

Brighton Rock (ABPC) d. John Boulting: William Hartnell, Wylie Watson, Richard Attenborough. Attenborough mesmeric as the doll-faced teenage hoodlum in Graham Greene's adaptation of his own novel

When the Bough Breaks (Gainsborough) d. Lawrence Huntington: Torin Thatcher, Patricia Roc. Honest attempt to deal with the problems of illegitimacy, marred by patronising class attitudes

Odd Man Out (Two Cities) d. Carol Reed: Elwyn Brook Jones, James Mason, F J McCormick. Mason is the wounded Irish gunman who is an unconscionable time dying, in rhythmic, ornate *tour de force*

Good Time Girl (Gainsborough) d. David Macdonald: Peter Glenville, Jean Kent. Lurid, highly entertaining chronicle of Kent's downward spiral from nightclub hostess to reluctant accomplice in murder

Holiday Camp (Gainsborough) d. Ken Annakin: Kathleen Harrison, Jack Warner. Compendium of late-40s social life contained in a holiday camp housing everyone from card sharps to sex murderers

Dancing with Crime (Coronet) d. John Paddy Carstairs: Richard Attenborough. Low-life saga very much of the period with taxi driver Attenborough on the trail of villains who murdered a wartime chum

Hue and Cry (Ealing) d.Charles Crichton: Jack Warner, Harry Fowler. Charming fantasy in which a gang of street urchins discover that some crooks are exchanging coded messages in their favourite comic

Root of all Evil (Gainsborough) d.Brock Williams: John McCallum, Phyllis Calvert. Calvert is the jilted woman who channels all her drive into founding a business empire, at the expense of her personal life

The Ghosts of Berkeley Square (British National) d.Vernon Sewell: Robert Morley, Felix Aylmer. Morley and Aylmer are a pair of ghosts condemned to haunt a house until it is visited by a reigning monarch

Men of Two Worlds (Two Cities) d.Thorold Dickinson: Phyllis Calvert, Eric Portman, Robert Adams. An African composer (Adams) returns from Europe and confronts a witch doctor

Broken Journey (Gainsborough) d.Ken Annakin: David Tomlinson, Margot Grahame, Phyllis Calvert, Raymond Huntley. Early group jeopardy film in which a Dakota crashes in the Alps

Le Diable au Corps (France) d.Claude Autant-Lara: Micheline Presle, Gérard Philipe. Romantic melodrama set at end of First War in which boy's affair with older woman has tragic consequences

Les Maudits (France) d.René Clement. A group of influential Nazis flee by U-boat to South America as Germany collapses, but only a few of them still believe they have a mission

Germany Year Zero (Italy) d.Roberto Rossellini: Edmund Moeschke. The ruins of Berlin provide the background to the tragic tale of a young boy. The interiors were shot in Rome

Quai des Orfèvres (France) d.H-G Clouzot: Suzy Delair, Bernard Blier. A pair of small-time music-hall artistes find themselves implicated in the murder of the lecherous head of a film company

Le Silence est d'Or (France) d.René Clair: Maurice Chevalier, Marcelle Derrien. Chevalier makes a return to the screen after an eight-year absence playing a raffish old-time movie director

1948

Cinema still clung to its position as the principal form of popular entertainment, but television was fast catching up. In the United States television sales quadrupled. In Britain there were still only about 300,000 television licence holders, but within ten years the number was to rise to 10.5 million.

With one hand Hollywood was fending off the small screen; with the other it was fighting increasing pressure from the US government for the major companies to shed their interests in theatre chains. Box office receipts continued to decline.

MGM was still feeling the pinch. Although the year's gross of $185 million was a new record for the studio, profits had slumped to $5 million, the lowest since the Depression year of 1932/33. Nevertheless, Louis B Mayer remained the highest paid man in the United States, at a salary of $733,024. During the summer the studio's President Nicholas Schenck persuaded RKO's boss Dore Schary – a former MGM writer and producer – to return to his old company as head of production.

Schary left a studio thrown into confusion by Howard Hughes' purchase of just under a million RKO shares in a move described as 'the biggest motion picture transaction since Twentieth Century took over Fox films'. RKO suffered a blow of a different kind when rising star Robert Mitchum was arrested on a drugs charge and sentenced to 60 days in jail. Far from wrecking Mitchum's career, however, the scandal helped to cement his rebellious 'Go To Hell' image, and by the end of the decade he was the studio's biggest asset.

Warner's profits fell by $10.2 million to $11,837,253, but the studio regained some of the prestige it had lost in recent years with *Johnny Belinda* , *Key Largo* and *The Treasure of the Sierra Madre*. Jane Wyman received the Best Actress Oscar for her moving performance as a deaf-mute victim of a brutal rape in *Johnny Belinda*. Claire Trevor's portrayal of gangster Edward G Robinson's drunken moll in *Key Largo* won her the Best Supporting Actress Oscar. Walter Huston's grizzled, quirky old-timer in *The Treasure of the Sierra Madre* gained him the Best Supporting Actor Award. The Oscar for Best Actor went to Laurence Olivier for *Hamlet*, which was also voted the year's Best Film.

Among the year's outstanding films were *The Snake Pit*, *The Search*, *Easter Parade* and *The Naked City*, Jules Dassin's punchy crime thriller whose hectoring commentary and dramatic location shooting prompted a string of imitators. These strident Hollywood approximations of realism make an interesting comparison with the more low-key efforts of the Italian school of neo-realism which produced de Sica's *Bicycle Thieves*, de Santis' *Bitter Rice* and Visconti's *Terra Trema*.

On 27 July David Wark Griffith died at Hollywood's Knickerbocker Hotel. He had hardly worked in the last 20 years of his life and had become an embittered, drunken spectator of the industry which he dominated until the growth of the studio system had thrust him on to the sidelines. In the Soviet Union silent cinema's greatest propagandist, Sergei M Eisenstein, died of a heart ailment. Other deaths included Warren William – Columbia's suave Lone Wolf – Dame May Whitty, King Baggot – who had collaborated with William S Hart on the masterly *Tumbleweeds* (1925) – C Aubrey Smith and Carole Landis, who in a fit of depression took her own life. Montgomery Clift made an impressive debut in *The Search*. Marilyn Monroe's beauty and talent were less apparent way down the cast list in *Dangerous Years*.

In Britain, Olivier's triumph in *Hamlet* partially obscured the crisis facing the film industry. J Arthur Rank's expansion programme had bitten deeply into his resources – as early as 1946 his losses in film production alone were over £1.5 million. To add to Rank's problems, the American Motion Picture Association replied to the British government's imposition of the *ad valorem* tax with an embargo on the export of new films to Britain. This dealt a heavy blow to Rank's theatre empire. The government then compounded the crisis by encouraging Rank and his great rival Alexander Korda to fill the gap caused by the embargo with an expanded British film programme. This spurred Rank into raising nearly £9.5 million for a wildly optimistic investment plan of 47 films. Korda came unstuck with a truly terrible epic, *Bonnie Prince Charlie*, which was savaged by the critics and ignored by the public. More happily, Korda handled the distribution of Herbert Wilcox's *Spring in Park Lane*, whose success at the box-office confirmed its independent producer-director's belief that in the late 1940s British audiences wanted 'films about nice people'. The nice people were Michael Wilding and Anna Neagle, decorating a featherweight confection in which Wilding played a peer masquerading as a footman. Dirk Bogarde had his first starring role in *Esther Waters*, one of a large number of costume melodramas produced in Britain towards the end of the decade.

ACTION

Sealed Verdict (Paramount) d.Lewis
Allen: Florence Marly, Broderick Crawford,
Ray Milland. Army lawyer Milland is
determined to settle the doubts
surrounding a war crimes trial

Saigon (Paramount) d.Leslie Fenton: Alan
Ladd, Douglas Dick, Veronica Lake. A
routine flight to Saigon brings with it a
forced landing, police investigation, love
and violent death

The Treasure of the Sierra Madre
(Warner) d.John Huston: Tim Holt, Humphrey Bogart, Walter Huston. Bogart superb
as paranoid all-time loser Fred C Dobbs
joining Holt and Huston in quest for gold

Rogues' Regiment (Universal) d.Robert
Florey: Dick Powell, Marta Toren. Action-
packed spy thriller with US Army
Intelligence man Powell scouring Indo-
China for escaped Nazi war criminal

Fighter Squadron (Warner) d.Raoul
Walsh: Edmond O'Brien, Robert Stack.
World War II drama of fighter pilots in the
build-up to D-Day. The sky is black with
clichés rather than Stukas

The Naked City (Universal) d.Jules Dassin:
Ralph Brooks, Arthur O'Connell, Barry
Fitzgerald. Shelley Winters the blonde in
the bath, Ted de Corsia the thug on the run,
Barry Fitzgerald the cop in charge

The Street with No Name (Fox) d.William
Keighley: Richard Widmark, Mark Stevens
(r). Bureau chief Lloyd Nolan sends
undercover agent Stevens on mission to
infiltrate gang led by slick Widmark

Iron Curtain (Fox) d.William Wellman:
Dana Andrews, Frederic Tozere. Andrews is
the Russian code clerk in Ottawa who
defects and asks for asylum. Semi-
documentary account of real-life story

ADVENTURE

The Gallant Blade (Columbia) d. Henry Levin: Larry Parks, Marguerite Chapman. Swordsman Parks has his work cut out protecting his general from the machinations of scheming Victor Jory

Tarzan and the Mermaids (RKO) d. Robert Florey: Linda Christian, Johnny Weissmuller, George Zucco. A tribe of pearl divers groan under the brutal heel of a white trader

Macbeth (Republic) d. Orson Welles: Orson Welles. Astonishing, narcissistic tour de force from Welles shot in just over three weeks on a very low budget. Some of the acting more in keeping with a B Western

Siren of Atlantis (UA) d. Gregg Tallas: Maria Montez, Jean-Pierre Aumont. Dennis O'Keefe and Aumont are the two Foreign Legionnaires who find Atlantis and its ruthless ruler Montez

The Adventures of Don Juan (Warner) d. Vincent Sherman: Errol Flynn. Tongue-in-cheek swashbuckler borrowed costumes from *Private Lives of Elizabeth and Essex* (1939), but Flynn's decline shows

Prince of Thieves (Columbia) d. Howard Bretherton: Michael Duane, Patricia Morison, Jon Hall. By this stage in his career Hall was getting a little porky to be an entirely convincing Robin Hood

The Fighting O'Flynn (Universal) d. Arthur Pierson: Richard Greene, Douglas Fairbanks, Jr. Singlehanded, Irish Musketeer Fairbanks prevents Napoleon's army from coming ashore in the Emerald Isle

The Three Musketeers (MGM) d. George Sidney: Van Heflin, Gig Young, Gene Kelly, Lana Turner. Kelly provides the most acrobatic of D'Artagnans in lavish Technicolor slice of period hokum

Man-Eater of Kumaon (Universal) d. Byron Haskin: Joanne Page, Sabu. Jungle melodrama in which a hunter stirs up trouble in a remote Indian village in his obsessive hunt for a tiger

Joan of Arc (RKO) d. Victor Fleming: Ingrid Bergman. Ingrid is no match for Falconetti in plodding, overupholstered epic which was a forerunner of the glut of wide-screen spectaculars clogging '50s cinema

MELODRAMA

So Evil My Love (Paramount) d.Lewis Allen: Ann Todd, Ray Milland. Caddish artist Milland lures missionary's widow Todd into pinning a murder charge on Geraldine Fitzgerald

The Loves of Carmen (Columbia) d.Charles Vidor: Glenn Ford, Rita Hayworth. Rita's exotic costume changes are a delight but only add to the artificiality of drama based on Merimée's story

Smart Woman (Allied Artists) d.Edward Blatt: Constance Bennett, Barry Sullivan. Hot shot lawyer Bennett is forced to defend her ex-husband and father of her son – a fact she has tried to keep a secret

To the Ends of the Earth (Columbia) d.Robert Stevenson: Maylia, Dick Powell, Signe Hasso. Pacy melodrama, with narcotics agent Powell covering half the globe to smash a dope ring

Night Has a Thousand Eyes (Paramount) d.John Farrow: Edward G Robinson. Edward G has the power of prophecy, foretells a woman's death and sees his own body there too

Road House (Fox) d.Jean Negulesco: Ida Lupino, Richard Widmark, Cornel Wilde. Roadhouse owner Widmark becomes unhinged when his singer Lupino falls in love with manager Wilde

Secret Beyond the Door (Universal) d.Fritz Lang: Michael Redgrave, Joan Bennett. Bennett discovers husband Redgrave is a schizophrenic with an extremely unhealthy interest in murder

Rope (Warner) d.Alfred Hitchcock: Farley Granger, James Stewart, John Dall. Hitchcock's first film in colour and famous for its 10-minute takes. Granger and Dall are a pair of sadistic young killers

Sorry, Wrong Number (Paramount) d.Anatole Litvak: Barbara Stanwyck, Burt Lancaster. Stanwyck is the bedridden neurotic who overhears a telephone conversation about her own murder

Portrait of Jennie (Selznick) d.William Dieterle: Joseph Cotten, Jennifer Jones. Impoverished artist Cotten becomes obsessed by his encounters with an ethereal young girl, who is a ghost

Moonrise (Republic) d.Frank Borzage: Dane Clark, Harry Morgan. Clark is the son of a murderer who is himself driven to kill by the taunts of a former schoolmate. Late masterpiece from Borzage

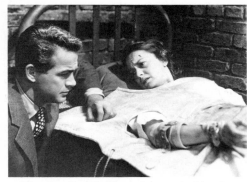

The Snake Pit (Fox) d.Anatole Litvak: Mark Stevens, Olivia de Havilland. De Havilland superb as an intelligent woman hovering on the edge of madness in an overcrowded state mental asylum

The Search (MGM) d.Fred Zinnemann: Ivan Jandl, Montgomery Clift, Aline MacMahon. Story of GI Clift rescuing World War II casualty in the US-occupied zone of Germany. Won Best Screenplay Award

Race Street (RKO) d.Edwin L Marin: William Bendix, George Raft, Marilyn Maxwell. San Francisco bookie Raft gets tough with the protection racketeers who bump off his best friend

Sleep My Love (UA) d.Douglas Sirk: Don Ameche, Claudette Colbert. Permanently, if Don has his way as he sets about using drugs and hypnosis to rid himself of bubbly wife Claudette

Hazard (Paramount) d.George Marshall: Macdonald Carey, Paulette Goddard, Fred Clark. Gambling-crazy Paulette offers herself as stakes in bet with Clark, then takes a powder pursued by gumshoe Carey

The Lady from Shanghai (Columbia) d.Orson Welles: Orson Welles, Rita Hayworth. Tangled tale of jealousy and intrigue speaks volumes for Hayworth's looks and Welles' ambivalence about her

Arch of Triumph (Enterprise) d.Lewis Milestone: Charles Boyer, Ingrid Bergman. Boyer is the refugee from Nazi brutality in pre-war Paris, Bergman the lost soul he temporarily saves

Beyond Glory (Paramount) d.John Farrow: Alan Ladd, Audie Murphy, Donna Reed. Murphy's screen debut in drama of rather elderly West Point cadet Ladd who is haunted by World War II incident

The Miracle of the Bells (RKO) d.Irving Pichel: Fred MacMurray, Frank Sinatra. A film actress's dying wish to be buried in her small mining town home is turned into a nationwide Press stunt by MacMurray

Pitfall (UA) d.Andre de Toth: Dick Powell, Lizabeth Scott. Glum tale in which Average Joe Powell's infatuation with gangster's moll Scott leads to murder. Doesn't it always?

Key Largo (Warner) d.John Huston: Lauren Bacall, Humphrey Bogart. A bunch of hoods take over a hotel during a storm and terrorize the inhabitants. Claire Trevor touching as the boss' alcoholic moll

Force of Evil (MGM) d. Abraham Polonsky: Sheldon Leonard, Roy Roberts, John Garfield. Lawyer Garfield's ambition to be a big wheel in the numbers racket leads to his brother's death

Larceny (Universal) d. George Sherman: Shelley Winters, John Payne, Joan Caulfield. Con-man Payne tries to cheat war hero's widow Caulfield out of money with phoney memorial scheme

Fighting Father Dunne (RKO) d. Ted Tetzlaff: Pat O'Brien, Darryl Hickman. O'Brien as priest struggling to find home for underprivileged newsboys. Hickman the rotten apple in the barrel

The Undercover Man (Columbia) d. Joseph H Lewis: Nina Foch, Glenn Ford. Efficient crime melo showing the work of US Treasury agents nailing a big-time racketeer for tax evasion

Hills of Home (MGM) d. Fred Wilcox: Edmund Gwenn. Kindly doctor Gwenn adopts failed sheepdog Lassie, who repays him by overcoming her fear of water to save his life

The Velvet Touch (RKO) d. John Gage: Rosalind Russell, Leon Ames. Temperamental actress Russell kills producer Ames in a tiff over casting. Then Claire Trevor is accused of the crime

Johnny Belinda (Warner) d. Jean Negulesco: Jane Wyman. Outstanding performances from Wyman and Lew Ayres as deaf mute victim of a brutal rape and the young doctor who becomes her protector

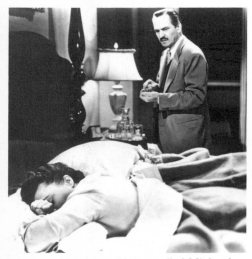

An Act of Murder (Universal) d. Michael Gordon: Florence Eldridge, Fredric March. 'Mercy killing' is the theme of drama in which judge March discovers his wife is suffering from an incurable disease

The Woman in White (Warner) d. Peter Godfrey: Sydney Greenstreet, Eleanor Parker. Feeble adaptation of Wilkie Collins' Gothic thriller but Greenstreet in commanding form as Count Fosco

The Walls of Jericho (Fox) d. John M Stahl: Ann Dvorak, Marjorie Rambeau, Linda Darnell, Cornel Wilde. Steamy goings-on in a small Kansas town in 1908 with Dvorak plugging husband Wilde

Cry of the City (Fox) d.Robert Siodmak: Victor Mature, Richard Conte. Vigorous direction and fluid camerawork underpin cop Mature's hunt for boyhood pal turned murderer Conte

Call Northside 777 (Fox) d.Henry Hathaway: Richard Conte, James Stewart. Chicago-set drama of crusading journalist Stewart's battle to clear falsely convicted Conte

Act of Violence (MGM) d.Fred Zinnemann: Van Heflin, Robert Ryan. Ryan erupts into Heflin's quiet life to settle an old prison camp score. Sizzling thriller with a marvellous performance from Mary Astor

Another Part of the Forest (Universal) d.Michael Gordon: Edmond O'Brien, Ann Blyth, Fredric March. Lillian Hellman's prequel to *The Little Foxes*, with an odious Southern family picking its collective scabs

All My Sons (Universal) d.Irving Reis: Louisa Horton, Edward G Robinson, Mady Christians, Burt Lancaster. Effective adaptation of Arthur Miller play. Robinson the war profiteer with terrible secret

The Decision of Christopher Blake (Warner) d.Peter Godfrey: Alexis Smith, Ted Donaldson, Robert Douglas. Poor little Ted is driven frantic by the constant bickering of parents Smith and Douglas

Big City (MGM) d.Norman Taurog: Lotte Lehmann, Danny Thomas, Margaret O'Brien. Maudlin musical melodrama. Orphan O'Brien acquires a clutch of ethnic guardians; Lehmann sings 'God Bless America'

The Big Clock (Paramount) d.John Farrow: Ray Milland, Charles Laughton. Publishing magnate Laughton murders his mistress, then tries to pin the blame on Milland, editor of 'Crimeways' Magazine

Berlin Express (RKO) d.Jacques Tourneur: Merle Oberon, Paul Lukas. Lukas is visionary German statesman whose life is threatened by a group of diehard Nazis. Effective location shooting in Germany

Deep Waters (Fox) d.Henry King: Dana Andrews, Jean Peters. Welfare worker Peters' concern for troubled orphan Dean Stockwell leads to an affair with lobster fisherman Dana Andrews

Command Decision (MGM) d.Sam Wood: Clark Gable. Drama set on an American airfield during the bombing of Germany. Should Gable do what is right or what looks best for public consumption ?

Caught (MGM) d.Max Ophuls: Barbara Bel Geddes, James Mason. Nasty Robert Ryan drives wife Bel Geddes into the arms of doctor Mason but it takes a death and a miscarriage to seal their relationship

Alias Nick Beal (Paramount) d.John Farrow: Audrey Totter, Thomas Mitchell, Ray Milland, Fred Clark. Milland in splendidly sinister form as Lucifer enlisting Totter's aid to corrupt Mitchell

The Fountainhead (Warner) d.King Vidor: Gary Cooper. Phallic imagery abounds in rip-roaring melodrama of rebellious architect Cooper, whose character was loosely based on Frank Lloyd Wright

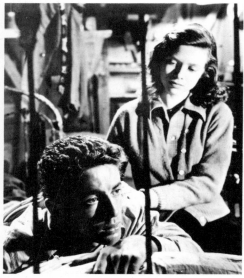

They Live by Night (RKO) d.Nicholas Ray: Farley Granger, Cathy O'Donnell. As a young couple flee from their past they build their own fantasy world. Brilliant debut by Ray. Remade as *Thieves Like Us* (1974)

Edward My Son (MGM) d.George Cukor: Deborah Kerr, Spencer Tracy. Tracy is the ruthless self-made tycoon and Kerr his neglected alcoholic wife, in adaptation of Robert Morley-Noel Langley play

The Boy with Green Hair (RKO) d.Joseph Losey: Dean Stockwell, Pat O'Brien. A war orphan's hair miraculously turns green in heavyhanded metaphor for the cruelty of warfare. Losey's first Hollywood film

Casbah (Universal) d.John Berry: Tony Martin, Yvonne De Carlo. Musical version of *Algiers* (1938) reveals Martin's limitations as an actor, but Yvonne is as bewitchingly camp as ever. Marta Toren's screen debut

Criss Cross (Universal) d.Robert Siodmak: Yvonne De Carlo, Burt Lancaster, Dan Duryea. Gangster Duryea finds armoured-truck guard with wife De Carlo and blackmails him into pulling a heist

Embraceable You (Warner) d.Felix Jacoves: Geraldine Brooks, Dane Clark. Clark fatally injures Brooks driving a getaway car after a murder. To pay for her treatment he resorts to blackmailing the murderer

COMEDY

The Bishop's Wife (RKO) d.Henry Koster: Cary Grant, David Niven, Loretta Young. Engaging Christmas fantasy in which infuriatingly suave angel Grant arrives on Earth to help Bishop Niven

I Remember Mama (RKO) d.George Stevens: Barbara O'Neill, Oscar Homolka. Indomitable Norwegian housewife Irene Dunne brings up her family in turn-of-the-century San Francisco

No Minor Vices (MGM) d.Lewis Milestone: Dana Andrews, Lilli Palmer. Doctor Dana Andrews brings home eccentric artist Louis Jourdan, who promptly falls in love with Palmer

My Girl Tisa (Warner) d.Elliott Nugent: Sam Wanamaker, Lilli Palmer. Overly sentimental tale of immigrant girl Palmer struggling to bring her elderly father to a new life in America the Beautiful

The Sainted Sisters (Paramount) d.William Russell: Joan Caulfield, Veronica Lake. Caulfield and Lake are two pretty confidence tricksters who are themselves conned into becoming public benefactors

A Letter to Three Wives (Fox) d.Joseph L Mankiewicz: Kirk Douglas, Ann Sothern, Jeanne Crain. Three wives each receive a letter from a flirt telling them that one of their husbands will run away with her

You Gotta Stay Happy (Universal) d.H C Potter: Joan Fontaine, Eddie Albert, James Stewart. Fontaine deserts dull husband on wedding day, persuades amiable pilot Stewart to fly her to California

The Noose Hangs High (Eagle) d.Charles Barton: Lou Costello, Bud Abbott. A & C are cack-handed delivery men who get mixed up with the Mob. Droll slapstick support from Leon Errol

A Southern Yankee (MGM) d.Edward Sedgwick: Red Skelton. Passable Skelton outing as hamfisted Yankee spy nosing around down South in Civil War is enlivened by Buster Keaton sight gags

Sitting Pretty (Fox) d.Walter Lang: Clifton Webb, Maureen O'Hara. Webb superb as the caustic, self-declared genius Lynn Belvedere who adds babysitting to his list of accomplishments

Romance on the High Seas (Warner) d.Michael Curtiz: Jack Carson, Doris Day. Breezy Caribbean-set musical comedy introduced Doris Day to the screen sweetly singing 'It's Magic'

Two Guys from Texas (Warner) d.David Butler: Dennis Morgan, Jack Carson. M & C play a couple of vaudevillians tangling with broads and crooks in easy-paced musical comedy

The Paleface (Paramount) d.Norman Z McLeod: Bob Hope. Bob is Painless Potter, timid dentist out West encountering Calamity Jane Russell's big guns. Oscar-winning song 'Buttons and Bows'

Mr Blandings Builds His Dream House (Selznick) d.H C Potter: Myrna Loy, Cary Grant, Melvyn Douglas. Faultless performances and direction as Grant and Loy set about building a house in the country

The Saxon Charm (Universal) d.Claude Binyon: Audrey Totter, Susan Hayward, John Payne, Robert Montgomery. Sophisticated comedy-drama dominated by Montgomery as heartless producer

State of the Union (MGM) d.Frank Capra: Katharine Hepburn, Spencer Tracy, Adolphe Menjou. Hepburn and Tracy patch up their differences when he is persuaded to run for President by fixer Menjou

Sorrowful Jones (Paramount) d.Sidney Lanfield: Mary Jane Saunders, Bob Hope. Hope is Damon Runyon's skinflint bookie forced to adopt a little girl whose father has been murdered by a race track combine

Good Sam (RKO) d.Leo McCarey: Gary Cooper, Ann Sheridan. Cooper is a saintly boob whose guileless attempts at charity inevitably lead to catastrophe. Sheridan excellent as harassed wife

Mr Peabody and the Mermaid (Universal) d.Irving Pichel: Ann Blyth, William Powell. Flimsy fantasy about a fisherman's encounter with a mermaid is sustained by Powell's quizzical charm

Let's Live a Little (Eagle Lion) d.Richard Wallace: Robert Cummings, Anna Sten. Mixed-up advertising executive Cummings consults psychiatrist (sic) Hedy Lamarr, then drives her nuts

The Girl from Manhattan (UA) d.Alfred E Green: Ernest Truex, Dorothy Lamour. Lamour returns to home town to find her uncle's boarding house is about to be pulled down to make way for a church

Dream Girl (Paramount) d.Mitchell Leisen: Betty Hutton. Betty is a fantasizing female version of Walter Mitty until brought down to earth by newspaperman boyfriend Macdonald Carey

June Bride (Warner) d.Bretaigne Windust: Bette Davis, Mary Wickes. Hot shot magazine editor Davis fences with former lover Robert Montgomery while attempting to set up a wedding as publicity stunt

On Our Merry Way (UA) d.King Vidor, Leslie Fenton: Henry Fonda, Burgess Meredith, James Stewart. Roving reporter Meredith pops the question, 'What influence has a little child had on your life?'

A Foreign Affair (Paramount) d.Billy Wilder: Jean Arthur, Marlene Dietrich. Arthur is starchy Congresswoman Phoebe Frost tangling with chanteuse Marlene over John Lund in postwar Berlin

Feudin', Fussin' and A-Fightin' (Universal) d.George Sherman: Percy Kilbride, Donald O'Connor, Marjorie Main. Uninhibited backwoods musical comedy with O'Connor as a hoofing salesman

For the Love of Mary (Universal) d.Frederick de Cordova: Deanna Durbin, Edmond O'Brien. The (unseen) US President helps White House telephonist Durbin untangle her love life

Mexican Hayride (Universal) d.Charles Barton: Susanna Ridgeway, Lou Costello. Dismal South of the Border romp very loosely based on Cole Porter's hit, but without any of his music. A pity

Miss Tatlock's Millions (Paramount) d.Richard Haydn: Wanda Hendrix, John Lund, Barry Fitzgerald. Stuntman Lund impersonates a family idiot and finds he has inherited a fortune

Family Honeymoon (Universal) d.Claude Binyon: Fred MacMurray, Claudette Colbert, Gigi Perreau. Fred finds new bride Claudette insists on bringing children of previous marriage on honeymoon

If You Knew Susie (RKO) d.Gordon Douglas: Eddie Cantor, Joan Davis. Cantor and Davis are vaudevillians whose discovery of an ancient document turns them into national celebrities

Julia Misbehaves (MGM) d.Jack Conway: Peter Lawford, Walter Pidgeon, Greer Garson, Elizabeth Taylor. Garson successfully tries slapstick in carefree romantic comedy

Unfaithfully Yours (Fox) d.Preston Sturges: Kurt Kreuger, Linda Darnell, Rex Harrison. Temperamental conductor Harrison imagines various lurid ways of dealing with Darnell's suspected infidelity

Wallflower (Warner) d.Frederick de Cordova: Janis Paige, Edward Arnold, Joyce Reynolds. Paige and Reynolds are both out to lassoo heart-throb Robert Hutton in frisky adaptation of stage hit

Abbott and Costello Meet Frankenstein (Universal) d.Charles Barton: Glenn Strange, Lou Costello, Bud Abbott, Lon Chaney, Jr. Bela Lugosi is after Costello's brain. Cruelty to monsters

A Date with Judy (MGM) d.Richard Thorpe: Elizabeth Taylor, Jane Powell. Taylor and Powell compete for Robert Stack in diverting musical comedy stolen (as ever) by Carmen Miranda

The Bride Goes Wild (MGM) d.Norman Taurog: Jackie 'Butch' Jenkins, Van Johnson. Drunken, kid-hating children's writer Johnson 'adopts' a son to retain services of prim illustrator June Allyson

Every Girl Should be Married (RKO) d.Don Hartman: Cary Grant, Betsy Drake, Franchot Tone. Salesgirl Drake mounts an elaborate campaign to win her predatory way into bemused baby doctor Grant's heart

Apartment for Peggy (Fox) d.George Seaton: Edmund Gwenn, Jeanne Crain, Griff Barnett. Gwenn walks away with film as kindly college professor taking in newlyweds Crain and William Holden

My Dear Secretary (UA) d.Charles Martin: Keenan Wynn, Helen Walker, Kirk Douglas. Laraine Day goes to work for dashing disorganised writer Kirk, but she's the one who writes the best-seller

The Beautiful Blonde from Bashful Bend (Fox) d.Preston Sturges: Rudy Vallee, Betty Grable. Strident Western farce with Grable in good form as a pistol-packin' schoolmarm, Vallee a fumbling suitor

Isn't it Romantic (Paramount) d.Norman Z McLeod: Veronica Lake, Billy de Wolfe. Unfortunately, no, but this turn-of-the-century comedy-drama has one charming sequence when Lake visits a nickelodeon

The Luck of the Irish (Fox) d.Henry Koster: Cecil Kellaway, Tyrone Power. American newspaperman Power goes to Ireland on holiday and is promptly adopted by leprechaun Cecil Kellaway

WESTERNS

Whispering Smith (Paramount) d.Leslie Fenton: Alan Ladd, Brenda Marshall, Robert Preston. Solid actioner with Ladd as railway detective pursuing Preston – a role first played by W S Hart

The Strawberry Roan (Columbia) d.John English: Gene Autry, Dick Jones. Autry's first film in colour and a big hit despite plot's close resemblance to Roy Rogers' *My Pal Trigger* (1946)

The Plunderers (Republic) d.Joseph Kane: Rod Cameron, Adrian Booth. Cameron infiltrates an outlaw gang but after its leader lets him escape he is reluctant to hand him over to the law

Panhandle (Allied Artists) d.Lesley Selander: Charles Judels, Rod Cameron. Rod buckles on his guns to avenge killing of his brother. Produced by Blake Edwards, who also plays a heavy

Belle Starr's Daughter (Fox) d.Lesley Selander: Rod Cameron, Ruth Roman. Roman in title role joins Cameron's outlaw gang before Marshal George Montgomery makes her see the error of her ways

Red River (Monterey) d.Howard Hawks: John Wayne, Montgomery Clift. Relaxed, epic storytelling, glorious set pieces, as Wayne and adopted son Clift tangle on a huge trail drive to Abilene. Masterpiece

Four Faces West (UA) d.Alfred E Green: Joel McCrea, Charles Bickford, Frances Dee. McCrea co-stars with wife Dee as easygoing outlaw who turns to banditry to save his father's ranch

Three Godfathers (MGM) d.John Ford: Harry Carey, Jr, Pedro Armendariz, John Wayne. Three outlaws (Wise Men) find baby (Christ child) abandoned in desert. Film was dedicated to Harry Carey

Return of the Badmen (RKO) d.Ray Enright: Randolph Scott. Oklahoma lawman Scott takes on the Youngers, Daltons, Billy the Kid and Wild Bill Doolin' in well-paced Western outing

Streets of Laredo (Paramount) d.Leslie Fenton: William Holden. Two former outlaws join the Texas Rangers and pursue a former partner. Remake of *Texas Rangers* (1936)

Thunderhoof (Columbia) d. Phil Karlson: William Bishop, Preston Foster, Mary Stuart. Classic 'psychological' B Western with trio in search of fabulous stallion, a kind of sagebrush Moby Dick

Station West (RKO) d. Sidney Lanfield: Dick Powell. Tongue-in-cheek 'tough guy' script enlivens tale of Powell investigating suspicious deaths and prowling around villainess Jane Greer

Coroner Creek (Producers-Actors) d. Ray Enright: George Macready, Marguerite Chapman. Interesting 'revenge' Western and an early collaboration between Randolph Scott and Harry Joe Brown

Yellow Sky (Fox) d. William Wellman: Robert Arthur, Gregory Peck. A gang of bank robbers led by Peck and Richard Widmark stumble on a desert ghost town in Western version of *The Tempest*

The Untamed Breed (Columbia) d. Charles Lamont: Barbara Britton, Brahma bull, Sonny Tufts. Sonny is the rancher determined to improve Texas cattle with his big-eared Brahma Bull. A load of...

Fury at Furnace Creek (Fox) d. H Bruce Humberstone: Glenn Langan, Victor Mature. Superior second feature with Mature and Langan as brothers determined to clear disgraced father's name

The Man from Colorado (Columbia) d. Henry Levin: William Holden, Glenn Ford. Ford is an army officer turned psychopath by Civil War experiences who is appointed Federal Judge

Black Bart (Universal) d. George Sherman: Dan Duryea, Yvonne De Carlo. The heroes are affably unrepentant villains Jeffrey Lynn and Duryea in engaging Western. De Carlo is Lola Montes

Fort Apache (RKO) d. John Ford: John Wayne, Henry Fonda. A remote outpost provides an idealized microcosm of America in masterly first film in Ford's great cavalry trilogy

Red Canyon (Universal) d. George Sherman: Jane Darwell, Ann Blyth. Rancher's daughter Blyth falls for horsethief's son Howard Duff in brisk Zane Grey adaptation

Blood on the Moon (RKO) d.Robert Wise: Robert Mitchum, Barbara Bel Geddes. Shadow-drenched noirish Western with gunman Mitchum switching sides to defend Bel Geddes against one-time friend

I Shot Jesse James (Lippert) d.Samuel Fuller: Barbara Britton, John Ireland. Frenzied close-ups characterize Fuller's directorial debut as he gleefully hacks away at the James legend

The Younger Brothers (Warner) d.Edwin L Marin: Wayne Morris, James Brown. Bruce Bennett and Robert Hutton complete the bad quartet trying to stay out of trouble and keep their freedom

ROMANCE

That Wonderful Urge (Fox) d.Robert Sinclair: Tyrone Power, Gene Tierney. Remake of *Love is News* (1937) with Power repeating role of busybody journalist. Tierney succeeds Loretta Young

B.F.'s Daughter (MGM) d.Robert Z Leonard: Van Heflin, Barbara Stanwyck, Margaret Lindsay. Strong-willed tycoon's daughter Stanwyck tries to mould husband Heflin in her own image

The Voice of the Turtle (Warner) d.Irving Rapper: Ronald Reagan, Eleanor Parker. Lonely soldier Reagan woos brokenhearted actress Parker in slick adaptation of John Van Druten romantic comedy

On an Island with You (MGM) d.Richard Thorpe: Cyd Charisse, Ricardo Montalban. Dripdry Esther Williams vehicle, with swimming star romancing pilot Peter Lawford against Honolulu backdrop

One Touch of Venus (Universal) d.William Seiter: Robert Walker, Ava Gardner. Ava is the department store statue of Venus which springs to life when kissed by window dresser Walker

Winter Meeting (Warner) d.Bretaigne Windust: James Davis, Bette Davis. Poet Bette Davis has tentative romance with war hero who wants to become a priest. Works on principle of jaw, jaw, not war, war

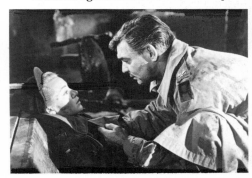

Homecoming (MGM) d.Mervyn Le Roy: Lana Turner, Clark Gable. Army surgeon Gable falls for nurse Lana during war service. Trouble is, there's wife Anne Baxter at home

Letter from an Unknown Woman (Universal) d.Max Ophuls: Joan Fontaine, Louis Jourdan. Sensitively handled tale of Fontaine's unrequited love for concert pianist Jourdan. Prepare to shed tears

Enchantment (RKO) d.Irving Reis: Teresa Wright, David Niven. Flashback story of thwarted love affair between Niven and Wright mingles with romance between Evelyn Keyes, Farley Granger

Britannia Mews (Fox) d.Jean Negulesco: Maureen O'Hara, Sybil Thorndike. Maureen is terrorized by old hag Thorndike and contrives to marry Dana Andrews twice. No wonder she looks worried

MUSICALS

A Song is Born (RKO) d.Howard Hawks: Danny Kaye, Virginia Mayo. Misfiring remake of *Ball of Fire* (also directed by Hawks) with Kaye/Mayo in the Cooper/ Stanwyck roles

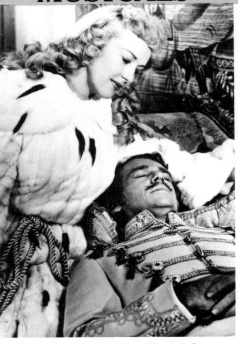

That Lady in Ermine (Fox) d.Otto Preminger: Betty Grable, Douglas Fairbanks, Jr. Ruritanian romance is remake of *Bride of the Regiment* (1930). Begun by Lubitsch, finished by Otto

The Pirate (MGM) d.Vincente Minnelli: Judy Garland, Gene Kelly. Highly stylized, frenetic vehicle for Kelly's braggadoccio as the strolling player pretending to be a Caribbean buccaneer

Luxury Liner (MGM) d.Richard Whorf: George Brent, Jane Powell. Interfering Little Jane is determined to marry off widower Brent in tuneful romantic Technicolor cruise

Three Daring Daughters (MGM) d.Fred Wilcox: Jane Powell, Ann Todd, Mary Eleanor Donahue, Jeanette MacDonald. Jeanette's three daughters object to new husband Jose Iturbi

The Kissing Bandit (MGM) d.Laszlo Benedek: Frank Sinatra, J Carrol Naish. Scrawny Frank has to step into father's role as womanizing desperado. Grayson, Miller, Charisse on hand

Melody Time (RKO) d.Clyde Geronimi, Wilfred Jackson, Hamilton Luske, Jack Kinney. String of animated musical numbers, this one 'Little Toot' with soundtrack from The Andrews Sisters

Lulu Belle (Columbia) d.Leslie Fenton: Dorothy Lamour. Mixture of music and melodrama as ruthless singer Lamour tramples on a succession of men on her way to the top

When My Baby Smiles at Me (Fox) d.Walter Lang: Betty Grable, Dan Dailey. Dailey steals the show as comic whose career hits the skids. Remake of *The Dance of Life* (1929), *Swing High Swing Low* (1937)

Words and Music (MGM) d.Norman Taurog: Vera-Ellen, Gene Kelly. Vera-Ellen and Kelly's 'Slaughter on Tenth Avenue' is best thing in biopic of Rodgers (Tom Drake, dreadful) and Hart (Mickey Rooney)

Up in Central Park (Universal) d.William Seiter: Deanna Durbin, Vincent Price. Not many songs as Deanna and reporter Dick Haymes uncover the crooked ways of Boss Tweed (Price) and his organization

April Showers (Warner) d.James Kern: Ann Sothern, Jack Carson, Bobby Ellis. Big Jack's drinking breaks up the family vaudeville act until a Broadway booking brings them together again

Easter Parade (MGM) d.Charles Walters: Fred Astaire, Judy Garland. Smash-hit backstage musical crammed with Irving Berlin evergreens including 'A Couple of Swells' (illustrated here)

The Emperor Waltz (Paramount) d.Billy Wilder: Bing Crosby, Joan Fontaine. Bing is the phonograph salesman wooing the Emperor Franz Joseph's niece (Fontaine) in smooth Tyrolean fantasy

Countess of Monte Cristo (Universal) d.Frederick de Cordova: Hugh French, Sonja Henie, Michael Kirby. Sonja and Olga San Juan land job in film studio and masquerade as countess and maid

Are You With It? (Universal) d.Jack Hively: Olga San Juan, Donald O'Connor. O'Connor is the maths genius who joins a carnival where he falls for pert little Olga Embarrassing ballet finale

Take Me Out to the Ball Game (MGM) d. Busby Berkeley: Frank Sinatra, Gene Kelly. Esther Williams is manager of the baseball team of which hoofing athletes Sinatra and Kelly are members

A Connecticut Yankee in King Arthur's Court (Paramount) d. Tay Garnett: Bing Crosby, Cedric Hardwicke. Sumptuous third screen version of Twain classic. Highlight is 'Busy Doing Nothing'

Variety Time (RKO) d. Hal Yates. Ultra-cheap compilation of skits, dance routines and other acts culled from a host of RKO features with Jack Paar acting as master of ceremonies

AMERICANA

The Time of Your Life (UA) d. H C Potter: Jeanne Cagney, William Bendix, James Cagney. A group of eccentric regulars fantasize and chew the fat in a waterfront bar, in adaptation of Saroyan play

The Tender Years (Fox) d. Harold Schuster: Joe E Brown, Richard Lyon. Kindly small-town minister Brown risks a charge of theft in a bid to put a stop to the sport of dog fighting

Tap Roots (Universal) d. George Marshall: Susan Hayward, Van Heflin, Ruby Dandridge. Torrid saga of the Dabney family's attempt to stay neutral in the Civil War. *Gone With the Wind* in diminuendo

One Sunday Afternoon (Warner) d. Raoul Walsh: Janis Paige, Dorothy Malone. Dennis Morgan, Paige and Malone step into the Cagney/Hayworth/de Havilland roles in remake of *The Strawberry Blonde* (1941)

So Dear to My Heart (RKO) d. Harold Schuster: Bobby Driscoll, Burl Ives. Country boy Driscoll's devotion to a black lamb leads to friction with crusty grandma Beulah Bondi in sentimental Disney tale

Scudda-Hoo! Scudda-Hay! (Fox) d. F Hugh Herbert: Lon McCallister, Walter Brennan. Boy-meets-mule tale in cheerful slice of rural Americana. Bit part by Marilyn Monroe ended on cutting room floor

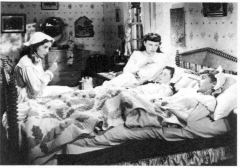

Little Women (MGM) d.Mervyn Le Roy:
Janet Leigh, June Allyson, Margaret O'Brien,
Elizabeth Taylor. Saccharine-soaked
adaptation of Louisa M Alcott story. C
Aubrey Smith's last film

Louisiana Story (Robert Flaherty)
d.Robert Flaherty: Joseph Boudreaux. Oil
men arrive to disturb the peace of the
Bayou Marshlands; seen through the eyes
of a 12-year-old boy

Blondie's Secret (Columbia) d.Edward
Bernds: Arthur Lake, Penny Singleton,
Jerome Cowan. Daisy the dog disturbs an
unusual burglar in series now looking very
rough around the edges

The Quiet One (Film Documents)
d.Sidney Meyers. Moving documentary of a
neglected black child with a commentary
by James Agee

B MOVIES

The Shanghai Chest (Mon) d.William
Beaudine: Victor Sen Yung, Mantan
Moreland, Roland Winters. Charlie Chan
investigates murders committed by a
criminal executed six months previously

I Love Trouble (Columbia) d. S Sylvan
Simon: Janet Blair, Franchot Tone. It
seemed like another routine assignment for
gumshoe Tone, but intrigue and murder lie
just around the corner

Raw Deal (Eagle Lion) d.Anthony Mann:
Claire Trevor, Marsha Hunt, Dennis
O'Keefe. O'Keefe breaks out of jail and flees
across country with girlfriend Trevor and
hostage Hunt. It all ends in tears

He Walked by Night (Eagle Lion) d.Alfred
Werker: Richard Basehart. Riveting
performance from Basehart as glacial
psychopath tracked down in the sewers of
Los Angeles

G-Men Never Forget (Republic) d.Yakima
Canutt, Fred C Brannon: David Sharpe (r). Jut-
jawed serial hero Clayton Moore joins forces
with Ramsay Ames in one of famous stuntman
Canutt's infrequent directing outings

Trapped by Boston Blackie (Columbia)
d.Seymour Friedman: Patricia White,
George E Stone, Chester Morris, June
Vincent. When a priceless pearl necklace is
lifted Blackie cracks the riddle

Appointment with Murder (Film Craft)
d.Jack Bernhard: John Calvert (r). Frozen-
faced Calvert as the Falcon investigating
stolen paintings and murder in Hollywood
and Italy.

Thirteen Lead Soldiers (Fox) d.Frank
McDonald: Tom Conway, Maria Palmer.
Conway as Bulldog Drummond tracking
Saxon toy soldiers which provide the key
to an ancient treasure trove

Night Wind (Fox) d.James Tinling: James
Burke, Charles Russell, Gary Gray, Flame.
Former army dog Flame can spot a
Commie atom spy at a hundred paces, so
we can sleep easy nights

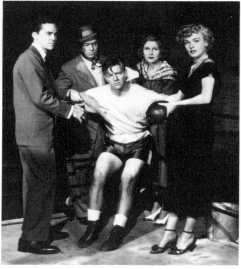

Trouble Preferred (Fox) d.James Tinling:
Peggy Knudsen, Charles Russell, Lynne
Roberts. A pair of female cops bend the
rules to obtain more exciting assignments

Mystery in Mexico (RKO) d.Robert Wise:
Jacqueline White (c). White co-stars with
William Lundigan in hunt for missing
insurance agent. Former silent star
Ricardo Cortez is also featured

Smuggler's Cove (Mon) d.William
Beaudine: Jacqueline Dalya, Martin Kosleck
(c). The Bowery Boys foil a plot to use a
Long Island mansion as a base for a
smuggling racket

The Creeper (Fox) d.Jean Yarbrough:
Onslow Stevens, Janis Wilson. Scientists
Stevens and Ralph Morgan discover serum
that changes humans into cats. Pity it can't
do something for Stevens' taste in ties

Ruthless (Eagle Lion) d.Edgar Ulmer:
Sydney Greenstreet, Lucille Bremer. Lizard-
like Zachary Scott is poor man's Citizen
Kane in gripping melodrama, Greenstreet
his nemesis

Congo Bill (Columbia) d.Spencer Bennet,
Thomas Carr: Don McGuire. Congo Bill
McGuire penetrates the backlot jungle
searching for missing circus heiress in
witless serial

Boston Blackie's Chinese Venture
(Columbia) d.Seymour Friedman: Maylia,
Richard Lane, Chester Morris (c). Boston
Blackie under suspicion for the last time,
this time for the murder of Chinaman

Whiplash (Warner) d.Lewis Seiler: Dane Clark, Douglas Kennedy. Artist Clark turns boxer for love of Alexis Smith. Zachary Scott his usually unpleasant self as crippled ex-champ

Bungalow 13 (Fox) d.Edward L Cahn: Tom Conway. Detective Conway's hunt for a valuable piece of jade leads to a string of murders. Conway imperturbable as ever in confusing mystery

Half-Past Midnight (Fox) d.William Claxton: Peggy Knudsen, Kent Taylor. Man about town Taylor clears Knudsen of the murder of a blackmailer. Comic relief from Joe Sawyer as boneheaded cop

The Counterfeiters (Fox) d.Peter Stewart: Pierre Watkin, Lon Chaney, Jr. Much doublecrossing afoot as Scotland Yard man (John Sutton) joins forces with US Secret Service to bust counterfeiting gang

Batman and Robin (Columbia) d.Spencer Bennet: John Duncan, Robert Lowery. Sagging tights and subliminal production values undermine Caped Crusaders' adventures in rock bottom serial

Superman (Columbia) d.Spencer Bennet, Thomas Carr: Tommy Bond, Kirk Alyn. Clark Kent alias Superperson tangles with the 'reducing ray' wielded by beautiful but deadly Spider Lady (Carol Forman)

BRITISH & FOREIGN

Hamlet (Two Cities) d.Laurence Olivier: Laurence Olivier. Bravura but rather hollow technical display. Jean Simmons is touching Ophelia, Stanley Holloway wry gravedigger

Anna Karenina (London) d.Julien Duvivier: Vivien Leigh, Kieron Moore. Leigh no match for Garbo. Ralph Richardson miscast as Karenin, Moore simply out of his depth

Quartet (Gainsborough) d.Ken Annakin, Arthur Crabtree, Harold French, Ralph Smart: Dirk Bogarde, Honor Blackman. Based on Somerset Maugham stories. Illustrated, 'The Alien Corn'

Oliver Twist (Cineguild) d.David Lean: Robert Newton, Alec Guinness. Guinness' portrayal of Fagin so upset Jewish groups in the US that the film was not shown there until 1951

Vice Versa (Two Cities) d.Peter Ustinov: Roger Livesey. Livesey is the pompous Victorian stockbroker who changes places with his son in lively adaptation of F Anstey's novel

The Winslow Boy (London) d.Anthony Asquith: Neil North, Robert Donat. Solidly built courtroom drama with an Edwardian setting and screenplay by Terence Rattigan

Saraband for Dead Lovers (Ealing) d.Basil Dearden: Flora Robson, Stewart Granger. The studio's first colour film and a handsome looking but laboured historical melodrama set in 18th-century Germany

Bonnie Prince Charlie (London) d.Anthony Kimmins: David Niven. Catastrophic attempt at an Errol Flynn-style swashbuckler with David Niven looking extremely ill at ease in the title role

The First Gentleman (Columbia) d.Alberto Cavalcanti: Joan Hopkins, Jean-Pierre Aumont, Cecil Parker. Parker plays the princely buffoon George IV to the hilt in mild drama over royal matchmaking

Esther Waters (Wessex) d.Ian Dalrymple, Peter Proud: Kathleen Ryan, Dirk Bogarde. Bogarde's first starring role as William Latch, the ne'er do well footman of George Moore's 19th-century novel

The History of Mr Polly (Two Cities) d.Anthony Pélissier: John Mills. Meandering version of the Wells novel with Mills excellent as the daydreaming draper and Megs Jenkins as the Plump Woman

Meet Me at Dawn (Fox) d.Thornton Freeland: William Eythe, Stanley Holloway. Mildly diverting turn-of-the-century comedy adventure in which Eythe plays a professional duellist

The Queen of Spades (World Screen Plays) d.Thorold Dickinson: Edith Evans. A young officer (Anton Walbrook) becomes obsessed with prising the secret of winning at cards from an aged countess (Evans)

Trottie True (Two Cities) d.Brian Desmond Hurst: Hattie Jacques, Jean Kent, Bill Owen. Cheerful tale of showgirl Kent who marries into the aristocracy and becomes a celebrity

Cardboard Cavalier (Two Cities) d. Walter Forde: Sid Field, Margaret Lockwood. Rumbustious historical farce finds barrow boy Field clowning around on a secret mission for the exiled Charles II

Portrait from Life (Gainsborough) d. Terence Fisher: Patrick Holt, Mai Zetterling, Guy Rolfe, Sybilla Binder. Zetterling is an amnesiac found by Rolfe in postwar refugee camp

Against the Wind (Ealing) d. Charles Crichton: Simone Signoret, Jack Warner. Warner is effectively cast against type as a treacherous member of an SOE group sent to help the Resistance in occupied Europe

The Small Back Room (London) d. Michael Powell: David Farrar. Gripping wartime *film noir* in which a crippled, alcoholic scientist (Farrar) must dismantle a German booby-trap bomb

London Belongs to Me (Individual) d. Sidney Gilliat: Richard Attenborough (r). Attenborough is the young tearaway on a murder charge in sprawling comedy-drama based on London boarding house

Escape (Fox) d. Joseph L Mankiewicz: Peggy Cummins, Rex Harrison. Former air ace Harrison escapes from prison after being found guilty of a murder he did not commit, falls in love with Cummins

The Guinea Pig (Pilgrim) d. Roy Boulting: Cecil Trouncer, Richard Attenborough. Dicky sheds a dozen years to play a working-class scholarship boy finding the going tough at a public school

Mine Own Executioner (London) d. Anthony Kimmins: Kieron Moore, Burgess Meredith. Mixed-up alienist Meredith treats violent schizophrenic Moore, with discouraging results

Snowbound (Gainsborough) d. David Macdonald: Dennis Price, Mila Parely, Robert Newton, Marcel Dalio. A none too lovely bunch find themselves cut off in a mountain chalet in search of Nazi gold

House of Darkness (International) d. Oswald Mitchell: Laurence Harvey, Leslie Osmond, John Teal. Weird haunted house fantasy introduced by George Melachrino and punctuated by 'The First Rhapsody'

Night Beat (British Lion) d. Harold Huth: Maxwell Reed, Christine Norden. Former commandos Ronald Howard, Hector Ross fall foul of Reed's black market gang

Dick Barton, Special Agent (Hammer-Marylebone) d.Alfred Goulding: Don Stannard, Geoffrey Wincott. 'You filthy swine – you won't get away with this!' Radio 'tec Barton foils evil spies

No Orchids for Miss Blandish (Renown) d.St. John L Clowes: Jack LaRue, Linden Travers. Hilarious attempt to film James Hadley Chase's risqué thriller. LaRue is mixed-up mobster Slim Grissom

End of the River (Archers) d.Derek Twist: Bibi Ferreira, James Hayter, Sabu. Sabu is the South American Indian boy exiled from his village and becoming a 'twig on the river of life'

Calling Paul Temple (Nettlefold) d.Maclean Rogers: Dinah Sheridan, John Bentley. Smooth sleuth Bentley and wife Steve (Sheridan) escape death by drowning and time bomb in murder chase

My Brother's Keeper (Renown) d.Alfred Roome: Jack Warner, George Cole, Jane Hylton. Old lag Warner and callow youth Cole make a jailbreak inconveniently handcuffed together

Miranda (Gainsborough) d.Ken Annakin: Griffith Jones, Glynis Johns. Jones meets a Cornish mermaid and takes her back to London – suitably draped in a wheelchair – to see the sights

The Blue Lagoon (Individual) d.Frank Launder: Jean Simmons, Donald Houston. Simmons achieves perfectly immaculate conception in discreet version of H de Vere Stacpoole's desert island tale

The Passionate Friends (Cineguild) d.David Lean: Ann Todd, Claude Rains. Upper-class version of *Brief Encounter*, updated by Eric Ambler from an H G Wells novel, given the customary Lean gloss

The Red Shoes (Archers) d.Michael Powell: Moira Shearer, Robert Helpmann. A young ballerina is torn between love and career. Remarkable fantasy, throbbing with colour and Powell's assault on 'total cinema'

My Brother Jonathan (ABPC) d.Harold French: Michael Denison, Dulcie Gray. Well-paced drama of self-sacrificing young doctor Denison's growing disillusionment with the pre-war medical system

Just William's Luck (Alliance) d. Val Guest: William Graham, Garry Marsh. The pint-sized suburban anarchist of Richmal Crompton's humorous novels succeeds in creating chaos for his long-suffering family

The Fallen Idol (London) d. Carol Reed: Bobby Henrey, Ralph Richardson, Michele Morgan. A young boy's attempt to help his hero after his wife's death succeeds in implicating him in murder

Easy Money (Gainsborough) d. Bernard Knowles: Dennis Price, Greta Gynt. Portmanteau film following the fortunes of football pools winners. Sultry Gynt seduces pools worker Price into fraud

Bond Street (World Screenplay) d. Gordon Parry: Jean Kent, Derek Farr. A Mayfair bride prepares for her wedding, and on each item in her outfit there hangs a tale in well-crafted portmanteau film

Vote for Huggett (Gainsborough) d. Ken Annakin: Petula Clark, Jack Warner, Susan Shaw. Local elections form background to Huggett family saga spun off from *Holiday Camp* (1947)

Another Shore (Ealing) d. Charles Crichton: Moira Lister, Robert Beatty, Michael Medwin. Dublin-set comedy with Beatty as a feckless fantasist dreaming of escape to the South Seas

Daughter of Darkness (Alliance) d. Lance Comfort: Siobhan McKenna. Overwrought melodrama in which Irish servant girl McKenna has somewhat violent way of showing affection to opposite sex

The Corridor of Mirrors (Apollo) d. Terence Young: Eric Portman, Edana Romney. Portman believes Romney is reincarnation of girl in 400-year-old painting, with gloomy and confusing results

Mr Perrin and Mr Traill (Two Cities) d. Lawrence Huntington: Marius Goring, David Farrar. A young public school master (Farrar) discovers that an older colleague (Goring) is his rival in love

Les Parents Terribles (France) d. Jean Cocteau: Jean Marais, Gabrielle Dorziat. Tragi-comedy of tangled family relationships including incest and suicide. Adapted from a stage work

Monsieur Vincent (France) d.Maurice
Cloche: The life and works of St Vincent de
Paul (Pierre Fresnay) and his struggle to
alleviate the suffering of the poor

Sotto il Sole di Roma (Italy) d.Renato
Castellani. Slightly phoney exercise in
neo-realism depicting a day in the life of
a Roman street gang towards the end of
the war

Jour de Fête (France) d.Jacques Tati:
Jacques Tati (c). A village postman decides
to adopt American methods to speed up
delivery. Captivating comedy by a master
of the genre

Hans Le Marin (France) d.Francois
Villiers: Jean-Pierre Aumont, Lilli Palmer.
Sailor Aumont has a lively time ashore in
Marseilles and ends up committing a
couple of murders.

Bicycle Thieves (Italy) d.Vittorio de Sica:
Enzo Staiola, Lamberto Maggiorani. A
municipal bill poster's bicycle is stolen and
he spends the day searching for it with his
son. Small masterpiece

L'Amore (Italy) d.Roberto Rossellini: Anna
Magnani. Two-part film starring
Magnani, the first part (illustrated)
adapted from the Cocteau monologue
La Voix Humaine

Bitter Rice (Italy) d.Giuseppe de Santis:
Silvana Mangano. Saga of exploited rice
workers introduced Mangano erupting
from the earth like a sexy proletarian
counterpart of Rita Hayworth

La Terra Trema (Italy) d.Luchino Visconti.
The harsh life of a family of poor fishermen
adapted from a novel by Giovanni Verga.
Superb photography by
G R Aldo

Berliner Ballade (Germany) d.R H
Stemmle: Gert Fröbe (r). The troubles
which beset an average law-abiding citizen
in postwar Berlin are laid out in an
engaging satire

The Pearl (Mexico) d.Emilio Fernandez:
Maria Elena Marques, Pedro Armendariz.
The story of a fisherman who finds
a huge pearl, and the misery it brings
in its wake

Drunken Angel (Japan) d.Akira Kurosawa:
Toshiro Mifune. Melodrama of an alcoholic
doctor trying to cure gangster Mifune
of tuberculosis. Mifune's first
starring role

1949

MGM celebrated its silver jubilee with a massive luncheon at which serried ranks of stars toyed with their chicken amid the popping of flash bulbs. The studio's profits crept back to $6.75 million, but overall the outlook remained unsettled.

During the course of the year the Hollywood majors – MGM, Paramount, Warner, Fox and RKO – agreed with the US government to split their theatre organizations from the production-distribution business. Although it did not come into immediate effect, the 'consent decree' spelt the end of the vertically integrated Hollywood empires, and within a few years led to the collapse of the studio system.

Having tackled anti-Semitism in 1948, Hollywood now turned its attention to the colour question in films like *Pinky*, *Home of the Brave* and *Intruder in the Dust*. A small clutch of classic *noir* B thrillers – *D.O.A.*, *Gun Crazy* and *C-Man* – provided an epitaph for the second feature, which was soon to be rendered redundant by television's sitcoms, cop shows and Western series.

The Academy voted Robert Rossen's *All the King's Men* the year's Best Film, as did the New York Critics. Broderick Crawford won the Best Actor Oscar for his blistering performance in the film as Willy Stark, a thinly disguised portrait of the charismatic, corrupt Louisiana 'Kingfisher' Huey Long. It was a part so perfectly suited to Crawford's belligerent, loudmouth style that it provided one of those infrequent examples of character and actor becoming completely one. The film also won Mercedes McCambridge the Best Supporting Actress Award and provided John Ireland with probably his best role as the jaundiced newspaperman who narrates the story. Olivia de Havilland won the Best Actress Award for *The Heiress*, as the gauche spinster who finally turns the tables on her calculating suitor Montgomery Clift. The Best Supporting Actor Award went to Dean Jagger for *Twelve O'Clock High*. Special Awards were also made to Fred Astaire, Cecil B DeMille and child star Bobby Driscoll.

A new comic team, Dean Martin and Jerry Lewis, made their debut in *My Friend Irma*. A longer-established team, Fred Astaire and Ginger Rogers, were reunited in *The Barkleys of Broadway*. Judy Garland had been slated to partner Astaire, but she simply failed to turn up and Ginger stepped into the breach. At the end of the film she danced with Fred to the strains of 'They Can't Take that Away from Me', reprised from RKO's *Shall We Dance* (1937).

Light years away from Astaire's thirties mannequin elegance was newcomer Tony Curtis' performance as a young hoodlum in *City Across the River*, the story of a street gang, The Amboy Dukes. Johnny Weissmuller hung up his loincloth and was replaced as Tarzan by Lex Barker. The new jungle hero told the press, 'If my muscles hold up and my waistline keeps down, I can play Tarzan till I'm 50.' Weissmuller's waistline had long been a problem, and it was with some relief that he turned to play the white hunter Jungle Jim in an ultra-low-budget adventure series produced by Sam Katzman – 'Tarzan with clothes on,' as one wag remarked.

Four significant Hollywood figures passed away: Richard Dix, the durable, stern-jawed hero who had bowed out with the 'Whistler' series at Columbia; Wallace Beery, typecast in later years as a purveyor of loveable roguery, but a far better actor than he was often given credit for; Sam Wood, director of *Goodbye Mr Chips* (1939), *Kitty Foyle* (1940), *The Pride of the Yankees* (1942) and *For Whom the Bell Tolls* (1943); and director Victor Fleming, whose flair for masculine adventure pictures overshadowed a sure touch with leading actresses, seen at its best in his handling of Harlow in *Red Dust* (1932) and *Bombshell* (1933).

Once again the British film industry had a prestige success to celebrate. The New York Critics chose Carol Reed as Best Director for *The Fallen Idol* (1948), a subtle tale of innocence and inexperience adapted by Graham Greene from one of his short stories. The collaboration between Reed and Greene reached a peak in *The Third Man*, a romantic thriller set in postwar Vienna and dominated by Orson Welles' Harry Lime, the Citizen Kane of the occupied city's black market. But these successes could not disguise the fact that the crisis in the industry had come to a head. Rank's debts were approaching £16 million and an accountant, John Davis, was called in to institute a policy of retrenchment. An edict went out that no film was to cost more than £150,000.

Ironically it was at this point that Ealing Studios produced the three classic comedies with which its name is always associated: Henry Cornelius' *Passport to Pimlico*, Alexander Mackendrick's *Whisky Galore* and Robert Hamer's *Kind Hearts and Coronets*. For Ealing, and its presiding genius Michael Balcon, 1949 was an *annus mirabilis*, a year in which three outstanding films bore witness to the studio's unique and peculiarly British structure and working methods. Nevertheless, in common with the film industry on both sides of the Atlantic, Ealing was to lose its way in the decade that was to follow.

ACTION

Sands of Iwo Jima (Republic) d.Allan Dwan: John Wayne (r). Wayne is pitiless Sergeant John M Stryker in flag-waving actioner anticipating jingoistic mood of the 1950s

Twelve O'Clock High (Fox) d.Henry King: Gregory Peck, Millard Mitchell. Peck is the hard-driving CO of US bomber group who restores morale to battle-fatigued unit at cost of a nervous breakdown

Battleground (MGM) d.William Wellman: John Hodiak, Van Johnson. Johnson is continually frustrated in attempts to scramble eggs in his helmet in gritty account of Battle of the Bulge

Malaya (MGM) d.Richard Thorpe: James Stewart, Spencer Tracy, Valentina Cortese, Sydney Greenstreet. Fine cast wasted in stilted wartime tale of adventurers stealing rubber from the Japanese

Sword in the Desert (Universal) d.George Sherman: Philip Friend, Hugh French, Dana Andrews. Cynical sea captain Andrews agrees to smuggle Jewish refugees into Palestine, then conscience strikes

White Heat (Warner) d.Raoul Walsh: James Cagney, Edmond O'Brien, Wally Cassell. Pinnacle of Cagney's career as the mother-fixated psychopathic gangster Cody Jarrett. Frenetic performance

Task Force (Warner) d.Delmer Daves: Gary Cooper. The story of naval commander Cooper's fight to establish the importance of aircraft carriers climaxes with the battles off Okinawa

Rope of Sand (Paramount) d.William Dieterle: Claude Rains, Burt Lancaster. Brutal, heavy-handed melodrama in which Lancaster goes through hell to retrieve a cache of diamonds in South Africa

Border Incident (MGM) d.Anthony Mann: Arnold Moss, Ricardo Montalban. Howard da Silva is brains behind smuggling of Mexican workers into US. Documentary gloss but basically 'cops and robbers' stuff

Down to the Sea in Ships (Fox) d.Henry Hathaway: Richard Widmark, Lionel Barrymore. Grizzled whaling captain Barrymore and first mate Widmark instil the manly virtues in young Dean Stockwell

Sand (Fox) d.Louis King: Mark Stevens, Colleen Gray. A prize stallion runs free after a railroad accident and threatens to become a killer. Based on a Will James novel

Chicago Deadline (Paramount) d.Lewis Allen: Alan Ladd, Arthur Kennedy. In a faint echo of *Laura*, reporter Ladd obsessively pieces together the story of a dead woman's life from list of phone numbers

Take One False Step (Universal) d.Chester Erskine: Marsha Hunt, William Powell, Shelley Winters. Staid professor Powell's ill-advised visit to predatory old flame Winters leads to a murder hunt

Roseanna McCoy (Goldwyn) d.Irving Reis: Farley Granger, Peter Miles, Joan Evans. Granger and Evans are the young lovers caught in the middle of the ferocious hillbilly blood feud

Champion (UA) d.Mark Robson: John Day, Kirk Douglas, Arthur Kennedy. Ferocious fight scenes belie soft-centred adaptation of Ring Lardner's bleak account of a boxer's rise and fall

Slattery's Hurricane (Fox) d.Andre de Toth: John Russell, Richard Widmark, Linda Darnell. Widmark in usual heel-hero role as a Navy pilot turned smuggler saving everyone's bacon in a Florida hurricane

The Black Hand (MGM) d.Richard Thorpe: Gene Kelly, J Carrol Naish. Kelly returns from Italy to avenge the killing of his father by the Mafia. Set in turn-of-the-century New York

ADVENTURE

Bagdad (Universal) d.Charles Lamont: Maureen O'Hara, Vincent Price. Sheik's daughter Maureen O'Hara returns from London to a threatened inheritance in parody of studio's 'tits and sand' cycle

Bride of Vengeance (Paramount) d.Mitchell Leisen: John Lund, Paulette Goddard. Paulette and Macdonald Carey have a stab at the roles of Lucretia and Cesare Borgia. Inane historical drama

Prince of Foxes (Fox) d.Henry King: Orson Welles, Tyrone Power. Welles enjoys himself hugely as scheming Cesare Borgia, Power the confederate who turns against him. Visually stunning although b/w

Christopher Columbus (Gainsborough)
d.David Macdonald: Fredric March, Derek
Bond. Dull British biopic gets bogged down
in court intrigue long before the great
navigator (March) sets sail

Mighty Joe Young (RKO) d.Ernest B
Schoedsack: Robert Armstrong (l). Crass
entrepreneur Armstrong turns Terry
Moore's monster pet ape into a nightclub
attraction. Then someone gives it a drink

Wake of the Red Witch (Republic)
d.Edward Ludwig: Gail Russell, John
Wayne. Full-blooded seafaring yarn with
deadly enemies Wayne and Luther Adler
after gold from a scuttled schooner

Samson and Delilah (Paramount) d.Cecil
B DeMille: Victor Mature, Hedy Lamarr.
Vic's glistening, be-thonged musculature
provides camp centrepiece to DeMille's
tuppence-coloured epic

Bomba The Jungle Boy (Mon) d.Ford
Beebe: Peggy Ann Garner, Johnny Sheffield.
Beefy Sheffield stars in own cut-rate jungle
series eked out with stock footage from
Africa Speaks (1930)

MELODRAMA

Under Capricorn (Transatlantic) d.Alfred
Hitchcock: Michael Wilding, Ingrid
Bergman, Joseph Cotten. Leaden triangle
love story set in an Australian penal
settlement. Everyone loses his way

Madame Bovary (MGM) d.Vincente
Minnelli: Louis Jourdan, Jennifer Jones.
Loose adaptation of Flaubert classic has
odd framing device in which the author is
tried for corrupting public morals

The Set-Up (RKO) d.Robert Wise: Robert
Ryan, Audrey Totter. Third-rate boxer Ryan
refuses to take a dive and must pay the
price. Gripping evocation of dingy lower
depths of the fight world

The Forsyte Saga (MGM) d.Compton Bennett: Greer Garson, Robert Young, Errol Flynn. Flynn may not be everybody's idea of Soames Forsyte but he is surprisingly good in handsome version of Galsworthy novel

The Great Sinner (MGM) d.Robert Siodmak: Gregory Peck, Walter Huston, Ava Gardner. Gambling mania unconvincingly overwhelms Peck in lumbering adaptation of Dostoievsky story

Knock on Any Door (Columbia) d.Nicholas Ray: John Derek, Humphrey Bogart: Derek's screen debut as the young punk who never had a chance, defended on a murder charge by lawyer Bogart

Undertow (Universal) d.William Castle: Scott Brady, Peggy Dow, John Russell. Brady's two-timing fiancée Dorothy Hart and former buddy Russell frame him on a murder rap

East Side, West Side (MGM) d.Mervyn Le'Roy: Barbara Stanwyck, James Mason. Stanwyck in her element as the wife Mason neglects while chasing after Ava Gardner. Excellent support from Gale Sondergaard

Beyond the Forest (Warner) d.King Vidor: Bette Davis, Joseph Cotten. Bette is the '12 o'clock girl in a 9 o'clock town' making life hell for Cotten. Absurd film marked end of Davis' stormy career at Warner

A Dangerous Profession (RKO) d.Ted Tetzlaff: Don Dillaway, Betty Underwood, George Raft. Paunchy rather than punchy melodrama with Raft and Pat O'Brien running a dodgy bail bond firm

Bad Boy (Allied Artists) d.Kurt Neumann: Audie Murphy. Mixed-up Audie causes a lot of trouble at reformatory ranch until it is discovered he did *not* poison his mother

Any Number Can Play (MGM) d.Mervyn Le Roy: Lewis Stone (c), Clark Gable. An evening of high emotion at Gable's gambling den including heart attacks, hold-ups and a run on the bank

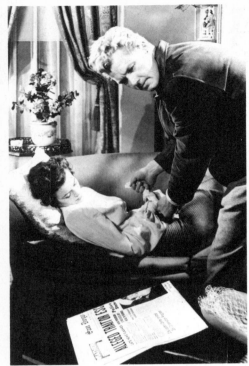

Clay Pigeon (RKO) d.Richard Fleischer: Barbara Hale, Bill Williams. Seaman Williams awakes from a coma in a Navy hospital to find that he is to stand trial for treason

The File on Thelma Jordan (Paramount) d.Robert Siodmak: Barbara Stanwyck, Wendell Corey. Stop-at-nothing Stanwyck lures naive DA Corey into a web of murder and deceit. Much underrated *film noir*

Flamingo Road (Warner) d.Michael Curtiz: Sydney Greenstreet, Joan Crawford. Carnival dancer Joan crosses the tracks and claws her way to the top in steamy tale of Southern chicanery

Conspirator (MGM) d.Victor Saville: Elizabeth Taylor, Robert Taylor. Warmed-over *Undercurrent* performance from Robert as Elizabeth's charming husband revealed as Communist spy

City Across the River (Universal) d.Maxwell Shane: Tony Curtis, Joshua Shelly, Al Ramsen. The Dead End Kids reincarnated as the Amboy Dukes in heart-on-its-sleeve tale of Brooklyn street gang

Johnny Stool Pigeon (Universal) d.William Castle: Shelley Winters, Howard Duff, Dan Duryea. Fearless Fed Duff strikes deal with Alcatraz inmate Duryea to bust open narcotics ring

Scene of the Crime (MGM) d.Roy Rowland: Leon Ames, Van Johnson. Hard, fast thriller in which Johnson finds himself temporarily handcuffed to a corpse before tracking down a robbery gang

Flaxy Martin (Warner) d.Richard Bare: Virginia Mayo, Zachary Scott. Zachary is the honest attorney trapped by the Mob and pleading guilty to a murder he didn't commit to protect predatory Mayo

Side Street (MGM) d.Anthony Mann: James Craig, Farley Granger. Part-time letter-carrier Granger stumbles on a suitcase with proceeds of blackmail gang. Brilliantly edited car chase climax

Tokyo Joe (Columbia) d.Stuart Heisler:
Humphrey Bogart. Bogie returns to postwar
Japan only to fall foul of black market
baron Sessue Hayakawa, who turned in one
of the best performances of his career

Shadow on the Wall (MGM) d.Pat
Jackson: Kristine Miller, Zachary Scott. A
child accidentally witnesses death of nasty
stepmother. Undergoes analysis to reveal
identity of killer

The Accused (Paramount) d.William
Dieterle: Sam Jaffe, Robert Cummings,
Loretta Young. Loretta plays Dr Wilma
Tuttle, a psychology professor who kills
one of her students when he gets fresh

Thieves' Highway (Fox) d.Jules Dassin:
Valentina Cortese, Richard Conte.
Picaresque tale of fruit market racketeers is
charged with sizzling sexual chemistry
between Cortese and Conte

The Story of Molly X (Universal) d.Crane
Wilbur: June Havoc, Cathy Lewis.
Gangster's moll Havoc is reformed by a
spell in prison, even confessing to a murder
she didn't commit

The Bribe (MGM) d.Robert Z Leonard:
Charles Laughton, Robert Taylor, Ava
Gardner. Government agent Taylor breaks
up Central American war-surplus racket.
Terrific fight with Vincent Price

Lost Boundaries (Film Classics) d.Alfred
Werker: Mel Ferrer, Beatrice Pearson. Study
of racial intolerance. Doctor Ferrer and wife
Pearson 'pass for white' in a small New
Hampshire town

A Woman's Secret (RKO) d.Nicholas Ray:
Maureen O'Hara, Gloria Grahame. Gloria
outstanding as the little slut groomed
obsessively for stardom by O'Hara. With
unfortunate results, as you can see

House of Strangers (Fox) d.Joseph L
Mankiewicz: Edward G Robinson, Richard
Conte. Appalling paterfamilias Robinson
presides over a disintegrating family who
eventually round on the old tyrant

Intruder in the Dust (MGM) d.Clarence
Brown: Juano Hernandez, David Brian.
Faulkner's novel brought vividly to life as a
small group of whites prevent the lynching
of an elderly black in a Southern town

The Lady Gambles (Universal) d.Michael Gordon: Barbara Stanwyck, Stephen McNally. Gambling frenzy seizes bored housewife Barbara, and leads to a beating-up and a suicide attempt

Home of the Brave (UA) d.Mark Robson: James Edwards, Lloyd Bridges, Frank Lovejoy. Edwards superb as the black soldier, beset with bigotry and his own hypersensitivity

Pinky (Fox) d.Elia Kazan: Ethel Waters, Jeanne Crain. Northern-trained nurse Crain 'passes for white', agonizes over marrying white doctor William Lundigan, while suffering the barbs of racialists

The Sun Comes Up (MGM) d.Richard Thorpe: Claude Jarman, Jr, Lassie, Jeanette MacDonald. Singing widow Jeanette retreats to the mountains where her life is brightened by an orphan and his dog

Easy Living (RKO) d.Jacques Tourneur: Victor Mature, Sonny Tufts, Lucille Ball. Grid-iron star Mature has a hard time coming to terms with a retirement forced by a heart condition

COMEDY

Miss Grant Takes Richmond (Columbia) d.Lloyd Bacon: Lucille Ball (c), William Holden (r). Crooked bookie Holden hires dumb broad Ball to front a phoney real estate business

Ma and Pa Kettle (Universal) d.Charles Lamont: Percy Kilbride, Marjorie Main. Two of the supporting characters from *The Egg and I* (1947) branch out into their own popular bucolic series

Free For All (Universal) d.Charles Barton: Ann Blyth, Robert Cummings, Percy Kilbride. Bright young inventor Bob finds a way of turning water into petrol but not the script into laughs

Francis (Universal) d.Arthur Lubin: Donald O'Connor, Francis. First in a moneyspinning series has loquacious quadruped coming to O'Connor's aid in a World War II spy romp

The Lady Takes a Sailor (Warner)
d.Michael Curtiz: Jane Wyman, Robert
Douglas, Eve Arden. Wyman's reputation
for honesty is put to the test when no-one
believes her strange story

Ma and Pa Kettle Go to Town (Universal)
d.Charles Lamont: Majorie Main, Percy
Kilbride. The Kettles visit the Big Apple and
wind up acting as bagmen for the Mob. OK
if you like this kind of thing

Holiday Affair (RKO) d.Don Hartman:
Robert Mitchum, Janet Leigh, Frank Mills.
Charming offbeat romantic comedy in
which happy-go-lucky engineer Mitchum
woos and wins young widow Leigh

Bride for Sale (RKO) d.William D Russell:
Claudette Colbert. Claudette is a tax expert
seeking a wealthy husband. George Brent
and Robert Young fight spiritedly for the
spoils

Africa Screams (UA) d.Charles Barton:
Bud Abbott, Lou Costello. A & C consigned
to darkest backlot Africa with chubby Lou
terrified of all the animals lurking therein.
Pretty dire

The Fan (Fox) d.Otto Preminger: Martita
Hunt, Richard Greene, Madeleine Carroll.
Much of Oscar Wilde's wit is junked for
amorous intrigue, but George Sanders
shimmers through as lecherous aristocrat

**Abbott and Costello Meet the Killer –
Boris Karloff** (Universal) d.Charles
Barton. Boris stalks warily around as
phoney swami trying to hypnotise Lou into
suicide. Alas, he fails

Champagne for Caesar (UA) d.Richard
Whorf: Ronald Colman. Colman is self-
assured know-all Beauregard Bottomley
bankrupting a soap company in their radio
quiz programme

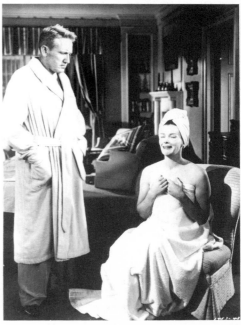

Adam's Rib (MGM) d.George Cukor:
Spencer Tracy, Katharine Hepburn. T & H
are the married lawyers at professional
loggerheads during Judy Holliday's trial for
husband-shooting. Holliday's debut

Everybody Does It (Fox) d.Edmund Goulding: Paul Douglas, Jane Hamilton, Linda Darnell. Celeste Holm wants to be an opera star but philistine husband Douglas is the one with the magnificent voice

Always Leave Them Laughing (Warner) d.Roy Del Ruth: Milton Berle. Comedy showcase for America's top funny man Milton Berle includes the sketch about fountain pens which write underwater

Father was a Fullback (Fox) d.John M Stahl: Maureen O'Hara, Natalie Wood, Fred MacMurray. Fred is the fumbling football coach whose disasters on the grid-iron are matched by chaotic family life

Once More My Darling (Universal) d.Robert Montgomery: Robert Montgomery, Ann Blyth. Ex-movie star Montgomery woos Blyth to acquire jewellery stolen by Nazis; then they elope to Las Vegas

The Yellow Cab Man (MGM) d.Jack Donohue: Red Skelton (r). Accident-prone inventor Skelton takes a job as a cabbie to secure demonstration of flexible windscreen glass. Some crooks want the formula

My Friend Irma (Paramount) d.George Marshall: Diana Lynn, Marie Wilson. Wilson is the ultimate dumb blonde, almost wrecking Lynn's chances of marriage in knockabout comedy outing

The Life of Riley (Universal) d.Irving Brecher: Lanny Rees, William Bendix, Meg Randall, Rosemary de Camp. Bendix's promotion at work gets mixed up with his daughter's love life

It Happens Every Spring (Fox) d.Lloyd Bacon: Paul Douglas, Ray Milland. Impecunious professor Milland makes a baseball wood-repellent, becomes the greatest pitcher of all time

It's a Great Feeling (Warner) d.David Butler: Dennis Morgan, Doris Day, Jack Carson. Nobody wants to direct a film with Jack Carson in it so he tries to direct it himself. Lots of star cameos

Mr Belvedere Goes to College (Fox)
d.Elliott Nugent: Shirley Temple, Clifton
Webb. Infallible, impeturbable Webb sails
through college to qualify for an award
given only to those with degrees

The Judge Steps Out (RKO) d.Boris
Ingster: Ian Wolfe, Alexander Knox. Jurist
Knox leaves his harassed life to become a
short-order cook at Ann Sothern's roadside
cafe

I was a Male War Bride (Fox) d.Howard
Hawks: Cary Grant, Ann Sheridan. Classic
comedy of humiliation as French officer
Grant takes roundabout route to marrying
spunky Sheridan

WESTERNS

Calamity Jane and Sam Bass (Universal)
d.George Sherman: Yvonne De Carlo.
Howard Duff is Sam Bass and De Carlo the
calamitous one. Willard Parker the lawman
on their trail

Trail's End (Mon) d.Lambert Hillyer:
Johnny Mack Brown (cr), Kay Morley.
Outlaws are after gold deposits on Morley's
ranch. Comic relief from Max Terhune as
'Alibi'

The Fighting Kentuckian (Republic)
d.George Waggner: Oliver Hardy, John
Wayne. Rare solo appearance by Hardy, as
trapper Wayne reluctantly romances Vera
Ralston. Photography by Lee Garmes

Ghost of Zorro (Republic) d.Fred C
Brannon: Pamela Blake, Clayton Moore.
Moore is the masked avenger in routine
serial marking the end of Republic's
association with Zorro

The Gal Who Took the West (Universal)
d.Frederick de Cordova: John Russell,
Yvonne De Carlo. Russell and Scott Brady
feud away over songbird De Carlo in
would-be satire on Westerns

Colorado Territory (Warner) d.Raoul
Walsh: Virginia Mayo, Joel McCrea.
Substitute McCrea for Bogart in visually
stunning reworking of *High Sierra* (1941).
Final shot a knockout

Down Dakota Way (Republic) d.William
Witney: Roy Rogers. Witney's arrival gave
the Rogers series a tougher edge. In this
one he avenges the killing of a friend

Riders in the Sky (Columbia) d.John English: Gene Autry, Gloria Henry. Autry takes on ex-Mesquiteer Robert Livingston who's trying to frame a friend for murder

The Golden Stallion (Republic) d.William Witney: Dale Evans, Roy Rogers. Trigger, Jr gallops to Roy's rescue in offbeat tale of diamond smuggling across the Mexican border

Loaded Pistols (Columbia) d.John English: Gene Autry, Barbara Britton. Action-packed outing with Gene investigating a case of murder while he's hiding the youngster accused

South of St Louis (Warner) d.Ray Enright: Joel McCrea, Zachary Scott, Bob Steele. Scott, McCrea and Douglas Kennedy are out to revenge the burning of their ranches by Victor Jory's Union guerrillas

Canadian Pacific (Fox) d.Edwin L Marin: Victor Jory, Randolph Scott. Highly fictitious account of railway pioneers. Jory the trapper determined to thwart line surveyor Scott's plans

Fighting Man of the Plains (Fox) d.Edwin L Marin: Randolph Scott. Gunfighter turned lawman Scott cleans up the town of Lanyard, with the help of Dale Robertson's Jesse James

She Wore a Yellow Ribbon (RKO) d.John Ford: Ben Johnson, Cliff Lyons, John Wayne. Ford's woozy romanticism almost undercuts Wayne's moving, melancholy performance as veteran cavalry officer

ROMANCE

Mother is a Freshman (Fox) d.Lloyd Bacon: Van Johnson, Loretta Young, Rudy Vallee. Widowed mother (Young) and daughter (Betty Lynn) attend the same college and fall for Johnson

The Doctor and the Girl (MGM) d.Curtis Bernhardt: Glenn Ford, Janet Leigh. Romantic medical melodrama with doctor Ford renouncing brilliant career to marry working girl and practise in a poor district

John Loves Mary (Warner) d.David Butler: Patricia Neal, Ronald Reagan. Soldier Reagan's marriage of convenience to British girl Virginia Field causes complications, not least with fiancée Neal

The Girl from Jones Beach (Warner)
d.Peter Godfrey: Ronald Reagan, Virginia
Mayo. Ronnie is commercial artist in
search of the perfect woman, who turns out
to be history teacher Mayo

Adventure in Baltimore (RKO) d.Richard
Wallace: Albert Sharpe, Shirley Temple.
Baltimore 1905, and the whole town's
talking about minister's daughter Temple
and her mildly daring antics

My Own True Love (Paramount)
d.Compton Bennett: Melvyn Douglas,
Phyllis Calvert. Widower Douglas,
struggling to readjust after the war, falls for
a woman twenty years his junior

The Heiress (Paramount) d.William
Wyler: Montgomery Clift, Olivia de
Havilland. Wyler manipulates Henry James
adaptation with great skill but de
Havilland's beauty defeats dowdy make-up

My Foolish Heart (RKO) d.Mark Robson:
Susan Hayward, Dana Andrews. Hayward
gets pregnant by playboy Andrews, then
marries a man she doesn't love when he's
killed in a wartime training accident

Come to the Stable (Fox) d.Henry Koster:
Celeste Holm, Loretta Young, Elsa
Lanchester. Charming tale of two nuns
employing a variety of unconventional
methods to raise money for a hospital

Key to the City (MGM) d.George Sidney:
Clark Gable, Loretta Young. Two-fisted
longshoreman Gable and prim lawyer
Young meet at San Francisco convention,
plunge into whirlwind romance

MUSICALS

Nancy Goes to Rio (MGM) d.Robert Z
Leonard: Carmen Miranda. 1940 Deanna
Durbin vehicle *It's a Date* dusted off for
Jane Powell, Ann Sothern. Carmen sings
'Cha Bomm Pa Pa'

Give My Regards to Broadway (Fox)
d.Lloyd Bacon: Charles Winninger, Barbara
Lawrence, Dan Dailey. Vaudevillian
Winninger nurses dreams of a comeback
and showbusiness careers for his children

Jolson Sings Again (Columbia) d.Henry
Levin: Larry Parks. An example of
Hollywood picking over its own entrails as
much of the film is devoted to the filming of
The Jolson Story (1946). Another big hit

Look for the Silver Lining (Warner) d.David Butler: The Wilde Twins. Clichéd biopic of Marilyn Miller features stand-out performance by Ray Bolger tap dancing to Jerome Kern's 'Who'

Oh You Beautiful Doll (Fox) d.John M Stahl: Mark Stevens, June Haver. Lively biopic of composer Fred Fisher (S Z 'Cuddles' Sakall). Stevens' voice dubbed by Bill Shirley

The Inspector General (Warner) d.Henry Koster: Walter Slezak, Danny Kaye. Musical farce owes more to the spirit of burlesque than to Gogol's black comedy of mistaken identity. A one-man show, really

That Midnight Kiss (MGM) d.Norman Taurog: Mario Lanza, Kathryn Grayson. Singing truck driver Lanza sweeps operatic heiress Grayson off her feet in schmaltzy, successful screen debut

Dancing in the Dark (Fox) d.Irving Reis: William Powell, Betsy Drake. Hollywood in-joke has studio head Adolphe Menjou despatching has-been ham Powell to find a leading lady for Broadway hit *Bandwagon*

Slightly French (Columbia) d.Douglas Sirk: Dorothy Lamour. Don Ameche transforms Irish colleen Lamour into a French actress in remake of *Let's Fall in Love* (1934), which starred Ann Sothern

Red Hot and Blue (Paramount) d.John Farrow: Betty Hutton. Musical comedy-thriller in which would-be actress Hutton discovers a murdered gangster. Cameo from Frank Loesser

On the Town (MGM) d.Gene Kelly, Stanley Donen: Frank Sinatra, Jules Munshin, Gene Kelly. *The* musical of the decade, combining location shooting and balletic inspiration. Flags towards the end

Neptune's Daughter (MGM) d.Edward Buzzell: Red Skelton. Swimwear tycoon Esther Williams is romanced by polo star Ricardo Montalban, joins Skelton, Betty Garrett to sing 'Baby It's Cold Outside'

The Barkleys of Broadway (MGM)
d.Charles Walters: Ginger Rogers, Fred
Astaire. Ginger and Fred reunited after a 10
year gap as husband-and-wife-dance team
who split up when Ginger tries to go legit

My Dream is Yours (Warner) d.Michael
Curtiz: Eve Arden, Doris Day, Jack Carson.
Girl-next-door Day is discovered by radio
talent scout Jack Carson. Includes a Bugs
Bunny sequence

Top O' The Morning (Paramount)
d.David Miller: Bing Crosby, Ann Blyth.
Insurance investigator Bing arrives in
Ireland to investigate disappearance of the
Blarney Stone. Barry Fitzgerald in there

Make Believe Ballroom (Columbia)
d.Joseph Santley: Nat King Cole. A string of
top singing stars are squeezed into slim
story of collegiate carhops entering a
musical quiz show

You're My Everything (Fox) d.Walter
Lang: Anne Baxter. Baxter is silent star –
'The Hotcha Girl' – who makes the
transition to sound in pleasantly paced
backstage/backlot outing

Cinderella (RKO) d.Wilfred Jackson,
Hamilton Luske, Clyde Geronimi. Most
memorable characters in Disney version of
Perrault fairy tale are the two mice Jacques
and Gus-Gus

In the Good Old Summertime (MGM)
d.Robert Z Leonard: Judy Garland.
Charming romance between Judy and Van
Johnson who are pen pals unaware that
they both work in the same music shop

Yes Sir, That's My Baby (Universal)
d.George Sherman: Donald O'Connor.
Donald is war veteran working his way
through college, Gloria de Haven the wife
objecting to his joining the football team

**The Adventures of Ichabod and Mr.
Toad** (RKO) d.Jack Kinney, Clyde
Geronimi, James Algar. Two-part Disney
feature, based on *Wind in the Willows* and
The Legend of Sleepy Hollow

AMERICANA

The Red Pony (Republic) d.Lewis Milestone: Peter Miles, Robert Mitchum. Unsentimental Steinbeck boy-and-horse tale with excellent performances from Mitchum and Myrna Loy

Chicken Every Sunday (Fox) d.George Seaton: Dan Dailey, Celeste Holm. Wistful tale of the tribulations of married life in turn-of-the century Tucson. Dailey good as a shiftless charmer

The Story of Seabiscuit (Warner) d.David Butler: Rosemary de Camp (l), Barry Fitzgerald (c). Story of legendary racehorse bolstered with romance between Shirley Temple and Lon McCallister

Big Jack (MGM) d.Richard Thorpe: Richard Conte, Wallace Beery. Outlaw Beery saves outspoken doctor Conte from lynching twice in his last film. He died shortly after its completion

Blondie Hits the Jackpot (Columbia) d.Edward Bernds: Arthur Lake, Penny Singleton, Jerome Cowan, Larry Sims. Dagwood gets promoted and Blondie enters and wins a radio quiz

Blondie's Big Deal (Columbia) d.Edward Bernds: Arthur Lake, Penny Singleton. Dagwood Bumstead invents a fireproof paint which is stolen by some unscrupulous rival contractors

All the King's Men (Columbia) d.Robert Rossen: Broderick Crawford. Crawford superb as the corrupt, bullying Southern political bigshot in fluent adaptation of novel by Robert Penn Warren

The Stratton Story (MGM) d.Sam Wood: James Stewart, June Allyson. Stewart affecting as the gangling Chicago White Sox pitcher who loses a leg in a hunting accident and then fights his way back

B MOVIES

The Big Steal (RKO) d.Don Siegel: Robert Mitchum, William Bendix. Entertaining South of the Border chase thriller with a neat twist at the end. Another effective pairing of Mitchum and Jane Greer

D.O.A. (UA) d.Rudolph Maté: Laurette Luez, Edmond O'Brien. Claustrophobic *film noir* with O'Brien succumbing to effects of slow-acting poison as he searches Los Angeles for his killer

Gun Crazy (King Bros) d.Joseph H Lewis: Peggy Cummins, John Dall. Cummins and Dall are 'Bonnie and Clyde' couple on the run in breathtaking stylish celebration of mad love. Lewis' finest film

Illegal Entry (Universal) d.Frederick de Cordova: Howard Duff (c). World War II veteran Duff is employed by immigration official George Brent as undercover agent to bust alien-smuggling racket

The House Across the Street (Warner) d.Richard Bare: Janis Paige, Wayne Morris. Yet another remake of *Hi Nellie!* (1934) with newsman Morris solving murder, romancing sob sister Paige

Crime Doctor's Diary (Columbia) d.Seymour Friedman: Robert Armstrong, Adele Jergens, Stephen Dunne. Warner Baxter as Dr Ordway clears parolee Dunne of murder rap in final series entry

Not Wanted (Film Classics) d.Elmer Clifton: Sally Forest (c). First film produced by Ida Lupino tackles problem of unmarried mothers and successfully avoids the usual pitfalls of sentimentality

Follow Me Quietly (RKO) d.Richard Fleischer: William Lundigan, Dorothy Patrick. Detective Lundigan follows a trail of corpses left by a psychopathic killer who signs himself 'The Judge'

Abandoned (Universal) d.Joseph M Newman: Will Kuluva, Marjorie Rambeau, Mike Mazurki, Gale Storm. Slightly less than searing exposé of the black-market baby racket

The Window (RKO) d.Ted Tetzlaff: Paul Stewart, Bobby Driscoll, Barbara Hale. Little Bobby is prone to fantasy, so when he witnesses a murder from his tenement fire escape no-one believes him. Absorbing

Homicide (Warner) d.Felix Jacoves: Robert Douglas. Detective Douglas poses as insurance investigator, tracks down killers of hitchhiker, who turn out to be sinister racetrack syndicate. Above-average

I Cheated the Law (Fox) d.Edward L Cahn: Steve Brodie, Tom Conway, Robert Osterloh, Tom Noonan. Lawyer Conway secures acquittal of guilty mobster Brodie, then cleverly traps him

Strange Bargain (RKO) d.Will Price: Martha Scott, Jeffrey Lynn. Hard-up Lynn is persuaded to agree to fake his boss's death to collect on insurance. But the best-laid schemes...

Night unto Night (Warner) d.Don Siegel: Ronald Reagan, Viveca Lindfors. Epileptic scientist Reagan shares gloom with widowed Lindfors in a project which might have worked if directed by Bergman

The Devil's Henchman (Columbia) d.Seymour Friedman: Peggy Converse, Warner Baxter. Insurance agent Baxter masquerades as a down-and-out to trap waterfront gang in so-so melodrama

Joe Palooka in the Big Fight (Mon) d.Cyril Endfield: David Bruce, Leon Errol, Joe Kirkwood. Kirkwood is the musclebrained fighter, Errol his wily manager. Based on comic strip

The Feathered Serpent (Mon) d.Lesley Selander: Roland Winters. Charlie Chan takes time off from Mexican holiday to find missing archaeologists, Lost Temple and a cache of ancient treasure

The Big Wheel (UA) d.Edward Ludwig: Mickey Rooney, Mary Hatcher. Rooney is son of racing driver following in father's wheeltracks with disastrous results. OK if you want to keep the neighbours awake

Search for Danger (Film Classics) d.Jack Bernhard: John Calvert, Myrna Dell, Albert Dekker. Inordinately complicated Falcon mystery with Calvert in title role endlessly recounting tangled plot

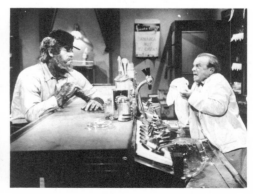

Master Minds (Mon) d.Jean Yarbrough: Glenn Strange, Bernard Gorcey. Bowery Boys farce in which Huntz Hall develops prophetic powers and is kidnapped by a mad scientist

Sky Dragon (Mon) d.Lesley Selander: Joel Marston, Noel Neill, Roland Winters, Elena Verdugo. The last of Winters' six impersonations of Chinese sleuth Charlie Chan. End of Monogram series

Miss Mink of 1949 (Fox) d.Glenn Tryon: June Storey, Richard Lane. Office clerk Lois Collier wins a mink coat in a radio contest but this expensive windfall causes her family nothing but trouble

King of the Rocket Men (Republic) d.Fred C Brannon: Tristram Coffin. Delightful serial in which jet propelled Coffin foils Dr Vulcan and prevents world disaster at the hands of the deadly 'decimator'

BRITISH & FOREIGN

The Third Man (London) d.Carol Reed: Joseph Cotten, Orson Welles. Orson gives Cotten a little lecture on Switzerland, democracy and cuckoo clocks as they ride a Viennese ferris wheel

Night and the City (Fox) d.Jules Dassin: Mike Mazurki (l), Richard Widmark. Strange cross between *Thieves' Highway* and *Oliver Twist* sets petty crook Widmark on doomed bid to sew up London's wrestling racket

Boys in Brown (Gainsborough) d.Montgomery Tully: Michael Medwin, John Blythe, Alfie Bass, Andrew Crawford, Dirk Bogarde, Robert Desmond, Richard Attenborough. Reform school drama

Silent Dust (Independent Sovereign) d.Lance Comfort: Nigel Patrick. Effective noirish thriller features Patrick as a 'war hero' who returns from the dead to reveal he is a blackmailing deserter

Obsession (Independent Sovereign) d.Edward Dmytryk: Robert Newton. macabre thriller in which doctor Newton imprisons his wife's American lover in a basement, with an acid bath in mind

The Glass Mountain (Victoria) d.Henry Cass: Valentina Cortese, Michael Denison. Composer Denison is shot down in the Dolomites during the war, joins partisans and writes an opera

Train of Events (Ealing) d.Sidney Cole, Charles Crichton, Basil Dearden: Mary Morris, Peter Finch. Flashback portmanteau film concentrating on three sets of people aboard a train heading for a crash

The Spider and the Fly (Mayflower) d.Robert Hamer: Guy Rolfe, Eric Portman, George Cole. Coolly ironic study of cracksman Rolfe and his rivalry with detective Portman

The Hasty Heart (ABPC) d.Vincent Sherman: Richard Todd, Patricia Neal. Prickly Scottish soldier Todd's discovery that he only has a short time to live brings him the first friendships of his life

The Last Days of Dolwyn (London) d.Emlyn Williams: Anthony James, Edith Evans. Williams also stars in overwrought tale of Welsh village threatened with flooding. Richard Burton's screen debut

Landfall (ABPC) d.Ken Annakin: Michael Denison, Patricia Plunkett. Competent study of Coastal Command in early days of the war is interspersed with some heavy-handed domestic comedy

Eureka Stockade (Ealing) d.Harry Watt: Chips Rafferty, Gordon Jackson. Robust Australian 'Western' set during the 1830s gold rush when rebellious miners clashed with British troops

Private Angelo (Pilgrim) d.Peter Ustinov: Peter Ustinov, Marjorie Rhodes, Maria Denis. Ustinov's flair for portraying whimsical continentals given full reign as the most reluctant of Italian soldiers

The Rocking Horse Winner (Two Cities) d.Anthony Pélissier: John Mills, John Howard Davies. D H Lawrence's tragic fantasy of a small boy driven to his death by the insatiable greed of his mother

Scott of the Antarctic (Ealing) d.Charles Frend: Derek Bond, Reginald Beckwith, John Mills, Harold Warrender. Reverential account of Scott's doomed journey. Fine score by Vaughan Williams

The Bad Lord Byron (Sydney Box) d.David Macdonald: Dennis Price, Raymond Lovell. Price looks the part in title role but film falls flat as a heavenly tribunal investigates poet's past

Idol of Paris (Premier) d.Leslie Arliss: Christine Norden, Beryl Baxter. Last gasp of 'Gainsborough Gothic' is enjoyably ludicrous account of rival courtesans in the court of Louis Napoleon

The Chiltern Hundreds (Two Cities) d.John Paddy Carstairs: A E Matthews, Cecil Parker, Marjorie Fielding. Well-turned version of stage hit in which butler Parker stands for Parliament as a Tory

Passport to Pimlico (Ealing) d.Henry Cornelius: Stanley Holloway, Betty Warren, Barbara Murray. Pointed social comedy in which a London street discovers it is part of the ancient kingdom of Burgundy

Whisky Galore (Ealing) d.Alexander Mackendrick: Basil Radford, Henry Mollison. A small Hebridean island's whisky famine ends when a steamer loaded with a huge export consignment runs aground

The Huggetts Abroad (Gainsborough) d.Ken Annakin: Jack Warner, Dinah Sheridan, Kathleen Harrison, Jimmy Hanley, Susan Shaw, Hugh McDermott. The comic Cockney family invade Africa

A Boy, A Girl, and a Bike (Gainsborough) d.Ralph Smart: Diana Dors (l), Patrick Holt, Honor Blackman, Megs Jenkins, Leslie Dwyer. Slight comedy built around romantic rivalries in a cycling club

Kind Hearts and Coronets (Ealing) d.Robert Hamer: Dennis Price, Valerie Hobson. Price murders his way to a title in elegant black comedy whose ironic surface barely conceals the passion pulsing beneath

Dear Mr Prohack (Wessex) d.Thornton Freeland: Cecil Parker, Heather Thatcher. Updated Arnold Bennett novel in which Treasury official Parker comes unstuck when he inherits a large private fortune

Murder at the Windmill (Grand National) d.Val Guest: Jack Livesey, Garry Marsh, Jon Pertwee. A body is found slumped in the stalls of London's famous revue theatre. Policemen Marsh and Pertwee investigate

It's Not Cricket (Gainsborough) d.Alfred Roome: Maurice Denham, Alan Wheatley. Denham is the runaway Nazi confusing the cricketing endeavours of Basil Radford and Naunton Wayne

The Perfect Woman (Two Cities)
d.Bernard Knowles: Patricia Roc, Stanley
Holloway, Nigel Patrick. Pat Roc changes
places with a robot invented by her uncle
Miles Malleson. Breezy comedy

Old Mother Riley's New Venture
(Reynolds) d.John Harlow: Sebastian
Cabot, Arthur Lucan. Outrageous
knockabout comedy in which the old Irish
termagant takes over an hotel

A Run for Your Money (Ealing) d.Charles
Frend: Alec Guinness. Guinness is the
gardening correspondent reluctantly
covering the visit to London of two
Stakhanovite Welsh miners

The Cure for Love (London) d.Robert
Donat: Dora Bryan, Robert Donat. Donat
repeats stage role as returning Eighth Army
sergeant in broad regional romantic
comedy written by Walter Greenwood

No Peace Among the Olives (Italy)
d.Giuseppe de Santis: Raf Vallone, Lucia
Boze. Melodramatic tale of sheep stealing
and rivalry in love filmed in the village
where de Santis was born

Stromboli (Italy) d.Roberto Rossellini:
Mario Vitale, Ingrid Bergman. To escape life
in a refugee camp Bergman marries an
Italian fisherman, who takes her home to
his island

Stray Dog (Japan) d.Akira Kurosawa:
Toshiro Mifune. Mifune chases his stolen
pistol through the lower strata of Tokyo,
presenting vivid picture of the city

The Broken Drum (Japan) d.Keisuke
Kinoshita: Tsumasaburo Brando,
Massayuki Mori. Examination of breakdown
of traditional Japanese concepts as a father
attempts to impose feudal ideas on family

Late Spring (Japan) d.Yasujiro Ozu:
Setsuko Hara (l). A father and daughter
have lived together for years, and now the
daughter must marry and leave him alone.
A film of immense, quiet charm

INDEX